How It Works®

Science and Technology

Third Edition

Marshall Cavendish
99 White Plains Road
Tarrytown, NY 10591

Website: www.marshallcavendish.com

Third edition updated by Brown Reference Group plc.

Library of Congress Cataloging-in-Publication Data
How it works: science and technology.—3rd ed.
p. cm.
Includes index.
ISBN 0-7614-7314-9 (set)   ISBN 0-7614-7315-7 (Vol. 1)
1. Technology—Encyclopedias. 2. Science—Encyclopedias.
[1. Technology—Encyclopedias. 2. Science—Encyclopedias.]
T9 .H738 2003
603—dc21   2001028771

Consultant: Donald R. Franceschetti, Ph.D., University of Memphis

Brown Reference Group
Editor: Wendy Horobin
Associate Editors: Paul Thompson, Martin Clowes, Lis Stedman
Managing Editor: Tim Cooke
Design: Alison Gardner
Picture Research: Becky Cox
Illustrations: Mark Walker

Marshall Cavendish
Project Editor: Peter Mavrikis
Production Manager: Alan Tsai
Editorial Director: Paul Bernabeo

Printed in Malaysia
Bound in the United States of America
08 07 06 05 04   6 5 4 3 2

Title picture: Stuart Little, the computer-designed mouse, see *Animation*

How It Works®

Science and Technology

Volume 1

Abrasive

Antiaircraft Gun

Marshall Cavendish

New York • London • Toronto • Sydney

Introduction

By Donald R. Franceschetti, Ph.D.
University of Memphis

Consulting Editor

This third edition of *How It Works* has been developed in response to the numerous technological changes that have affected daily life since the last edition. By far the greatest driver of change has been the rapid pace of developments in the area of microelectronics for information processing. Computers have become not just more powerful and faster but also cheaper and easier to use. Electronic mail has grown in volume to compete with mail carried by the world's postal services, and the World Wide Web brings into the reach of ordinary individuals information resources that have never before been available in one place. Television antennas have begun to disappear as cable television has all but supplanted broadcast television in one community after another. Computer image processing has changed forever what moviegoers accept as realistic.

Advances in medical and biotechnology have also been revolutionary. Magnetic resonance imaging and fiber-optic techniques have made it possible to image the human anatomy and to make many surgical repairs with only the most minimal amount of cutting of healthy tissues. The cloning of large animals and genetic modification of plants and microbes offer the possibility of enhanced health and well-being in the future.

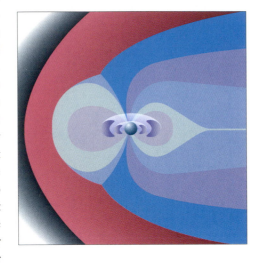

▲ Diagrammatic representation of the magnetosphere that surrounds Earth. Earth's magnetic field protects us from the worst effects of the solar wind by deflecting ionized particles into outer space. See *Radiation Belt*.

Technology, however, did not begin a decade ago or even a century ago. This reference work covers a continuous stream of technical development that began in ancient Babylonia, evolved in the scriptoria of medieval monasteries, and passed through the invention of printing with movable type by Johannes Gutenberg, to photography, lithography, and computer desktop publishing. Examples of the continuity of technological development are everywhere. The new computer eagerly awaited by a biotechnology research group might have been shipped over hundred-year-old waterways. The breeding of desirable traits in plants and animals—the original biotechnology—is as old as farming itself.

How It Works is intended as a reference for students and other readers who want to learn more about the technologies that are critical to modern life but who may not have the scientific background to understand the more technical literature. This reference work includes many articles about the scientific bases on which technologies are built. While no single set of volumes could cover every aspect of every technology, the authors, editors, and publishers believe that this new edition will prove useful in the vast majority of cases for those who want to know *How It Works*.

▼ Scientists can now image the ozone hole that appears over Antarctica every fall. See *Climatology*.

▼ The mechanism of a piano key works by a system of levers and dampers hitting a metal string. See *Piano*.

▼ A hidden black hole is revealed by a jet of X rays escaping from its center. See *Matter, Properties of*.

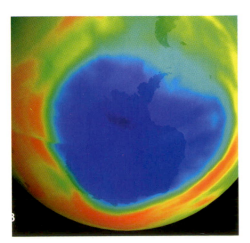

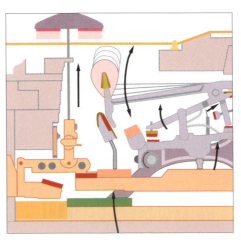

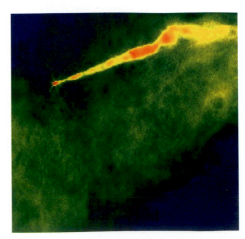

Reader's Guide

This newly revised and substantially updated edition of *How It Works* contains a number of features designed to make these volumes easy to use.

Volumes 1 to 19 cover more than 800 main subject entries in letter-by-letter alphabetical order. Article headings containing more than one word are alphabetized as if they are one word up to the punctuation mark. Words appearing in parentheses are not considered part of the heading for purposes of alphabetization. Thus:

Cable, Power
Cable, Submarine
Cable and Rope Manufacture
Cable Network

Each volume is prefaced with a contents list and contains an average of 40 entries, varying in length from one to eight complete pages. Many of the entries include Fact File boxes containing a number of historical, unusual, or improbable items of fascinating fact.

Reference facilities

To find entries rapidly, there is a running head at the top of the page and page numbers at the bottom throughout volumes 1 to 19. All entries are followed by an alphabetical list of cross references to other articles, allowing a reader to find further information about a subject without turning to the index. For example, the entry "Antifouling Techniques" ends with the following:

> **SEE ALSO:** CORROSION PREVENTION • METAL • SHIP • WARSHIP

Volume 20 contains a variety of indexes arranged alphabetically and the-

▲ The astronaut Michael Gernhardt holds on to the remote manipulator arm of the space shuttle as it orbits over the northern coast of Cyprus during an operation to extend the International Space Station. See *Space Photography, Space Probe, Space Shuttle, Space Suit,* and *Space Station*.

matically. Also included are a glossary of technical terms used in the encyclopedia, a list of websites that provide further useful information on subjects covered, and helpful conversion tables between U.S. and metric units.

Weights and measures

Weights and measures are given in both U.S. and (in parentheses) metric equivalents, except where convention demands a universal unit or the measurement is extremely small.

Contents of the Set

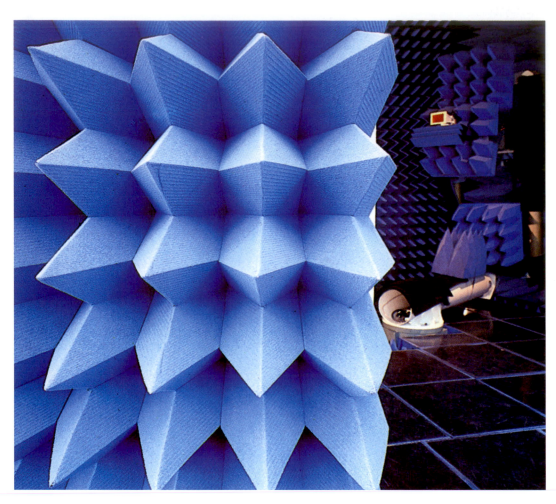

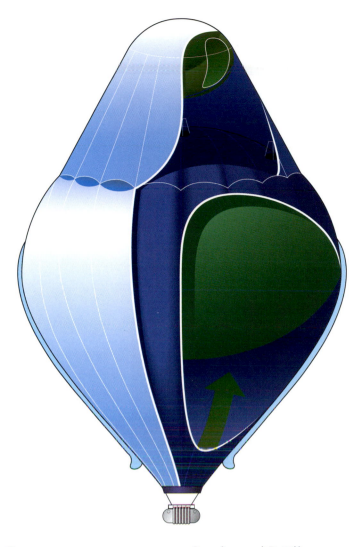

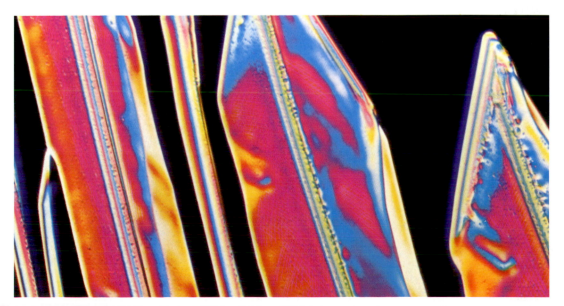

Volume 6

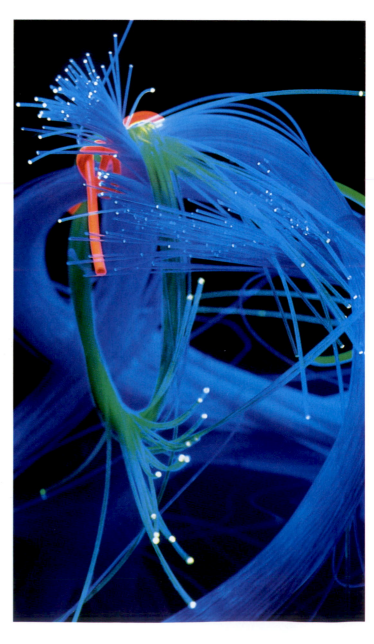

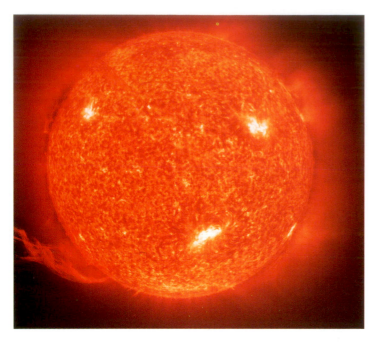

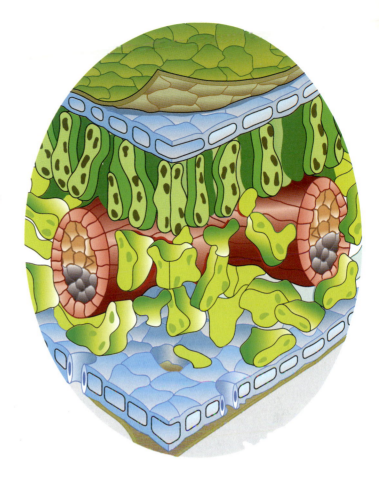

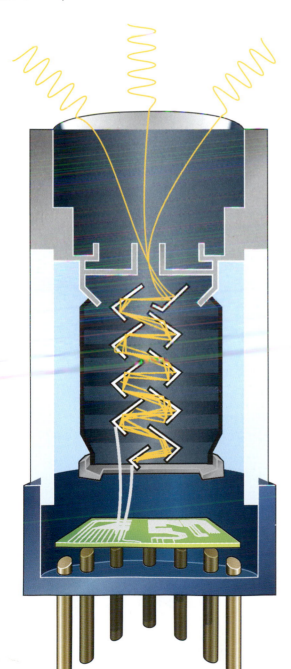

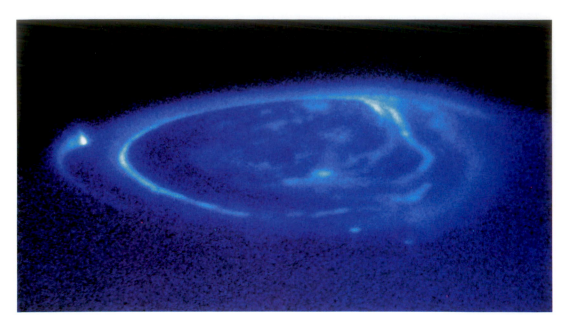

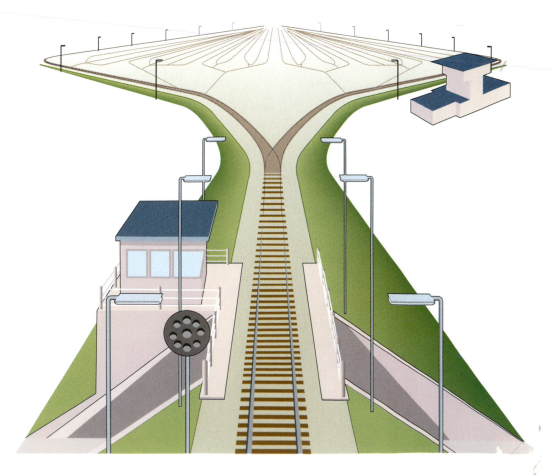

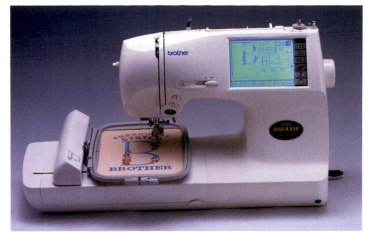

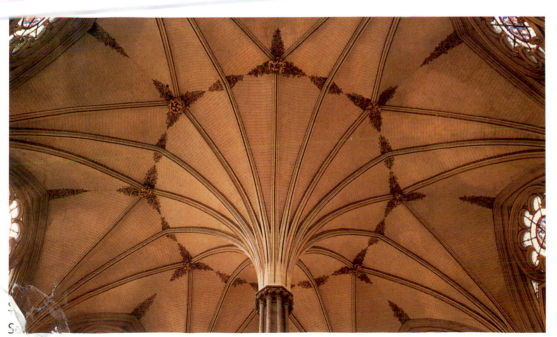

Contents

Volume 1

mobility aid. One very helpful device of this type, the Mark II Binaural Sensory aid, is built into spectacle frames. It uses frequency-modulated (FM) ultrasonic waves sent out from a transmitter built into the bridge alongside two microphones.

In operation, a beam of sound waves 60 degrees wide probes the space ahead for a distance of about 10 ft. (3 m) and detects obstacles or guide surfaces, such as buildings. It then bounces echoes back to be picked up by the aid's twin receivers. The FM waves have a frequency of 90 kHz, pulsing four times per second, and slight differences in the beat frequency of returned echoes from obstacles are electronically converted and heard as audio tones in twin earpieces. The tones are directly related to the distance of the reflecting object in the path, and the traveler learns eventually to relate pitch to the relative distance of a hazard ahead.

The aid is used in conjunction with a long cane, because the beam of sound waves is only 30 degrees in elevation, that is, from waist to head height, and thus, hazards at ground level are not detected. Nevertheless, a traveler's awareness of the near environment is still heightened by a significant amount.

Thousands of blind people use a long cane to aid their mobility as an alternative to the guide dog. The cane, which is about 40 percent longer than an ordinary walking stick, is scanned from side to side, the tip contacting the ground one pace ahead of the user.

In the United States, one advance on this basic model has been the incorporation of three laser beams into a modified long cane. The lasers, mounted near the crook of the handle, direct their beams in three well-defined locations: below ground level, to detect sudden drops; in the main direction, up to three or four paces ahead; and above, for head-height obstacles. At about 1.5 ft. (0.5 m) down the cane, three photodetecting diodes gather information about any hazards, which reflect the laser probing beam back to the cane. Sudden drops in the terrain are signaled by a low audio tone from an amplifier at the end of the crook handle. High tones indicate head-high overhanging obstacles, while the main beam gives warning by vibrating a small stud on which the index finger rests when using the cane. The laser's pencil-thin beams are given width by virtue of the lateral scanning action of the cane, which picks up information about level one pace ahead.

All these kinds of mobility aids may become outdated if the predictions of some farsighted workers in the field of robotics come true. For instance, there may come a day when devices such as ʼisor worn by Geordie in *Star Trek: Next*

Generation become reality. A number of prototypes are already being tested. Recent scientific experiments, capitalizing on increased knowledge of the areas of the brain that control various functions, have enabled a man to be fitted with electronic sensors sited in a pair of spectacles. These sensors relay basic information on location: they provide a crude black and white image of the area being scanned. This information is then relayed directly via a ribbonlike cable—not unlike those used within computers—through the skull, where the signal directly stimulates the area of the brain used to interpret visual images, the visual cortex. Although this device is in the early stages of development, the blind user has reported significant ability to interpret these signals as a picture of the world around him.

Industrial aids

To help blind or partially sighted workers in an industrial environment, various devices have been developed. The Braille micrometer caliper, for instance, is a highly successful adaptation of the most widely used measuring instrument for precision engineering components. The usual visual scales are replaced by embossed calibrations and Braille numerals on two integrally geared drums. When a component is checked between the anvils in the caliper, the measurement is read by touch against an embossed datum line on the nonrotatable center drum. The pinion-to-gear ratio between the drums is 40:1, and there are 25 and 40 divisions, respectively, to give a 0.001 in. (0.025 mm) resolution. Four-decimal-place resolution is provided on a five-division Vernier scale

▼ Products such as this lightwriter have been designed for people with communication difficulties. They are small, portable, and run on batteries. The user types in what he or she wants to say, and the words are displayed on a small digital screen.

adjacent to the datum line. The usual micrometer screw thread pitch is retained to advance or retract the measuring drum assembly when checking a component. This adaptation has been made to micrometers measuring up to 6 in. (15 cm) and to depth gauges and, with appropriate calibrations, to high-resolution bevel protractors. Developments such as these have enabled blind people to do types of work previously open only to sighted people.

Aids for other disabilities

There are many other aids available to help those with a range of disabilities to lead a full life. Among these are small portable text-to-speech communication aids designed to meet the needs of people with speech disabilities.

These aids can also help those with other disabilities, such as poor motor control, tremor, muscle weakness, spasticity, impaired vision, and deafness. Some have dual displays, one facing the user, who can then see what he or she is typing and a second turned outward to allow communication face to face.

Such devices also often have a range of internal speech synthesisers so that any word typed in will be spoken aloud. They may also be connected to printers and computers to provide a written output. A variation on this device uses scanning to help people unable to use a keyboard.

The alphabet is displayed on a screen on which a selector box moves automatically from letter to letter. When the box reaches the desired letter, the user presses a switch to select it. Other devices use touch screens, predictive spelling, and simple icons to enable those with some mobility to communicate using digitized speech.

For the deaf, there are a variety of aids, including ultrasonic bone-conduction hearing aids, which are placed behind the ear on the mastoid bone and allow the profoundly deaf to hear sounds. This technique is also being investigated for the elimination of tinnitus, an unpleasant condition in which the sufferer experiences permanent noises in the ear.

Digital technology has also helped in the development of improved hearing aids. Digital hearing aids utilize true digital signal processing. Users are able to understand speech better because the digital technology enables sound to be precisely customized to the individual ear. In a noisy environment, the difference is marked, as noise suppression allows speech to be filtered out from the background.

In recent years, the development of devices known as tele-loop, or inductive-loop, amplifiers, enable the hard of hearing to hear sounds in

public places that would normally present challenges for conventional hearing aids. With these devices, an aerial cord placed along the walls of a room enables the user of a hearing aid with the switch in the "T" position to listen to religious services, theater, the radio, TV, CD players, or other sound sources.

The Laryngophone was developed to help those with speech problems—for instance, individuals who have had their vocal chords removed. It operates in the same way as a real larynx, using the vibration in the windpipe to provide, with practice, a close approximation of speech.

There is also a variety of devices to help the disabled in their daily routines—for instance, an alarm clock with a vibrator instead of a bell or buzzer specially designed for those unable to respond to a conventional alarm clock. Visual baby alarms are also available for deaf couples unable to hear their baby crying. Telephone amplifiers, with volume controls that can be placed on the telephone handset, enable those with partial hearing to amplify an incoming call.

Similarly, doorbells are available that flash rather than ring, and there are even trained hearing dogs, who alert their owners to the presence of sounds, such as those made by the telephone or doorbell. There is also a speech synthesizer available that can send typed messages by phone and translate the response back into type so that a deaf recipient is able to carry on a normal conversation by telephone.

▲ This lightwriter has a second display unit so that anybody facing the person trying to communicate can see what they are saying without turning the keyboard. Further refinements of these devices include scanners for people unable to type—when a cursor moving over the alphabet reaches the required letter, the user selects it by pressing a switch.

SEE ALSO: Bioengineering • Digital display • Eye • Hearing • Mobility aid • Optical scanner • Sound • Speech and language • Voice recognition and synthesis

Acid and Alkali

Acids are substances that tend to react with bases and metals to form salts and water (with bases) or hydrogen (with metals). Common acids are protonic acids—their molecules can dissociate to release protons (hydrogen ions, H^+), which form hydronium ions (H_3O^+) with water.

Protonic acids include hydrochloric, nitric, and sulfuric acids (HCl, HNO_3, and H_2SO_4) and organic (carbon-based) acids, such as ethanoic acid (acetic acid, CH_3COOH). Some organic acids occur in nature; others are synthetic.

Some substances, called Lewis acids, react with bases even though they contain no hydrogen; such substances include aluminum chloride ($AlCl_3$), and they are characterized by their ability to form bonds by accepting electron pairs from Lewis bases, which include ammonia (NH_3).

Alkalis are water-soluble substances that release hydroxide ions (OH^-) when they dissolve in water and react with acids to form salts and water. Alkalis include the hydroxides of certain metals, notably sodium and potassium hydroxides ($NaOH$ and KOH), and ammonia. They are a subgroup of bases; nonalkaline bases react with acids in the same way as alkalis do, but they do not dissolve in water to any appreciable extent.

Acids and alkalis are important products and raw materials of the chemical industry. The manufacture of caustic soda (sodium hydroxide) was one of the earliest industrial chemical processes, and caustic soda is used to manufacture a wide range of products, including bleach, paper, and soap. Acids, such as phosphoric acid (H_3PO_4) and sulfuric acid, are important industrial catalysts.

Acid and base strengths

When some acids dissolve in water, they completely dissociate into hydrogen ions and anions. Hydrochloric acid is a strong acid, for example, so it forms a solution of oxonium ions and chloride ions (Cl^-) in water (H_2O):

$$HCl + H_2O \rightarrow H_3O^+ + Cl^-$$

Thus a 1 mol/l solution of hydrochloric acid is really a solution of 1 mol/l hydrogen ions and 1 mol/l chloride ions. Acids that dissociate completely in this way are called strong acids.

Not all acids are strong, however. Weak acids remain largely in molecular form when they dissolve in water, and the concentration of hydrogen ions they produce is much less than that produced by strong acids. Ethanoic acid is an example of a weak acid. When it dissolves in water, only a small proportion of ethanoic acid molecules react to

form hydronium ions and ethanoate ions according to the following equation:

$$CH_3COOH + H_2O \leftrightarrow H_3O^+ + CH_3COO^-$$

Approximately four in every thousand molecules dissociate in water at room temperature. In fact, a 1 mol/l solution of ethanoic acid contains only 0.0042 mol/l of hydrogen ions (and the same concentration of ethanoate ions).

Just as acids may be strong or weak, bases (and therefore alkalis) can be classified as strong or weak. Sodium hydroxide is an example of a strong alkali, whereas ammonia is weak.

Sulfuric acid, H_2SO_4

Concentrated sulfuric acid is a clear, oily liquid that is corrosive to skin and to metals. Apart from being fiercely acidic, it is a powerful oxidant.

The principal starting material for sulfuric acid is elemental sulfur—sulfur is one of the few elements that occur uncombined in nature. Sulfur burns in air to produce sulfur dioxide (SO_2) in the first stage of manufacture. Alternative starting materials include metal sulfides, which occur as ores or are by-products of industrial processes, such as the desulfurization of natural gas and petroleum. Roasting a metal sulfide in air produces sulfur dioxide and the metal oxide.

The two industrial processes for making sulfuric acid from sulfur dioxide are the chamber process and the contact process. The original and

▲ A sulfuric acid manufacturing plant. The complex pipework is made of steel, and the acid is contained by the noncorrodible linings.

traditional method is the chamber process, so called because sulfur dioxide reacts with air and steam in a lead-lined chamber. Oxides of nitrogen are also present as catalysts. The reaction is complex, on account of the involvement of catalysts, but is basically an oxidation reaction that produces chamber acid—an impure solution of around 65 percent sulfuric acid in water:

$$2SO_2 + 2H_2O + O_2 \rightarrow 2H_2SO_4$$

The chamber process now produces less than 20 percent of all sulfuric acid, since the process has been largely supplanted by the more efficient contact process (see the box below).

The contact process can produce pure sulfuric acid at any concentration by the addition of the appropriate amount of water. An intermediate product is oleum ($H_2S_2O_7$), a derivative of sulfuric acid that is intensely corrosive and oxidizing and a useful substance in its own right.

Of the sulfuric acid produced, about one-third goes to make fertilizers. Other important uses are the production of paints, pigments, fibers, detergents, and plastics, as well as pickling—the preparation of metal surfaces by oxide removal.

Nitric acid, HNO_3

Nitric acid is a colorless liquid when pure, but it soon acquires a yellow or brownish-red color and produces brown fumes when exposed to air. The color is caused by a mixture of nitrogen oxides that forms as a result of the action of light and heat. Concentrated nitric acid is extremely corrosive and oxidizing and is capable of causing severe skin burns. Nitric acid can also cause readily combustible materials to ignite.

The laboratory preparation of nitric acid—and formerly the industrial method—is the treatment of sodium nitrate (Chile saltpeter, $NaNO_3$) with sulfuric acid. Distillation separates the

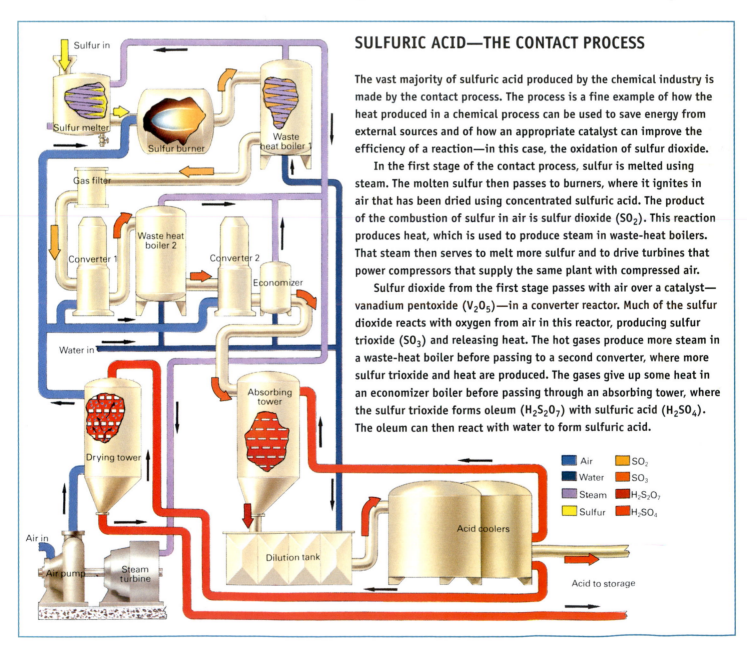

SULFURIC ACID—THE CONTACT PROCESS

The vast majority of sulfuric acid produced by the chemical industry is made by the contact process. The process is a fine example of how the heat produced in a chemical process can be used to save energy from external sources and of how an appropriate catalyst can improve the efficiency of a reaction—in this case, the oxidation of sulfur dioxide.

In the first stage of the contact process, sulfur is melted using steam. The molten sulfur then passes to burners, where it ignites in air that has been dried using concentrated sulfuric acid. The product of the combustion of sulfur in air is sulfur dioxide (SO_2). This reaction produces heat, which is used to produce steam in waste-heat boilers. That steam then serves to melt more sulfur and to drive turbines that power compressors that supply the same plant with compressed air.

Sulfur dioxide from the first stage passes with air over a catalyst—vanadium pentoxide (V_2O_5)—in a converter reactor. Much of the sulfur dioxide reacts with oxygen from air in this reactor, producing sulfur trioxide (SO_3) and releasing heat. The hot gases produce more steam in a waste-heat boiler before passing to a second converter, where more sulfur trioxide and heat are produced. The gases give up some heat in an economizer boiler before passing through an absorbing tower, where the sulfur trioxide forms oleum ($H_2S_2O_7$) with sulfuric acid (H_2SO_4). The oleum can then react with water to form sulfuric acid.

volatile acid from nonvolatile sodium hydrogen-sulfate ($NaHSO_4$) solution:

$$NaNO_3 + H_2SO_4 \rightarrow HNO_3 + NaHSO_4$$

The usual industrial synthesis of nitric acid is by the oxidation of ammonia using oxygen from air and a platinum-rhodium catalyst. The initial product is nitric oxide (NO). Subsequent oxidations and reaction with water produce nitrogen dioxide (NO_2) and finally nitric acid:

$$4NH_3 + 5O_2 \rightarrow 4NO + 6H_2O$$
$$2NO + O_2 \rightarrow 2NO_2$$
$$4NO_2 + 2H_2O + O_2 \rightarrow 4HNO_3$$

Nitric acid is used to make nitrate fertilizers and organic nitro compounds for explosives, dyes, and drugs. Nitric acid dissolves most metals, making it useful for etching, and aqua regia—a mixture of one part nitric acid to three parts hydrochloric acid—dissolves even gold.

Hydrochloric acid, HCl

Hydrochloric acid is produced by dissolving hydrogen chloride gas in water. Hydrogen chloride is a by-product of the chlorination of hydrocarbons and may also be produced by treating sodium chloride with sulfuric acid or by the reaction between hydrogen and chlorine produced as by-products of the electrolysis of sodium chloride solution for sodium hydroxide production.

Concentrated hydrochloric acid is extremely corrosive and must be transported in glass- or polymer-lined tanks. It differs from nitric and sulfuric acids in that it is not an oxidizing agent.

Hydrochloric acid is used for pickling steel before it is galvanized (zinc plated), for decomposing bones to make gelatin, in the manufacture of dyes and rayon, for refining oils, fats, and waxes, and for tanning leather.

Carboxylic acids

The majority of organic acids owe their acidity to the presence of one or more carboxylic acid (–COOH) groups in their molecules. This group dissociates to some extent in water to form hydrogen ions and carboxylate ions. The simplest of these acids is methanoic acid (formic acid, HCOOH), a corrosive substance responsible for the "sting" of certain types of ants.

Simple carboxylic acids are made by a number of chemical and biochemical routes. Ethanoic acid (CH_3COOH), for example, can be made by a catalytic reaction between methanol (CH_3OH) and carbon monoxide (CO), by chemical oxidation of ethanal (CH_3CHO), or by air oxidation of ethanol (CH_3CH_2OH) in the presence of certain bacteria (the method that turns wine to vinegar).

More complex carboxylic acids are made as salts by saponification (alkaline hydrolysis) of natural esters, which contain the –CO–O– linkage; alcohols are by-products of this process. Fats and oils, whose molecules are triesters of glycerol ($CH_2(OH)CH(OH)CH_2(OH)$), yield mixtures of long-chain carboxylate salts.

Simple carboxylic acids are used to make esters as monomers and plasticizers for plastics and as scents and flavorings. Complex carboxylic acids are used as their soaps (metal salts) for cleaning and as driers for some paints.

Caustic alkalis

The caustic alkalis—sodium hydroxide (NaOH) and potassium hydroxide (NaOH)—are made as solutions by electrolysis of solutions in water of the appropriate chlorides. Hydrogen and chlorine are important by-products:

$$2NaCl + 2H_2O \rightarrow 2NaOH + H_2 + Cl_2$$

The caustic alkalis are corrosive substances that are used in a number of industrial processes, including the manufacture of soaps and paper. The reaction of sodium hydroxide with chlorine produces sodium hypochlorite (NaOCl), the active component of household bleach.

Ammonia, NH$_3$

Pure ammonia is a pungent and corrosive gas. It is manufactured by the Haber process, which combines hydrogen and nitrogen in the presence of an iron catalyst. Ammonia is extremely soluble in water. It is used to make ammonium fertilizers and, in pure or dissolved form, as a reagent in a vast range of chemical processes.

▲ The alkali lime (calcium hydroxide, $Ca(OH)_2$) being used to restore the pH of a lake in Sweden that has become acidic as a consequence of acid rain. Lime is made by roasting limestone ($CaCO_3$) to produce quicklime (CaO) and then adding water in a process called slaking.

SEE ALSO: Alcohol • Alkali metals • Ammonia manufacture • Chemistry, inorganic • Chemistry, organic • Fertilizer • Nitrogen • pH measurement • Salt, chemical

Acoustics

Acoustics is the science of sound: its various branches deal with the production, transmission, reproduction, and recording of sound as well as the way it propagates and the effect enclosed spaces have upon the way we experience it.

Being a wave motion of air molecules in the atmosphere, sound obeys the rules of reflection, diffraction, and dispersion in a similar fashion to the far shorter wavelength electromagnetic waves, such as those in the visible spectrum, but obviously from and through different materials. The wavelength difference is, in fact, crucial. Sound waves are generally long enough to be diffracted quite severely by everyday objects, because their wavelengths are usually similar in size to the objects.

The wave nature of sound is particularly important in architectural acoustics, where the detailed design of a concert or lecture hall depends crucially on how the designers wish sound to propagate through it. Other branches of acoustics deal with the design of sound recording and reproduction systems (engineering acoustics) and the highly specialized field of musical instruments (musical acoustics). Perhaps the most interesting and latest field of acoustic research, psychoacoustics deals with the way we actually perceive sound. Collaboration between engineers and psychoacousticians has led to some very sophisticated hi-fi systems that can fool a listener—via headphones or specially designed loudspeaker arrays—into thinking that he or she is hearing sounds that are not really there.

Hi-fi systems and psychoacoustics

Hi-fi originally stood for high fidelity, and the primary aim of hi-fi systems was to reproduce as faithfully as possible the listening experience of a live performance. With the advent of purely electric instruments, such as the electric guitar and the synthesizer, the aims of the hi-fi designers changed slightly. Much modern music is recorded as a collection of separate tracks on a studio master tape, and the aim of the new generation of hi-fi equipment has been to reproduce the recorded information (which has probably never been performed live, with all the instruments playing together) as accurately as possible and as lifelike.

So today the demands put upon a music reproduction system are twofold: it must be able to re-create live music recorded in undoctored acoustical surroundings, conveying something of the sense of space and reverberation that resonates through such performances, and it must

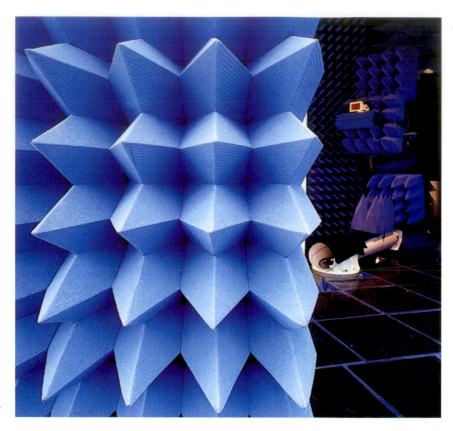

also be able to handle program sources that have been created only on tape and generally have all sorts of added reverberation and tonal doctoring.

No system can be perfect. In order to capture a live performance through a microphone or a direct electric input from, say, a synthesizer, the input signal must be processed by electronics, which inevitably introduce distortion into the original signal. Indeed, the microphone and eventually the loudspeaker often add more unwanted components to the signal than the amplifier does. The original signal can be recorded on tape as a series of varying magnetized stripes in an oxide coating, on record as a wavy groove in the surface plastic, or today most commonly, as a series of digital pulses encoded on a special light-reflecting disc scanned by the laser of a compact disc player to recapture the original signal. Digitally encoded music, recorded direct, offers the purest signal. The electronics that decode the series of pulses, which are turned eventually into sound waves, allow none of the distortion signals that are associated with other analog types of recording.

Modern hi-fi systems accept a variety of input sources, such as tape, compact disc, AM radio, and FM radio. It is in the reproduction of the recorded signal that the psychoacoustician makes a significant contribution—although if material is originally recorded with multidirectional microphones to produce a set of signals that can be subsequently processed electronically, the task of the hi-fi system can be made simpler.

▲ Absorptive interior of an anechoic chamber, used for acoustical research. Sound is absorbed by glass-fiber wedges, leaving a minimum of echoes and reverberations.

The simplest such technique is stereophony. Original music is recorded with two microphones set at an angle to each other, so they pick up slightly different signals. If the music is electronic in origin, pseudo-stereo parallel tracks can be produced. The two signals are recorded and amplified separately and fed to two loudspeakers spaced some distance apart in the listening room. Because the phase of the sound waves coming from each speaker is different—the waves from one speaker are slightly out of step with those from the other—the ear is fooled into hearing a complete sound image spread between the two speakers, with different instruments and singers apparently coming from different directions, much like a 3-D image. Further developments of this technique have used four or more speakers.

Architectural acoustics

In any auditorium, the whole audience must be able to hear clearly the performer or musician on the stage without undue echoes. For some types of music, notably choral and organ music, a degree of echo or reverberation actually makes the sound more pleasant, but to hear speech clearly, this reverberation must be kept to a minimum. The reverberation time (RT) of a concert hall—the time taken for an initial burst of sound to fall to half of its original level—depends on its shape and the materials of which it is made. Auditoriums designed for large-scale orchestral works are generally oblong shaped, so there are plenty of reflections from the sides of the hall into the audience. This reverberant field combines with the directly radiated sound from the musicians to create a quality of sound that is pleasing to the listener. For speech, the reverberation time

of a hall should be less than one second; for chamber music, around one to two seconds; and for full orchestras, over two seconds.

Rock concerts provide a great problem for many concert halls. The sound energy produced is enormous and usually has artificial reverberation components added electronically. The reverberation field in some parts of conventional auditoriums can easily swamp the detail in the music. The best type of hall for this sort of music is a fan-shaped arrangement, like the old movie theaters. The rock band can then concentrate their output into direct beams covering parts of the hall without much reflection from the side walls, which create reverberation.

Even in conventional concert halls the reverberation time can be controlled by moveable absorbers and reflectors. Some venues can even alter their acoustics by recycling the original sound through arrays of loudspeakers placed strategically throughout the auditorium.

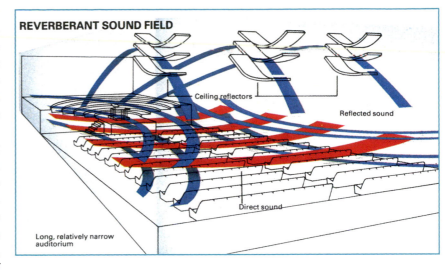

REVERBERANT SOUND FIELD

Ceiling reflectors

Reflected sound

Direct sound

Long, relatively narrow auditorium

▲ The acoustics of a concert hall are determined by its shape and the way sound is reflected around inside it. In this example, where length exceeds width, reflections from the walls and ceiling provide a reverberant sound field superimposed upon the direct sound (red) from the stage.

▼ Fan-shaped auditoriums are most suitable for speech and directionally amplified material. The walls are lined with sound-absorbing material to keep reflections to a minimum.

FACT FILE

- Acoustic detection is used to guide acoustical torpedoes onto their targets. Sounds from the engine, propeller, and other attributes of the target are picked up, or else the detector emits sonar pulses. Once in the target area, the detector controls the torpedo servomechanisms.

- Nondestructive testing, which employs high-frequency sound waves along with powerful microcomputers, helps engineers to monitor invisible pipeline welds, the condition of pressure vessels inside nuclear reactors, and hidden faults deep inside metal components.

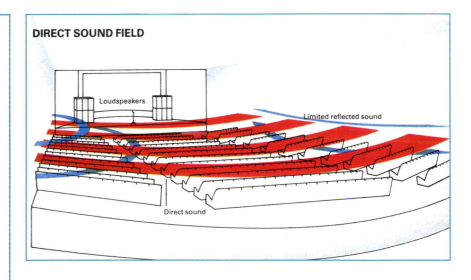

DIRECT SOUND FIELD

Loudspeakers

Limited reflected sound

Direct sound

SEE ALSO: AIR • COMPACT DISC, AUDIO • HEARING • HI-FI SYSTEMS • LOUDSPEAKER • SOUND • SOUNDPROOFING • WAVE MOTION

Adhesive and Sealant

Adhesives are substances used for bonding materials together, while sealants form a seal between materials in order to prevent the passage of a gas or liquid. In practice, the distinction between adhesives and sealants is not clear, since many sealants also act as adhesives and vice versa.

Until the 20th century, the only adhesives available were derived from natural sources, such as bones and plant saps. With the development of synthetic polymers, however, an enormous diversity of new adhesives became available. Today, adhesives range from the gum on postage stamps to the epoxy resins used in aircraft and bridge building.

Adhesives work in several ways; adsorption, in which adhesion takes place through intermolecular forces between the surfaces of the adhesive and the adherend; interdiffusion, which is the dissolving of the adherend surface by a liquid adhesive, causing the two surfaces to become mixed together; mechanical interlocking, which occurs as a result of the adhesive flowing into small pores in the surface of the adherend; and a combination of adsorption and surface reactions, in which chemical reactions occur between the adhesive and the surface of the adherend. In practice, more than one of these processes is likely to be involved in any particular adhesive reaction.

An adhesive must normally be applied to both surfaces that are to be joined together, because no matter how smooth they seem, they will be full of irregularities at a molecular level and must be evened out if the process is to be successful.

Design of joints

A normal adhesive joint has five parts, which may be considered five links in a chain—the joint being as strong as the weakest link. They are the inherent strength of one material, the strength of the bond of the adhesive to it, the inherent strength of the adhesive itself, the strength of its bond to the other material, and the strength of the other material.

With most types of adhesives, the strength of the bond between adhesive and adherend is stronger than the cohesion of the adhesive itself. For this reason, it is important to keep the adhesive film as thin as possible to prevent the joint from failing. The joining surfaces of the adherends must therefore fit together exactly. They must also have a large enough area and the right shape so as not to overstress the joint. Adhesive joints resist shearing (sideways) forces and tension as well but do not stand up to peeling forces, where there is tension at one edge of the joint that can cause a split to form and spread.

More and more joints in manufactured goods of all types are being made with adhesives instead of more traditional methods, such as bolting or welding. These joints even include metal-to-metal joints: for example, aluminum chair leg assemblies and certain parts of aircraft, where honeycomb structures of light alloy are bonded between two aluminum panels. In joints of this type, the adhesive cannot normally be used as direct replacement for the earlier fastening method; the joint has to be redesigned from scratch. Sometimes adhesive is used as a supplement to mechanical fastening: parts are spot-welded together and the space between the welds filled with adhesive to steady the parts against vibration.

It is important to choose the right adhesive for a job. For example, joints between flexible materials must be made with a flexible adhesive. In industry, other factors are also important, for example, setting time. It is no use cutting manufacturing costs by using adhesive joints instead of more expensive fastenings if the whole industrial process is held up while everyone waits for the adhesive to set.

Types of adhesives

Natural adhesives may come from animal, vegetable, or mineral sources. They may be hot-melt adhesives, which come in solid form, melt on heating, and harden on cooling. They may be water-soluble: adhesives of this type may be in the form of liquids or powders that dissolve in water; either kind remains soluble even after it has dried, so they are not water resistant. The adhesive may also be dissolved in an organic solvent that evaporates faster than water, thus allowing it to set quickly. This type of adhesive is normally water resistant.

The word *glue* is widely used for any type of adhesive but strictly speaking applies only to protein derivatives, that is, gelatin-like adhesives made from animal or vegetable protein. Scotch glue and similar types of woodworking glue are made by the traditional method of boiling down bones. They are hot-melt adhesives. A newer type of glue, soybean glue, is made of vegetable protein. Casein glue is a water-soluble woodworking adhesive made from milk.

Natural starches, cellulose, and gums from various plants are used to make light, inexpensive water-soluble adhesives. These are much used in the paper industry and also in the home as wall-

▲ Epoxy adhesive grout may be used to bond precast concrete sections such as these being used to build a bridge in northern England.

▶ Sealing compound oozes from the join of an auto engine block and head. The compound ensures complete contact between the sides of the gasket and the surface of the head and block.

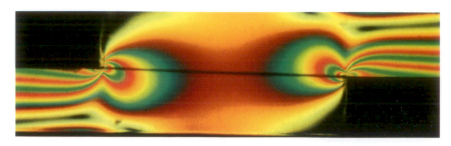

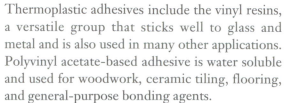

Thermoplastic adhesives include the vinyl resins, a versatile group that sticks well to glass and metal and is also used in many other applications. Polyvinyl acetate-based adhesive is water soluble and used for woodwork, ceramic tiling, flooring, and general-purpose bonding agents.

Other types of adhesives have organic solvents or are hot-melt types, such as the resin that is sandwiched between two thin layers of glass to make laminated safety glass stronger and safer for automobile windshields.

Acrylic resins

There are several types of acrylic resin adhesives, one- and two-part adhesives, both cured by adding chemicals. They can develop very strong bonds and are more transparent than other types of adhesives. Objects are often embedded in clear acrylic resin for protection or display. One unusual type is the popular "superglue" that cures to a high strength in a few seconds. This quality makes it useful for production lines.

paper paste, office paste, and gum. The adhesive on stamps and envelopes is gum arabic, an adhesive derived from a species of acacia tree.

Natural rubber, generally dissolved in air-drying organic solvents, makes adhesives that are used in industry for gluing rubber and leather and in building for attaching wall and floor coverings.

Natural resins and bitumens include blacktop, which is used to bind aggregate (gravel) in road making and similar applications. Marine glue is a natural resin in an organic solvent. It is not a true glue; true glues are not water resistant enough for marine use. Sealing wax is a hot-melt resin made from beeswax, Venice turpentine, and coloring.

All the previously mentioned adhesives are organic in origin. There is one inorganic natural adhesive: water glass (sodium silicate), which is used in the paper industry.

Most modern proprietary adhesives are based on synthetic rubber–resin formulations. Synthetic adhesives are generally called synthetic resins, because the natural adhesives they most resemble are the resin types. There are many variations, including one not found in natural adhesives: the two-part adhesive, where the adhesive is mixed with a separate hardener or catalyst to make it set. Synthetic resins are normally classed as thermoplastic (they melt when heated) and thermosetting (heat speeds hardening).

▲ Polarized light shining through two clear plastic sheets shows clearly the stress concentrations around an adhesive bond.

▼ Brake linings are glued together with complex phenolic resins.

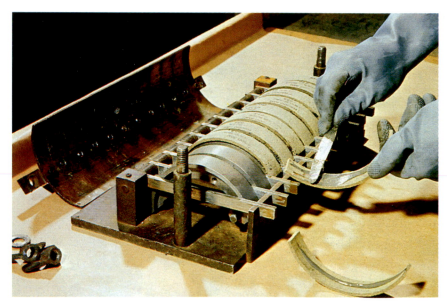

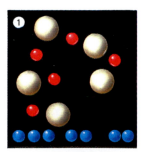

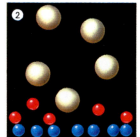

◄ The molecular life of a superglue from tube to fully hardened adhesive. (1) Acidic stabilizer (red) stops adhesive molecules (white) from linking and keeps adhesive in liquid state. (2) Water (blue) in surfaces to be joined neutralizes stabilizer. (3) Adhesive molecules join and curing begins. (4) Adhesive molecules build up on surfaces and interweave.

Cellulose adhesives consist of chemicals derived from cellulose (such as cellulose acetate) in an air-drying organic solvent; they are not the same as the water-based natural cellulose pastes mentioned above. They are quick drying and water resistant.

Other thermosetting resins include the phenolics, which are available both as chemical solvent resins and in thin, solid, pressure-sensitive sheets, which are used by the plywood industry for gluing layers of wood together.

Thermosetting adhesives include epoxide resins, among the strongest of all adhesives. Some types will withstand a shearing stress of up to 7,000 lbs. per sq. in. (500 kg/cm^2) in correctly designed joints.

Polyester resins are cheaper than epoxy resins and are therefore suitable for use in bulk. Their commonest use is with glass fiber to make glass-reinforced plastics.

Synthetic rubber is used with organic solvents and with water to make many types of adhesives. The pressure-sensitive adhesives that are used on adhesive tape can also be of this type. Synthetic rubber adhesives are widely used in automobiles for attaching interior trim panels.

Two products that do not fit into any of these categories, but which are nonetheless adhesives, are solder and hydraulic cement.

Medical uses

During the Vietnam War, doctors were faced with massive numbers of casualties—many with horrifyingly severe internal wounds and in imminent danger of bleeding to death. The task of the surgeon was to treat each casualty effectively but quickly in order to move on to the next patient. This need led to the development of tissue adhesive or surgical glue, applied by spraying. Surgical glue proved highly valuable in dealing with serious hemorrhaging under pressure of time.

The first surgical glue to be approved by the Federal Drug Administration, however, was an adhesive called Tisseel, which gained approval in 1998. Made from the blood proteins fibrinogen and thrombin, this glue causes blood to clot and is used to stop bleeding at the site of an injury as well as during various kinds of surgery. Most surgical glues so far developed, however, are based around a family of compounds known as cyano-acrylates from which superglue is made. These are organic compounds that are compatible with the biochemistry of living systems and that are more or less nontoxic to living cells. In the pres-

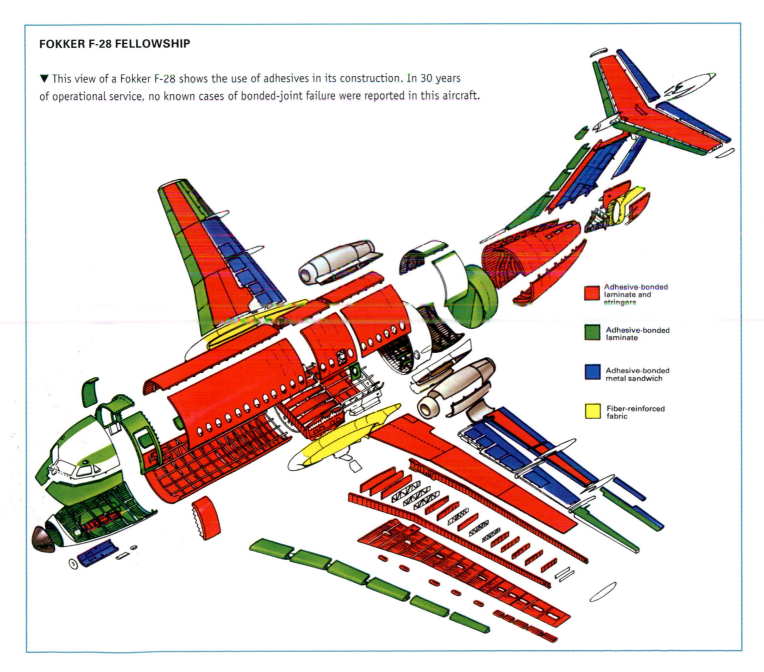

FOKKER F-28 FELLOWSHIP

▼ This view of a Fokker F-28 shows the use of adhesives in its construction. In 30 years of operational service, no known cases of bonded-joint failure were reported in this aircraft.

- Adhesive-bonded laminate and stringers
- Adhesive-bonded laminate
- Adhesive-bonded metal sandwich
- Fiber-reinforced fabric

ence of moisture, these compounds undergo a rapid reaction as strong chemical bonds are formed between individual cyanoacrylate molecules. This reaction—called polymerization—changes the compound from a liquid into a semisolid gel with considerable strength. Extra bonds are also formed between individual cyanoacrylate molecules and the surrounding tissue. The result is a tough lattice of molecular chains firmly fixed at the site of application. These glues are particularly useful for plastic surgery as they reduce the level of scarring.

provide watertight seals in areas such as kitchens, showers, and bathtubs. These sealants need to be resistant not only to water but also to high humidity and the growth of mildew and mold.

Nonsilicone sealants are used in the automobile industry to provide fast and highly flexible bonds between the wide variety of materials found in a motor vehicle. These sealants must be particularly resistant to the effects of vibration, expansion, and contraction as well as wide temperature differences. It must also be possible to paint over the seal.

Sealants are available that protect tires against the risk of puncture. A sealant is pumped inside the tire so that if a puncture occurs, the sealant is forced into the hole, where it forms a long-lasting plug preventing the tire from deflating.

Concrete sealants form a protective layer over the surface of concrete. When the sealant is applied to the concrete, it penetrates the surface and reacts chemically with alkalis naturally present in concrete. This reaction forms a gel that expands to seal cracks and pores and thus prevents any further penetration by moisture. This gel has the added effect of preventing harmful radioactive radon buildup in buildings that are built on areas overlying granitic rocks.

Another use for sealants is in dentistry. Plastic sealants may be coated onto the indented chewing surface of molar teeth. The indented areas are particularly prone to attack by plaque, so the seal provides a protective barrier.

Sealants

Many sealants are made from silicones, more properly called polysiloxanes. They are polymers that are basically formed from alternating silicon and oxygen atoms. Certain polysiloxanes have adhesive properties, which, combined with their resistance to water, hot and cold temperatures, and oxidation, make them ideal as sealants.

In buildings, the point where two external materials meet may be vulnerable to water penetration and heat loss. One way of solving this problem is by using a sealant that is resistant to water, variations in temperature, and also perhaps ultraviolet radiation. Some sealants, such as those used in close proximity to heavy machinery, may also need to be resistant to vibration.

The natural elasticity of silicone rubber-based sealants make them useful in many roles, since they can be made to cure quickly and are also flexible enough to expand and contract with the natural movement of a building. Glass and metal sealants, for example, are able to form weathertight seals between panes of glass and metal frames. Similarly, sealants may be used indoors to

▶ Cutaway of a bearing retainer and thread lock sealed with an anaerobic adhesive, which hardens in the presence of metal and absence of air.

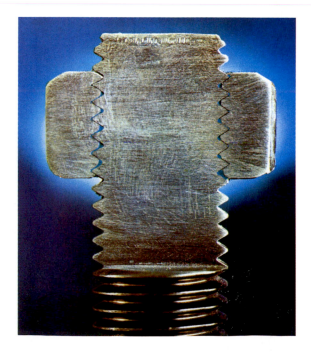

SEE ALSO: CATALYST • CHEMICAL BONDING AND VALENCY • GLASS FIBER • PLASTICS • POLYMER AND POLYMERIZATION • ROAD CONSTRUCTION • RUBBER, NATURAL • RUBBER, SYNTHETIC

Aerial Photography

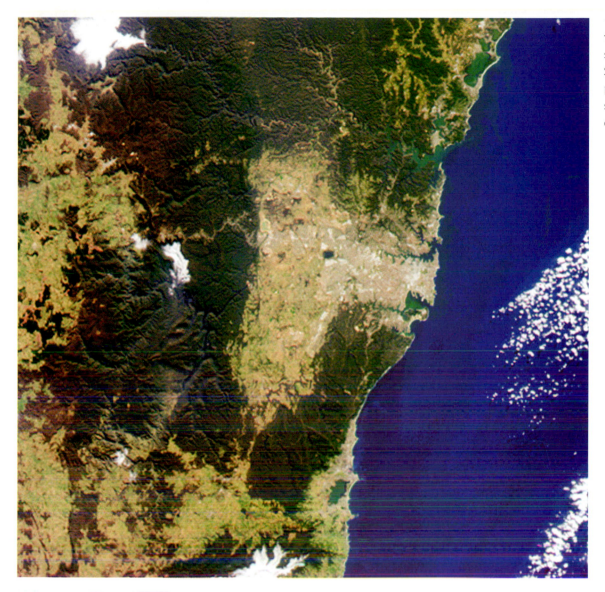

◄ This photograph, taken by the *Terra* satellite, shows the area around Sydney (the central pale region) on the southeastern coast of Australia.

Aerial photography—taking photographs of the surface of Earth from the air—has many important civil uses, such as mapping and crop surveying, as well as military applications, which include spying and battlefield reconnaissance.

History and development

Photographs have been taken from the air almost since the beginnings of photography itself. The first aerial photograph known was taken from the basket of a balloon over France in 1856. By the 1880s, photographs were being taken from balloons, kites, and even rockets in the course of experiments in Europe and, in 1909, from aircraft both in France and the United States.

The French were early pioneers in both aviation and photography. At the outbreak of World War I, they already had some aerial photographs taken in peacetime of the very places the German army was invading.

The French photographs provided the inspiration for improved methods of aerial photography. J. T. C. Moore Brabazon (later Lord Brabazon), a keen photographer in charge of the British Army's air reconnaissance team, experimented with old-fashioned bellows cameras but found them impractical for aerial photography, because they could not be kept still in the slipstream of an aircraft flying at 80 mph (130 km/h). So Brabazon designed a camera for insertion in the floor of an airplane—the first aerial photography camera built especially for that purpose. By the end of the war, these aerial cameras had developed into huge devices with focal lengths as great as 6 ft. (1.83 m) to give fine detail.

Brabazon also introduced a stereoscope to view pairs of pictures taken from slightly different points. In exaggerating the three-dimensional effect, the process allowed the height of objects taken from above to be measured.

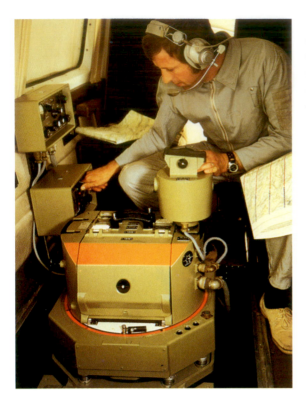

◀ A large, custom-built aerial photography camera. This type of camera is fixed to the floor of the aircraft and is used for vertical photography.

From spying to mapping

At the end of World War I, the newly developed techniques of aerial photography were applied to peaceful uses—though use in spying still continued. The main applications were mapmaking and surveying, but there were other uses. In Canada, for example, forests being grown for timber were photographed from the air as early as 1921. This was an ideal way of checking on trees.

Another use of aerial photography was discovered in the United States in the 1920s and 1930s. The Agricultural Production and Marketing Board regularly photographed farms from the air to check what crops were being grown. In this way, they were able not only to compile statistics but also to detect false claims made by farmers for the subsidies that were paid for growing certain crops. This unusual peacetime spying made them extremely unpopular.

By 1938, it had become obvious to everyone that Germany was preparing for war. In Britain, the Royal Air Force commissioned the renowned Australian aerial photographer Sidney Cotton to get as many pictures of military installations as he could without attracting attention.

Cotton had been taking aerial photographs since the early 1920s. His method of tackling the job was most ingenious. First of all, he used RAF funds to buy a Lockheed Electra, a fast civil airplane that he modified by installing three cameras under the floor; the cameras were hidden by a close-fitting sliding panel when not in use. He also arranged for a stream of warm air to be blown into the camera compartment inside the

▼ An infrared picture of the San Francisco Bay area and the Golden Gate Bridge taken from an aircraft flying at a height of 60,000 ft. (18,000 m).

airplane. The ventilation prevented the camera from fogging up or freezing at high altitudes and low temperatures, a problem that had dogged aerial photographers for years.

Regular aerial photography proved vital during World War II, when Sidney Cotton was given the job of organizing and running the first British photographic reconnaissance unit. Frequent pictures enabled a reference file on a place to be built up so that troop movements, new buildings, and unusual events could all be observed.

Current techniques

Today, aerial photographs may be taken using either an airplane or satellite. In airplane aerial photography, there are two basic techniques, oblique and vertical. Oblique photography is the simpler—it involves flying over a site in a small plane while a photographer on board takes pictures using a handheld camera through an open window, where the line of sight is at an angle to the ground. Such pictures are used mainly for their pictorial value or for illustrating various types of land forms.

Vertical photography is a much more exacting technique and uses large custom-built cameras mounted in the floor of the aircraft. As the term suggests, the cameras look vertically downward.

A typical camera has a high-quality lens of 6 in. (15 cm) focal length, carefully designed so as not to introduce distortions into the image. The camera uses a 250 ft. (76 m) roll of film 9 in.

(23 cm) wide and has a suction back to pull the film flat while the pictures are being taken. Exposure times vary from 1/200 to 1/1000 of a second, depending on light conditions and the movement of the image being photographed.

The heights used for aerial surveys vary with local conditions and requirements but are usually well above 1,300 ft. (400 m). The rate at which photographs are taken varies with the image speed, since the aim is to make each shot overlap the former by around 60 percent. In this way, stereoscopic views are taken. Picture-taking rates vary from a few seconds to one taken every couple of minutes.

Survey photographs may be taken in black and white on panchromatic film or on film sensitive to the infrared wavelengths. Infrared radiation penetrates haze much better than visible light, which makes photographs taken from high altitudes much clearer. In addition, the amount of infrared radiation emitted by an object changes with its temperature. Therefore, it is possible, for example, to distinguish between warm and cold water so that the discharges from factories into rivers can be monitored to make sure they are not overheating the water. In addition, the amount of heat absorbed from the Sun by living and dead vegetation is different, so the state of a field or forest can easily be seen at a glance.

Because infrared pictures cannot be printed in infrared, false-color film is generally used. This film renders infrared as red, red as green, and green as blue and is insensitive to blue light. Another device, the airscan thermograph, uses an electronic scanner similar to a television camera to record infrared radiation only, ignoring visible colors altogether.

More detailed information can be obtained with the multiband camera, a device that takes nine simultaneous photographic images of the same scene. It is loaded with nine combinations of film and color filters.

Pictures can also be taken with side-looking airborne radar (SLAR), which has the advantage that it works in complete darkness or fog, making it particularly suitable for military use. Unfortunately, the quality of the picture is not very good, though it is steadily being improved.

Pictures from space

Since the war, the rapid growth in space technology has led to enormous advances in vertical photography and mapping using high-resolution equipment in satellites.

By 1984, no less than seven meteorological satellites were in orbit around Earth at an altitude of around 22,000 miles (35,000 km). Their orbits

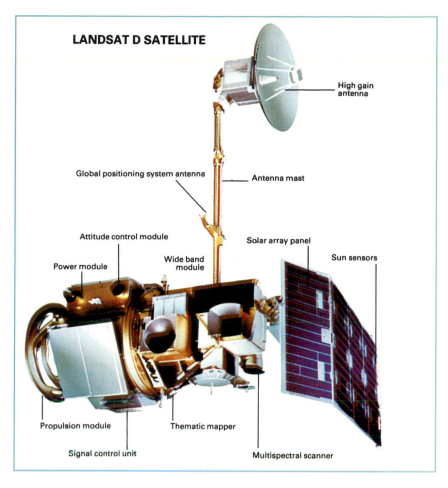

LANDSAT D SATELLITE

High gain antenna

Global positioning system antenna

Antenna mast

Attitude control module

Power module

Wide band module

Solar array panel

Sun sensors

Propulsion module

Thematic mapper

Signal control unit

Multispectral scanner

were synchronized with the rotation of Earth so that they appeared to hover motionless over their allotted sectors of the planet beaming down meteorological information as part of a joint World Weather Watch system.

In 1972, the United States launched the first of a series of Landsat satellites designed to take high resolution photographs of Earth. The latest addition to this series is *Landsat 7*, launched in April 1999, which orbits Earth 14 times per day taking a variety of different photographic images used in mapping, global-change research, and land-cover monitoring. This satellite is designed to regularly monitor its own performance and correct any problems, such as when the scanning mirror and scanning mechanisms lose synchronization.

With the advent of the reusable space shuttle, these applications have become cheaper and easier to maintain and are already taking over many of the tasks previously carried out by conventional high-altitude aircraft. In addition, digital cameras and the digitizing of images have further developed the methods for making and disseminating aerial photographic images.

▲ On each orbit of 35 minutes, *Landsat D* traced a path 114 miles (185 km) wide over Earth's surface. It carried a wideband communications system using NASA tracking and data-relay satellites (TDRS) and ground-based stations. *Landsat 7*, the latest satellite in this series, orbits Earth every 99 minutes.

SEE ALSO: AIRCRAFT DESIGN • CAMERA • ELECTROMAGNETIC RADIATION • LENS • PHOTOGRAPHIC FILM AND PROCESSING • SATELLITE, ARTIFICIAL

Aerodynamics

Aerodynamics (like hydrodynamics) is a branch of fluid dynamics, which is the study of fluids in motion. The fundamental laws governing the movements of gases, such as air, and liquids, such as water, are identical. The equations representing these natural laws are, however, so complex that, although formulated more than 100 years ago, they cannot be easily solved to account for all systems and conditions.

Even today, it takes the most powerful computers to solve the complex equations that govern the flow of fluids around irregularly shaped objects. It is a sobering thought to realize that we may be able to design craft that can enter space and glide back to Earth, but the detailed description of the way a river erodes its banks and changes course still relies a great deal on experiment rather than calculation.

Aerodynamics is of crucial importance in the design of jet engines, the turbines that drive electricity generators, and even the family automobile. Reducing aerodynamic drag on anything that moves through the atmosphere, be it a car, an airplane, or a train, means greater efficiency and less fuel consumption. The study of aerodynamics in the modern world has received a huge boost from the need to conserve energy.

Air is by no means as insubstantial as it might at first appear. At sea level on a mild day, the density of air is about 0.077 lbs. per cu. ft. (1.23 kg/m²). A large sedan car of about 20 sq. ft. (1.9 m²) cross section moving at 30 mph (50 km/h) must displace about 71 lbs. (32 kg) of air every second. Good aerodynamic design helps the air flow over and around a car in a smooth controlled sweep, minimizing the distance each molecule of air must be moved and thus minimizing drag forces.

The equations that describe in a general fashion the motion of fluids were first developed by C. L. M. H. Navier in 1820 and subsequently perfected by the Irish physicist George Stokes in 1845. These equations, now called the Navier–Stokes equations, relate velocity, density, pressure, compressibility, viscosity, and spatial dimensions of fluid. Because of the number of variables involved, the subject of fluid dynamics has been broken down into a number of subdivisions where certain conditions predominate and others can be ignored. The result is a whole series of solutions—each applying in a limited range of circumstances. Historically, hydrodynamics came first and includes the greater number of assumptions. Water is, however, almost incompressible, that is, the density of water does not change with the pressure applied to it. This property of water and other liquids simplifies the original Navier–Stokes equations.

Aerodynamic principles

At the beginning of the present century, aerodynamics, with the possibility of flight in air, began to attract more attention than hydrodynamics.

Because of the concentration of effort, aerodynamics, based on the same assumptions as hydrodynamics, soon outstripped its parent. The German physicist Ludwig Prandtl showed that the effect of viscosity for flow around streamlined (smooth) bodies was confined to a thin layer immediately adjacent to the body. This region is called the boundary layer. Outside the boundary layer, viscous forces are negligible, and consequently, potential flow theories apply. The analysis of streamlined bodies enabled airfoil design to advance rapidly.

Whereas smooth, streamlined bodies have an unbroken and stable boundary layer, bluff (unstreamlined) bodies do not. The flow starts to separate because of misbehavior of the boundary layer, and potential flow solutions, even away from the body, become inaccurate. Even today, no complete theory for low-speed flow around bluff bodies exists, but an understanding of what happens physically has been built up over the years. As aircraft speeds increased, it was found that the assumption of incompressibility introduced errors. The reason for this phenomenon can be explained by Bernoulli's equation.

Bernoulli's equation (derived by the Swiss physicist Daniel Bernoulli, who did much early work in hydrodynamics) is a statement of energy conservation in a fluid. A fluid, like any moving body, has kinetic energy through its motion and potential energy because of its potential to move under the influence of Earth's gravitation. At all points in a fluid, there is a static pressure proportional to the height of fluid above that point—this pressure is a measure of the potential energy of the fluid at that point. The kinetic energy of the fluid is proportional to the square of the velocity and gives rise to a dynamic pressure. If no energy is added to or taken away from the fluid stream, total energy will be conserved even if there is an

▶ Computer-aided design programs can help engineers develop an aerodynamically efficient shape for new trains, automobiles, and airplanes before expensive prototypes are built.

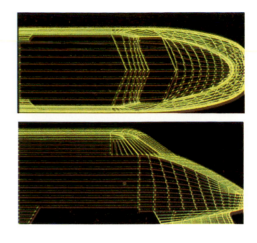

interchange between kinetic energy (dynamic pressure) and potential energy (static pressure)—this is the principle behind Bernoulli's equation.

Because dynamic pressure is proportional to the square of the fluid velocity, the rate at which pressure changes with increasing velocity will depend on the absolute velocity as well as its rate of change. Consequently, the higher the speeds involved, the larger will be the pressure changes and the greater the density changes because of compressibility. Below 126 mph (210 km/h), the density changes can be ignored and air can be treated as incompressible, but above this airspeed, the assumption becomes increasingly inaccurate.

Mach numbers and the speed of sound

Sound is a pressure wave of small magnitude, and its speed of propagation in the fluid is called the speed of sound. The airflow around a body creates higher air pressures in the vicinity that travel upstream, giving advance warning of the presence of the body. Because of this pressure wave, the air moves in a curved path ahead of the body, passing around it with the minimum of disturbance.

If the airspeed is greater than the speed of sound, these warning signals cannot propagate upstream at all, and no warning is given—this phenomenon is called supersonic flow. In this situation, the air must change direction suddenly when it encounters the body. If the deviation asked of it is small, it does so, producing a small-amplitude shock wave attached to the body. If the deviation is large, a large-amplitude shock wave can move ahead of the body (large-amplitude waves travel faster), and behind this shock wave, the air is slowed to subsonic speed. These shock waves are commonly called sonic booms.

With such different flow systems on either side of the speed of sound, it becomes imperative to know whether the airspeed is above or below this value. Unfortunately, the speed of sound does

◀ A BMW automobile body undergoes trials in the manufacturer's wind tunnel. It is through such testing at all stages of the design process that the necessary aerodynamic improvements can be incorporated in the final production model.

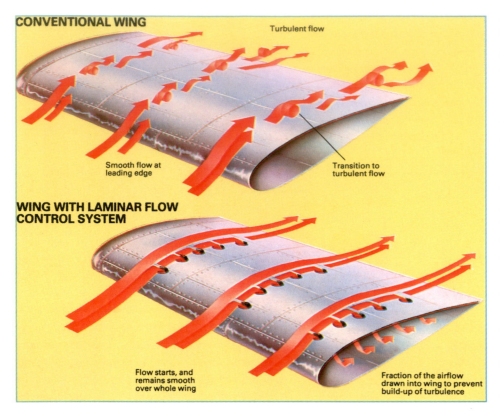

CONVENTIONAL WING

Turbulent flow

Smooth flow at
leading edge

Transition to
turbulent flow

**WING WITH LAMINAR FLOW
CONTROL SYSTEM**

Flow starts, and
remains smooth
over whole wing

Fraction of the airflow
drawn into wing to prevent
build-up of turbulence

Lift and drag

For an airplane to get off the ground, it must produce enough lift under its wings to support the weight of the aircraft and enable it to climb into the sky. Lift is a force that acts at right angles to the direction of motion and arises from the difference in the speed of the air flowing along the upper and lower surfaces of the wing. Airplane wings typically have a rounded leading (front) edge and a sharp trailing edge. As the air meets the front edge, it splits into two streams, one going over the wing, the other under. To produce lift, the flows, which must both be asymmetrical, can be created by curving the wing surfaces and setting the wing at a slight angle to the fuselage. As a result, a faster flow is created along the upper surface, reducing the air pressure upon it and lifting the wing into the air.

Drag is the force that resists the forward motion of an object and is influenced by its shape. Designers try to reduce drag by streamlining the contours of trains, automobiles, and airplanes so that they present a profile that air can flow over smoothly. There are three types of drag: friction drag, which occurs in the boundary layer around the surface of an object; form drag, where the air flowing past the object breaks away to form eddies that take energy away from the object and slow it down; and induced drag, which occurs as a consequence of lift and causes vortices to form behind the wing tips of airplanes.

The supercritical wing is among the most influential advances in aerodynamics. Its aerofoil section shape delays the increase in drag that begins when shock waves form, allowing the aircraft to fly faster and more efficiently. The winglet has been equally widely exploited. This wingtip aerofoil turns wasted energy in the vortex of air cast off by the wing into useful thrust and also offsets the drag that accompanies lift.

The key to significantly reducing subsonic aircraft drag lies in achieving laminar flow—a smooth flow, with no eddies. The airflow over a wing is generally turbulent, except near the leading edge, where it is still laminar. Laminar flow is fragile as it exists only in a layer a few millimeters thick close to the wing surface.

not have a unique value but varies with temperature. In this situation, it becomes convenient to divide the airspeed by the speed of sound—this ratio is named the Mach number, for Ernest Mach, an Austrian scientist who studied the flight of bullets. Jet fighters have been capable of reaching speeds up to Mach 5 since the 1960s.

When airspeeds increase still further, the rise in temperature and pressure behind shock waves becomes so large that the air dissociates, that is, some of the air's nitrogen and oxygen molecules break down into atoms. Behind the body, temperatures and pressures decrease and the molecules reform—a process called hypersonic flow.

Slip flow

Atmospheric pressure at sea level is caused by the weight of air above the point of measurement. Consequently, at higher altitudes, pressure and density decrease. There comes a height—over 50 miles (80 km) above sea level—where the density is so low that the mean free path (the average distance between collisions of the molecules) is the same order of magnitude as the body under consideration. Air no longer behaves as an entity (usually called a continuum), and pressure and forces become the result of individual molecular collisions with the body surface. This part of the subject is called free molecular, or Newtonian, flow. There is no sharp division between continuum and molecular flow, rather a progressive change, and this part of the subject is called the slip flow.

▲ Turbulent airflow over an airplane wing is reduced by the incorporation of a laminar flow control system, whereby some of the airflow close to the surface that would otherwise become turbulent on contact can be drawn off via holes to improve aerodynamic performance and thus save fuel.

▼ By introducing smoke into a wind tunnel, designers can see where areas of turbulence are forming along an aircraft's fuselage.

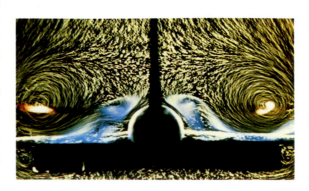

◀ Familiar objects can be redesigned through the application of aerodynamic techniques. This helmet has been designed to help competitive skiers present a smoother profile while racing.

◀ The prototype HiMAT all-purpose fighter aircraft included a number of upright fins to help reduce the formation of vortices behind the wings.

Certain airfoil sections can sustain laminar flow over more of the wing, at least while the aircraft is cruising. Natural laminar flow, as this technology is called, has been applied already to business jets to reduce drag. However, preventing turbulent flow is difficult during takeoff and landing, when the wing is working hard.

Large aircraft, such as commercial airliners and military transports, pose a greater problem. Their large wings generally have movable leading edges to increase lift during takeoff and landing. When these devices retract during the flight, they leave gaps that can trigger turbulent flow.

The answer is to sustain laminar flow artificially by suction. Called hybrid laminar flow control, this technique damps out disturbances in the thin layer of smooth airflow, delaying the transition to turbulent flow. The turbulent air is siphoned off through thousands of tiny, laser-drilled holes in the forward part of the wing surface.

Problems with laminar flow control

Laminar flow can be disrupted by small imperfections in the wing surface, such as ice and insects, which can also block the suction holes. Wings will require regular cleaning, possibly before every flight. The wing profile must be smooth, requiring very tight tolerances during manufacture.

Questions remain over the range of wing sizes, sweep angles, and aircraft speeds at which natural laminar flow can be maintained and those at which hybrid laminar flow control will be required. Supersonic laminar flow control is another area currently being explored by designers. NASA has fitted two arrow-wing F-16XL fighters with a test surface, or "glove," on the inner, highly swept sections of their left wings. These gloves are covered with laser-drilled holes through which the turbulent flow is siphoned off. Flight test results from these planes show that laminar flow can be sustained at supersonic speeds.

A new wing design

In studies over a number of years, a configuration has been evolved for the next generation of aircraft that uses an "arrow" wing. The inner part of the wing is much like that of Concorde, broad and highly swept. The outer sections on each side are more like a conventional wing. The resulting wing is shaped like an arrowhead.

One design using this shape is the blended-wing body, which is being developed by McDonnell Douglas. The engines, wings, and body have been integrated into a single thick airfoil-shaped wing capable of carrying 800 passengers at a speed of around 600 mph (960 km/h). Because all-wing designs experience substantial aerodynamic drag at these speeds, the airflow over the wing is carefully simulated on computers during the design stage. One method of reducing drag is to move the center of gravity toward the back of the airplane. Another method under investigation is to divert the air flowing over or near the surface of the wing through the engines, though this idea will require tests to determine how turbulence will affect the engine inlet.

▶ This recumbent bicycle features a curved windshield and is set very low on the ground to make it aerodynamically efficient.

SEE ALSO: Air • Aircraft design • Airliner • Ballistics • Dynamics • Glider • Hydrodynamics • Space shuttle • Supersonic flight • Ultralight aircraft • Wind tunnel

Aerosol

First patented in the United States in 1941, aerosol spray cans have been used as convenient packages for an ever-increasing range of products, including paints, cosmetics, insecticides, adhesives, and foodstuffs.

Today, most aerosol cans are made of aluminum and are monobloc in construction—the base and sides are stamped in one piece. Some cans, however, are still made of tin plate with soldered seams. At the top of an aerosol can, there is a simple plastic valve to control the spray. From the bottom of the valve, a flexible dip tube runs down to the bottom of the can. The can is filled with the product to be sprayed and the propellant, a compressed gas such as butane. The gas is partly liquefied by the pressure in the can, but there is a layer of free gas above the liquid. As the can empties, liquefied gas vaporizes to fill the space.

The valve is normally held shut by the pressure in the can and by the coil spring directly below the valve stem. When the push button is pressed, it forces the valve stem down in its housing, uncovering a small hole that leads up through the stem to the nozzle in the button and allowing the product to be forced up the dip tube by the gas pressure in the can. The nozzle is shaped to give a spray or a continuous stream.

To produce a fine mist, a propellant is used that mixes with the product. The two leave the nozzle together, and the propellant evaporates as soon as it reaches the air, breaking the product into tiny droplets. The same technique used with a more viscous liquid and a wider nozzle results in a foam. For a continuous stream of liquid or more viscous material, a nonmixing propellant is used, and the dip tube reaches into the product.

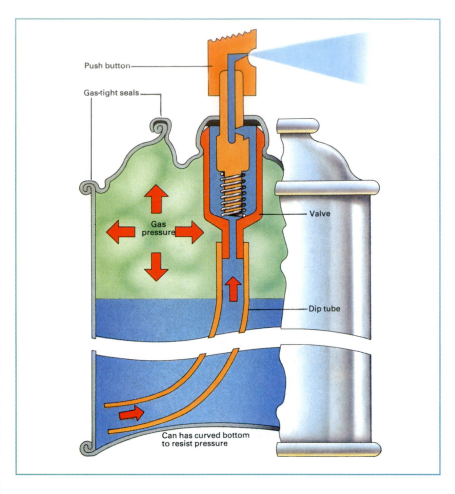

▲ Section through an aerosol can. Gas pressure created by the propellant forces liquid down the can and up the dip tube, emerging from the nozzle as a spray.

A different arrangement is used in cans containing very viscous substances. The product is enclosed in a plastic bag attached to the underside of the valve, and the propellant fills the space between the bag and the can, thus stopping the product from sticking to the sides of the can.

Dangers

The widespread use of aerosol cans using chlorofluorocarbons (CFCs) as the propellant led scientists to believe by the late 1970s that the ozone layer in the upper atmosphere, which filters out harmful ultraviolet radiation from the sun, could be destroyed by the large quantities of CFCs in the gas being released into the air. In 1978, federal controls were introduced to ban the use of CFCs, and today CFCs are banned throughout many countries of the world. Other propellants are now employed, notably butane, which, however, is dangerously flammable. Alternative propellants include compressed air and blends of water, alcohol, and ether.

FACT FILE

- *The aerosol spraying system has important medical uses. It is possible to dissolve drugs in an aqueous solution that can be atomized in an inhaler. The particles of the drug solution are sufficiently small to enable a wide distribution over the internal surfaces of the lungs.*

- *In ink-jet printing, a combination of aerosol technique and electric charging of the droplets results in very accurate printing that can be carried out at high speed.*

SEE ALSO: CANNING AND BOTTLING • FOOD PRESERVATION AND PACKAGING • SPRAY GUN • VALVE, MECHANICAL • VENTURI EFFECT

Aerospace Industry

◄ NASA's reusable space shuttles span the scope of aerospace engineering. They are designed to fly under rocket propulsion in airless space and to use aerodynamic lift when they fly through air in Earth's atmosphere. Unlike other spacecraft, space shuttles end their missions by landing on runways in the same way as conventional aircraft, but with the use of parachutes to reduce stopping distances.

The aerospace industry designs, constructs, and maintains civil and military aircraft, spacecraft, and missiles. It has been at the forefront in the introduction of new technologies—from mass production to computer-aided design—and in pioneering new materials, such as heat-resistant ceramics, high-strength lightweight alloys, and high-performance polymers. Constant endeavors to improve the performance and efficiency of aerospace vehicles have stimulated an ever deeper understanding of aerodynamics and the development of novel propulsion systems.

Mass production

In the early years of the 20th century, aircraft were built from wood and canvas by skilled individuals, many of whom were drawn from other woodworking trades. Each aircraft was unique, and was the product of one person's thoughts on how best to achieve flight.

The outbreak of World War I in 1914 was soon followed by a sudden need for thousands of aircraft for airborne combat. The response of the fledgling aircraft-building industry was to adopt mass-production techniques developed in 1913 by the U.S. industrialist Henry Ford for the automobile industry. Dedicated factories were built for the large-scale manufacture of components and assembly of aircraft using streamlined mass-production techniques and capable of being staffed by unskilled workers.

By 1918—the end of World War I—the British manufacturer Sopwith had made more than 9,000 units of its Camel aircraft by mass-production techniques. French and German manufacturers achieved similar feats, and while the United States entered the war only in its last year, the embryonic U.S. aerospace industry supplied many aircraft during the conflict, including the Curtiss Jenny.

The 1920s and 1930s saw gradual changes in aircraft design and construction. Wood and canvas gave way to aluminum as the principal structural material, and monoplanes (with one wing on either side of the fuselage) gained favor over biplanes. The power and reliability of aircraft engines increased, and aircraft became more widely used for passenger transport as ranges and payloads increased and comfort improved.

Rearmament in the late 1930s and the outbreak of World War II further stimulated the manufacture of aircraft and airborne weapons in Europe, the United States, and Japan. The aerospace industry had by this point spread worldwide and would change dramatically by the end of the war in 1945. Aero engines became more powerful and sophisticated and were made in vast numbers, the jet engine was developed and tested, and the German V-2 missiles provided practical demonstrations of rocket-powered flight. Also, the introduction of radar and other navigational techniques established the avionics industry.

The huge demand for aircraft during wartime meant that aircraft manufacturers grew enormously. By 1945, the U.S. aerospace industry alone had produced more than 300,000 aircraft for the war effort. When the war ended, production capacity far exceeded demand. Many aircraft producers went out of business; others amalgamated or reduced capacity to suit the market.

Diversification

The aircraft manufacturers that survived the postwar shrinkage of the aerospace market adjusted the focus of their businesses. Whereas the worldwide market for military aircraft had diminished, civil aviation using jet-powered airliners started to grow in the early 1950s.

Those manufacturers that stayed in the military market started to develop more sophisticated aircraft, such as supersonic jet fighters and helicopters. The main markets for such aircraft were in the countries of NATO (the North Atlantic Treaty Organization) and the Warsaw Pact.

The space race

The late 1950s also saw the postwar struggle for military and technological supremacy between East and West shift its focus to space. Both the United States and the USSR wanted to be first to launch a satellite into space, then to launch piloted vehicles into space, and ultimately to fly humans to the Moon and back.

While the most obvious goal of these efforts was prestige, it was also clear that a country that could launch a satellite into orbit would also be capable of producing intercontinental ballistic missiles—ICBMs. Fear of losing supremacy in the development of weapons that could carry

▼ An assembly hangar at McDonnell Douglas' factory in Long Beach, California. Five C-17 Globemaster III transport planes can be seen in various stages of production.

high-yield nuclear warheads over huge distances was therefore a major driving force in the development of aerospace technology.

Both Soviet and U.S. rocket research teams included scientists who had worked on the German V-2 during the war. Prominent among these scientists was Wernher von Braun, who worked for the United States from the end of World War II.

The Soviets were the first to launch satellites into space: *Sputnik 1* on October 4, 1957, and *Sputnik 2* on November 3 of the same year. The United States followed with *Explorer 1*, launched January 31, 1958, and *Vanguard 2*, launched March 17, 1958. These early satellites measured solar radiation, cosmic rays, and magnetic fields, and they transmitted their measurements to Earth as radio signals. *Sputnik 2* also sent measurements from probes attached to Laika, a dog.

The first probe to reach the Moon was the Soviet *Luna 2*, which was launched September 12, 1959, and crashed into the Moon's surface after a 36-hour journey. After several moon shots by both Soviet and U.S. governments, *Luna 9*—launched January 31, 1966—became the first probe to make a soft landing, one of the prerequisites for human flight to the Moon.

Meanwhile, other programs were putting humans into space. The first man in space, the Soviet cosmonaut Yuri Gagarin, made one orbit of Earth in *Vostok 1* on April 12, 1961; the first woman in space was the Soviet cosmonaut Valentina Tereshkova, who occupied *Vostok 6* for 48 Earth orbits after its launch on June 16, 1963. The first U.S. astronaut in space was Alan Shepard, Jr., who on May 5, 1961, flew the *Freedom 7* Mercury spacecraft on a 15-minute suborbital flight. In December 1968, the U.S. spacecraft *Apollo 8* made 10 Moon orbits with three astronauts on board, and on July 20, 1969, the U.S. astronauts Edwin Aldrin, Jr., and Neil Armstrong landed on the surface of the Moon in the lunar module of *Apollo 11* before returning safely to Earth with colleague Michael Collins.

The last humans visited the Moon with *Apollo 17* in December 1972. Since then, long-range space flight has turned to crewless flights to more distant bodies in our solar system. Probes have landed on Mars and Venus, and they have flown close to Jupiter, Mercury, Neptune, Saturn, and Uranus, observing the planets and their moons and transmitting their observations to Earth.

Satellites and space stations

From the early days of space travel, satellites have been used to observe Earth's surface and atmosphere for military reconnaissance, meteorological studies and geological surveys. Satellite-borne observatories have been used to detect nonvisible radiation that is obscured from terrestrial observatories by Earth's atmosphere. The development of onboard solar and nuclear power sources has greatly prolonged the satellites' working lives, making them useful as permanent relays for telecommunications and beacons for navigational systems, such as the U.S. Defense Department's global positioning system.

Space stations are orbital vehicles that serve as accommodation for crew, who perform experiments that take advantage of the weightless conditions in orbit. The first space station was the Soviet *Salyut 1*, launched on April 19, 1971, and boarded for 24 days in June 1971. *Salyut 1* had a mass of 20.5 tons (18.6 tonnes). Six more Salyut space stations were launched by 1991.

The first U.S. space station—*Skylab*—was much larger than the Salyuts, with a mass of 98 tons (89 tonnes) when it was launched on May 25, 1973. *Skylab* served as a platform for solar observations, experiments into crystal growth in weightless conditions, and studies of the effects of long-term weightlessness on human health. *Skylab* disintegrated on its reentry in July 1979.

Skylab started a tradition for international collaboration in space travel. Germany and Italy, for example, contributed some of the modules needed to provide living and working space for the scientists and astronauts taking part, and Britain developed a platform for experiments.

The next development in space stations was *Mir*, a vehicle that was launched by the USSR on February 20, 1986 and stayed in orbit until late March, 2001. During its 25 years in orbit, *Mir* was augmented by the addition of four laboratory modules and a utilities module. One of the core module's six docking stations remained free to accept visiting space vehicles that delivered supplies and carried crews to and from the station.

The next great space station to go into space was the International Space Station (ISS), whose first element was launched on November 20, 1998. A collaboration between the United States, 11 European nations, Brazil, Canada, Japan, and Russia, the ISS will comprise around 100 elements by 2004, when some 44 construction missions are expected to have been completed. The ISS will by then have a mass of around 450 tons (408 tonnes) and will have a working and living space with a volume of 46,000 cu. ft. (1,300 m³)— greater than that of the largest model Boeing 747 aircraft. The International Space Station will have two robot arms that it will use for its own assembly and repairs: one 58 ft. (17.7 m) in length, the other 12 ft. (3.7 m) in length.

▲ Super lightweight composite-material wings for the highly maneuverable Grumman X29 fighter plane are made as a single component on an old-fashioned jig but use the very latest in aerospace technology to achieve high degrees of tolerance.

Space shuttles

NASA started to develop its Space Transportation System—the "space shuttles"—in response to the growing demand for transport to put satellites and space stations in orbit and to maintain and supply them once in place. The space shuttles are unique craft: they are launched with the assistance of huge solid-rocket boosters (SRBs), maneuvered in space using rocket propulsion, and steered back through the atmosphere to an aircraft-style runway landing on Earth.

The first shuttle, *Columbia*, was test flown on April 12, 1981, and entered working duty in November 1982, when it put two telecommunications satellites into orbit. Since then, NASA's fleet of space shuttles have played key roles in the deployment, repair, maintenance, and retrieval of numerous satellites and space stations.

During the 1970s, when the space shuttle was in development, the European Space Agency developed the Ariane expendable launch vessel. Although not reusable, Ariane has proved to be a relatively low-cost means for delivering satellites and their associated supplies into space.

Computers in aviation

Many recent advances in aviation are directly attributable to the use of computers and electronic control systems. The influence of computers starts at the design stage of a new aircraft, when computers are used to assess the aerodynamic properties of a design. Computer-aided design (CAD) and computer-aided manufacturing (CAM) help prepare for construction.

Sophisticated avionics (aviation electronics) is a major feature of modern aircraft and accounts for around 25 percent of the cost of a finished aircraft. Digital computers manage the information from navigation equipment, control systems, and engine sensors and display the status of the craft on monitor screens or on head-up displays. The specialist companies that develop and produce avionics equipment now represent a vital and growing segment of the industry.

Another important application of control electronics is in the fly-by-wire (FBW) system, pioneered by Airbus Industrie in its A320. In FBW aircraft, the motions of a joystick are converted into signals that actuate the servomotors to move the plane's control surfaces. This system replaces mechanical and hydraulic linkages.

New materials

An important aspect of the aerospace industry is the impetus it has given to the development of new materials for use in atmospheric and spaceflight. In some cases, the value of appropriate high-performance materials for aerospace applications can offset development costs that would be excessive for other fields of application.

One of the earliest materials innovations in aerospace was the adoption in the 1930s of aluminum alloys for aircraft construction. These alloys are well suited to the task, since they combine great tensile strength with low density. Modern alloys include high-strength combinations of aluminum and lithium. Structural elements that must bear intense stress tend to be made from ultra-high-strength steel, whereas components that must withstand heavy loads at high temperatures—turbine blades, for example—are made using titanium alloys.

Other materials that present good combinations of high strength and low density include the aromatic polyamide Kevlar—a high-tech relative of nylon—and carbon fiber. These fibrous materials and fiberglass are sometimes used in composites. Since 1966, increasing numbers of components have been made by laying sheets of fibers in molds, impregnating them with thermosetting resin, and then curing (setting) the molded composite in huge ovens or autoclaves.

Construction using composites rather than alloys reduces overall weight and practically eliminates the risk of structural fatigue problems. Furthermore, several conventional components can be unified in relatively few composite-made parts, so the number of components can be reduced dramatically. The entire wing of the *Harrier II* jump jet is made of a carbon-fiber composite material. Airbus pioneered carbon-fiber composites for civilian aircraft with the carbon tail fin of its A310 wide-body; the entire tail ends of the A320, A330, and A340 aircraft are carbon-fiber composites.

Developments in materials for spaceflight include the heat-resistant ceramic tiles used on NASA's space shuttles. These tiles become hot through friction during reentry, but they radiate their heat and protect the hull from overheating.

Structural developments

Modern passenger jets have to be designed to withstand 60,000 or more hours of bending and flexing in rough air. Not only does the structure have to resist fatigue, but there also have to be duplicate load paths. This safety feature ensures that if one part cracks, another will still carry the load until the cracked part is replaced.

Future developments might include large single-crystal metal components. Single crystals of a given material have outstanding strength and fatigue resistance when compared with multicrystal samples of the same material, as has been demonstrated in single-crystal jet turbine blades. If components such as wings could be made from single crystals, they would be thinner, lighter, and therefore more efficient than current components.

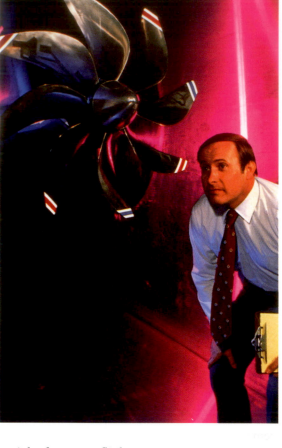

▲ The propeller makes a comeback. This propfan developed by the U.S. space agency NASA is an advanced means of propulsion that could pull an airplane through the air at speeds of nearly Mach 0.8. Each blade is designed to simulate a high-performance swept wing and is in fact a cross between a turbine, a wing, and a propeller.

SEE ALSO: AIRCRAFT-CONTROL ENGINEERING • AIRCRAFT DESIGN • AIRCRAFT ENGINE • AIRLINER • AIRPORT • AIR-TRAFFIC CONTROL • HEAD-UP DISPLAY • INERTIAL GUIDANCE • MATERIALS SCIENCE • MISSILE • PILOTLESS AIRCRAFT • SPACE SHUTTLE • SPACE STATION

Agricultural Machinery

◄ Combine harvesters often work in convoys to cover the vast plains of North America. The paddle wheel on the front of the vehicle turns and pushes the crop against a cutting bar. The crop enters the harvester and is threshed to separate the grain from the rest of the plant.

Of all the machines to be found on even the most technologically advanced farm today, the tractor remains the most versatile. Since the first self-propelled models began superseding the horse on farms at the begining of the 20th century, the tractor and its many derivatives have revolutionized farming methods and changed the face of the landscape throughout the world.

Tractor

The early tractors functioned chiefly for the purpose of heavy work, but the introduction of the light tricycle tractor in 1924, with its ability for easy maneuver, paved the way for greater versatility in tractor design, so they became useful in crop cultivation as well. This development heralded a new era for farming, and it signaled the demise of the workhorse on farms.

The most radical alteration in design was made by Harry Ferguson, who in the 1930s introduced the hydraulically controlled mounted implement. By the use of three linkage arms, the plow or cultivator effectively became part of the tractor. The resistance of the soil to the implement was transferred through the upper link and became a downward force onto the tractor, providing much additional grip and stability.

Almost without exception, tractors are powered by diesel engines. The engines have from one to eight cylinders, and turbochargers can be used to increase power output. Tractors have a heavy-duty type of clutch, and because of the wide range of operations, many of which have to be carried out at precise speeds, a four-speed gearbox is commonly used. This gearbox is often augmented by an epicyclic system to double the number of gears available.

If the tractor is to be used with a front loader or forklift gear, a torque converter, which allows extremely fast changing from forward to reverse, is often fitted. If the vehicle is mainly for use on rough terrain, a three-forward, one-reverse transmission is often used in conjunction with an automatic power-shift torque converter. This arrangement allows fast clutchless changes while on the move.

There are three main types of tractors in common use today. The row-crop tractor is a lightweight design, featuring high ground clearance, adjustable wheel track widths, a small turning circle, and good visibility, and as its name suggests, these features are especially useful for the operating of hoeing machinery close to row crops. Its engine power ranges between 30 to 45 horsepower. The general-purpose tractor is heavier and more powerful (around 50–100 horsepower) and is used for most work on arable and livestock farms. It generally has heavy-duty hydraulics and a drawbar for lifting considerable loads. The third type is the four-wheel-drive tractor. These can be of two sorts. It may be big and powerful (up to 200 horsepower) with four equally large wheels. These models are best suited to plowing and heavy cultivation. The other four-wheel-drive model has small front wheels, a less powerful engine (70–90 horsepower), and can be used as a general-purpose tractor. The advantages of a four-wheel-drive model are its ability to use more power and the improved traction, flotation, and stability it offers, making it an ideal tractor for wet and slippery weather conditions. In the United States and Canada, large articulated four-wheel drives are commonly used. They work fast, having engine powers of up to 350 horsepower, and they can handle a wide range of implements.

Implements are usually controlled through a three-point linkage. The linkage consists of one upper link—usually under compression—and two lower links—usually under tension. Sensing may be applied through the top link or through the bottom links, although the latter version is the more common system today.

Response control smooths out the draft control system's reactions, preventing loss of traction or loss of contact with the ground. Automatic position control makes adjustments to the implement's position so that they remain constant relative to the ground in changing working conditions. Pressure control enables the driver to control the pressure within the implement's lift cylinder in the tractor's hydraulic system. With pressure control, the driver can control the degree of weight transfer onto the tractor wheels when towing an implement.

Plow

The most important implement of tillage is the plow, which performs like the spade in that it loosens the oversoil, breaking it up and exposing new surfaces to the atmosphere. At the same time, it turns the soil over, burying any trash. A modern plow can turn more soil in a few minutes than a person working with a spade can in a whole day. A great deal of energy is expended in plowing, and a large-furrow plow needs to be attached to a tractor of 100 horsepower or more.

There are three types of plows. The fixed plow, which carries its moldboards on the right-hand side; the reversible plow, which has moldboards on both sides of the plow body that can turn on the frame, either mechanically or hydraulically; and the disk plow. The reversible plow can plow up and down in the same furrow. Although expensive to buy, it saves time both in marking out and at the ends of the fields and it leaves a level field, lessening the work to be done in seedbed preparation. The disk plows are the most popular types in the United States, where erosion by wind and water is often a prob-

lem. The disks, whether mounted on the right or reversible, replace the heavy-duty tillage of the moldboards and simply stir the soil, leaving it as well bound together as possible. In disk plowing, three or four sets of disks are mounted vertically on an axle at a fixed angle of 45 degrees to the soil surface. They do not completely bury the top growth, and therefore, they are suitable for dry conditions. Naturally, this shallow tillage is less effective in burying weeds or crop residue.

Where conservation of water and soil are a priority, the practice of postharvest plowing is sometimes replaced entirely by a stubbling mulching sweep, which draws several knives through the ground, cutting roots but leaving the soil barely affected. In some such cases, it is considered wiser to leave the soil altogether undisturbed and plant directly into it. Intercropping is yet another technique used to combat the effects of erosion.

The diamond plow, so named because the inverted furrow slice is diamond shaped rather than rectangular, is a recent innovation in moldboard plows and has a number of particularly interesting features. It has no coulters; the furrow wall is cut by the leading edge of the moldboard and, instead of being vertical, is curved. The skimmers, which could be described as small plows fitted in front of the moldboard to take the trash off the top of the slice and push it into the

▼ The Ford FW four-wheel drive articulated tractor, typical of the type of versatile, general purpose workhorses particularly suited to the large-scale farming of the United States and Canada. Most North American all-wheel drive machines have equalized large-diameter wheels to give maximum grip for heavy pulling work across vast acreages.

1 Insulated cab	7 Axles
2 Air conditioning	8 Battery
3 Diesel engine	9 Transfer case
4 Instrumentation	10 Drive shaft
5 Gear selectors	11 Hitch
6 Transmission	12 High-traction tires

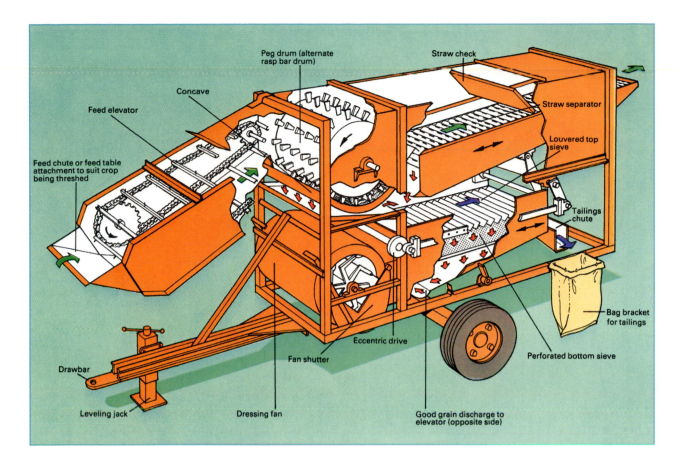

Peg drum (alternate rasp bar drum)

Straw check

Concave

Feed elevator

Straw separator

Feed chute or feed table attachment to suit crop being threshed

Louvered top sieve

Tailings chute

Bag bracket for tailings

Drawbar

Perforated bottom sieve

Eccentric drive

Leveling jack

Fan shutter

Dressing fan

Good grain discharge to elevator (opposite side)

furrow ahead of the moldboard, are fitted to the side of the moldboard. It is easier to pull than conventional designs.

Cultivator

Before World War I, farmers practiced cultivation by drawing a steel chisel or tine (similar to the prongs of a fork) through the upturned furrows of plowed land to work the soil down to a soft powdery consistency in which seeds could be successfully sown.

Today, powered cultivation is widely used not only to work down plowed and fallow ground into seedbed condition but also often to replace the task of first plowing the land. The machines used for this job are called rotary cultivators, because they work by a series of revolving blades chopping up the land. Most rotary cultivators cut the soil by means of L-shaped or curved hoe blades bolted to a robust central axle, which is either driven by the machine's own motor or by the power-takeoff drive shaft on the tractor on which the cultivator is mounted.

Tractor-mounted or hand-controlled rotary cultivators are rarely used to dig deeper than 8 in. (20 cm), as seeds are never sown that deep. Ideally, a seedbed should have deep soil fractures that break down into small lumps below the surface, reducing to even smaller friable lumps and free soil on the top. By varying the rotor speed with the rate of forward travel, a farmer is able to get the degree of coarseness into the tilth or seedbed that is required. Another advantage of the rotary cultivator is that it will chop unwanted crop residues into a mulch (a mixture of stalk, leaves, and straw) or compost of decomposing vegetation that will manure the ensuing crop and boost the yield.

A modern trend has been to combine the seeding and drilling machine (for drilling seed holes) with the tractor drawn variety of rotary cultivator. In this way, the farmer is saved from making a second journey over the ground drilling the seed. The drill, which is usually fixed above the cultivator hood, feeds its seeds into the freshly prepared earth via spouts that discharge just behind the rotating hoe blades. A further time- and labor-saving improvement that has been made is the splitting of the drill's hopper into two compartments, one holding seed and the other holding artificial fertilizer.

Naturally, a machine that performs three separate functions while making one pass over the ground must be accurately calibrated to deliver the correct amounts of seed and fertilizer into land that the machine has adequately prepared for sowing, or the whole benefit from combining two or more jobs will be lost. Jobs that are combined in this way are described by farmers as a minimum tillage (cultivation) system.

One minimum tillage machine, an Italian design, is a tractor-drawn giant rotary cultivator

▲ The Alvan Blanch minor thresher can process up to 4,400 lbs. (2,000 kg) of wheat per hour.

47

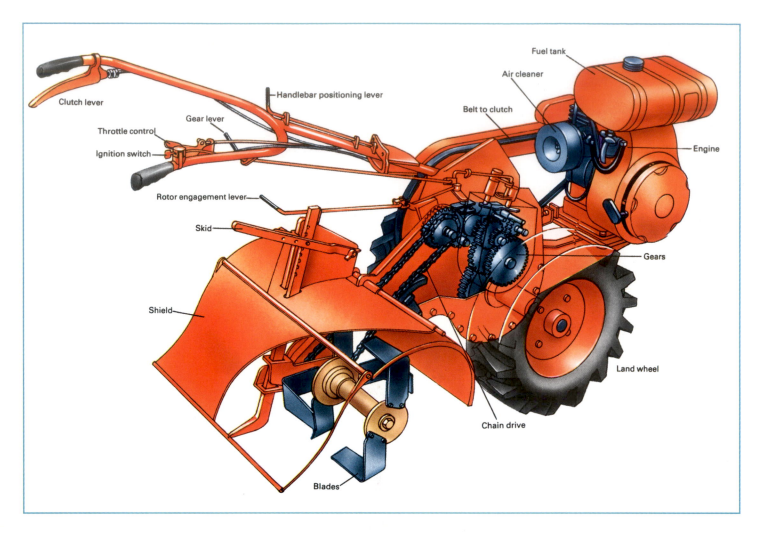

Fuel tank
Air cleaner
Belt to clutch
Engine
Handlebar positioning lever
Clutch lever
Gear lever
Throttle control
Ignition switch
Rotor engagement lever
Skid
Gears
Shield
Land wheel
Chain drive
Blades

that is powered by its own 315 horsepower diesel engine. It is 12 ft. (3.6 m) wide and capable of performing seven tasks. They include burying trash, cultivating the seedbed, applying pesticides, sowing seeds, applying fertilizer, covering and firming seeds, and applying weed killer. These tasks are normally undertaken separately, but with this type of machine, smallholding farmers could hire one to come and do all the field work needed for the year in an afternoon.

Seeding techniques

Almost every farmer growing crops in the Western world now uses seed drills rather than relying on the ancient practice of broadcasting, where seed distribution is quite random. The seed drill has been designed in order to avoid wastage of either seed or land. It consists of a hopper, which is filled with seeds, a series of tubes into which the seeds are mechanically channeled, and a matching number of coulters, which cut small hollows in the ground into which the seeds are dropped. The seeds are generally gravity fed, but pneumatic feeding, whereby the seed is guided by an airflow, is now considered to have advantages in distribution. Many farmers favor the use of the combine drill, which drops seed and fertilizer

together into a single cut. The dual operation can also be applied to no-till or direct drilling methods, when the seed is being planted into unplowed or uncultivated ground.

With such heavy demands on the land to produce high and frequent yields, intensive fertilizing is necessary. Systematic elimination of harmful pests or diseases is also fundamental to modern farming techniques. Chemicals for these purposes are distributed by sprayers, which consist of a tank, a pump, a control valve, and a boom, along which are a number of nozzles. Liquid from the tank passes into the pump, which when attached to a tractor may be driven by its power takeoff or by a hydraulic motor. Pressure can be set by an adjustable relief valve to give the required application, and excess liquid is returned to the tank, keeping the flow of chemicals and water well mixed. Filters are located throughout the mechanism and are designed to prevent blockages at the nozzles. Electronically controlled switches in the cab can regulate the application through the nozzles. Spray booms, which may be as wide as 60 ft. (18 m), generally fold on spring-loaded hinges, which give when the boom hits an obstruction, thus reducing possible damage to the sprayer. Some sprayers are self-propelled, and still others

▲ A small domestic rotary cultivator used in nurseries or large backyards. It has a four-stroke, 5-horsepower engine with four forward gears and two reverse gears. Its maximum speed is 5 mph (8km/h). This type of small cultivator works on the same principle as the larger agricultural ones, and its blades must also be made of the strongest steel. These machines are essential labor- and time-savers for tending the grounds on large estates and in public parks. For a homeowner, they make it possible to turn an unused, overgrown plot of land into useable soil for a lawn or garden.

are carried by helicopter or airplane. Aerial application is particularly suited to very large farms, but difficulties encountered in maintaining a uniform height can increase the risks of spray drift, causing possible damage to neighboring crops and water. Chemical firms are at present experimenting with electrodynamic spraying techniques that are designed to aim droplets more accurately from a nozzle to a target crop, thus reducing spray drift.

Combine harvester

One of the largest and most important farm machines seen in the fields is the combine harvester. It represents 150 years in the development of machinery to ease the labor of harvesting and to improve farm efficiency. Since the production of the first self-propelled cereal combine harvester in 1938, this impressive-looking machine has proved by far the most popular method of harvesting in the West. Despite its high capital outlay, farmers have found it a worthwhile investment, or they have been prepared to employ combine custom operators to cut their crop for them for a set fee per acre. Some operators follow the harvesting season from Texas to Canada, carrying their enormous combines on flatbed trucks wherever road transport is necessary. The basic operating principle of today's machines is much the same as that of earlier models.

Rotating sails pull the crop onto a reciprocating knife bar, which cuts it off at stubble height. The crop falls onto the cutter table (header) and is swept to the center by rotating augers. A central elevator gathers the cut crop and conveys it into the body of the machine, where it is threshed by the drum, which is an open cylinder of beater bars rotating at a high speed that rub, or knock, the grain out of the heads. The straw is conveyed to the back of the machine by jog-trough straw walkers for disposal back onto the ground, while the grain and the chaff fall onto sieves or screens that sort out the large pieces and then pass through a winnowing blast of air that blows away the chaff (small pieces of straw, husks, and other nongrain particles). The separated grain is now in the bottom of the machine and is side-augered across to a chain-and-flight elevator that carries it to a tank on top. Another auger inside a conveyor can push the grain into a truck.

A modern combine has a tank that can hold up to 5 tons (4.5 tonnes) of grain, allowing it to work for about a quarter of an hour without being relieved by the grain truck. Under ideal conditions, the machine can harvest 7 to 8 acres per hour, and one acre of land may yield four or more tons of grain. In Britain and certain other parts of the world the harvest season is very short, and so high-capacity machines are necessary, having engines rated at over 200 horsepower. The power required depends on the amount of machinery to be operated; machines that will chop the straw before depositing it back on the ground will require about 25 horsepower extra. The width of the cut produced by the harvester varies; in countries such as the United States and Canada, where access to fields is easy, the cut may be up to 30 ft. (9 m) wide. On the other hand, because of rainfall or the condition of the soil, the crop may not be as thick, so the output of the combine will not necessarily be greater than that produced by a narrower width of cut in a more lush field.

The largest modern combines have hydrostatic oil-drive fluid transmissions for the drives, power steering (combines steer with the rear wheels), and an air-conditioned cab to protect the driver from dust and sunstroke. The controls may include electronic monitoring of many of the machine's functions and performance monitoring.

Threshing machine

The earliest method of threshing was to beat out the grain with sticks or flails. Threshing was a very labor-intensive job that required strong men, so it was not surprising that during the industrial revolution various machines began to be developed. The first threshing machine was invented in 1786 and comprised a drum with four longitudinal iron beater bars on its surface that was rotated within an iron concave by means of a waterwheel. By the turn of the century, horse power was being used.

▼ A swivel plow, which has two sets of blades used in alternate directions to plow successive furrows that overlap evenly. Plows are marketed in a wide range of sizes to suit the power of the tractor, the toughness of the soil, the type of weather conditions, and the acreage. In the United States, large capacity is important to plow the vast acreage quickly and efficiently.

The threshing mechanism of a modern combine harvester (and also of a separate thresher) is still based on the drum and concave principle but with various refinements. The drum has a much more open design and consists of a shaft with several disks along its length to which are attached the beater bars. There may be from four to six beater bars, which are slotted. The concave is also very open in form, having a number of ridges against which the grain is rubbed off, and in the spaces between the ridges, there are sieves through which the grain falls together with some chaff. The straw is dealt with by the stripper beater at the rear of the concave. The distance between the drum and concave can be adjusted for different crops, which may need a fine thresh or a heavy thresh, depending on their thickness. In addition, the speed of the drum may be varied between 800 and 1,400 rpm.

Mechanized farming

Mechanization now extends into every aspect of modern farming. There are power-driven machines for driving fencing posts into the ground and for clearing manure from farm buildings. Farmyard equipment, such as grain driers and food mixers for animal feed, can be run by main electric power (which is usually cheaper at night) or by a farm's own generator.

Most livestock and poultry farming these days operates on a huge scale and is highly automated. With confinement and controlled conditions for animals and mechanized feeding systems operated from a single control shed, the farmer has virtually no labor costs to contend with, and production is generally high. Dairy farming still requires rather more daily care and attention, though udder washing can now be done by automated spray jets, and a cluster system (on milk machines) can disengage and hang itself up when milk flow ceases.

However, the high cost of mechanization to the farmer has encouraged specialization on the farm, and the trend for large farms, monoculture, and intensive farming techniques may well have reached its peak. In many parts of the West, overproduction of livestock and crops and their consequential drop in price on the world market are presenting new problems. The demand for more powerful machinery would appear to be at the point of giving way to a new concern: that of waste. Recent developments would seem to reflect this concern.

Electronic controls

Where there is greater power, it is possible to achieve higher speeds of operation, but for high-speed operations, there must be a high degree of precision too. This function can be achieved by the use of electronic equipment, and it is in this area that the greatest technological advances are at present being made for farm machinery. By means of sensors and monitors, it has now become possible to gauge the maximum speed at

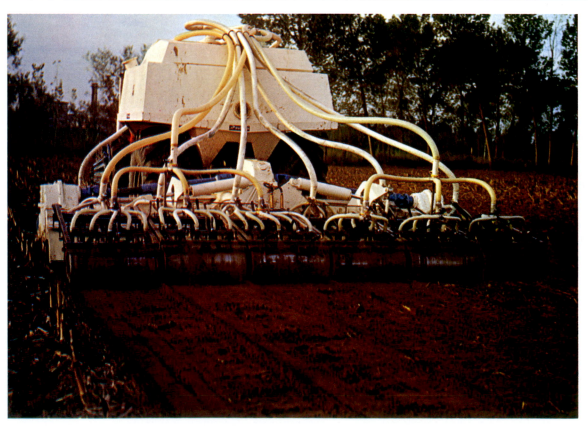

◀ The Italian Supercoltivatrice is among the best of the minimum cultivation systems. In a single run, it will chop the residue of a previous crop and prepare the ground to receive the next one. It can precision-sow rows of crops, such as corn, that need one seed every 4 in. (10 cm). In addition, this machine applies fertilizers, pesticides, and weed killer, and placement rollers cover the seed out of sight of birds. Finally, it sprays a weed killer to keep the soil clear for seedlings.

which a machine can move before its efficiency is impaired. The calculation is a complex one, depending on many factors. For example, ground speed, which until recently took no account of wheel slip in wet weather, was assessed simply by the number of wheel revolutions. This mistake led to inaccuracies in many areas, including seed drilling. A sensor, which is unaffected by wheel slip, can now be fitted to the wheel of any self-propelled machine and transmit a true measurement of ground speed to the speedometer fitted in the cab. This information can then be linked to, for example, a seed-drill operation. This, in turn, maximizes the efficiency of the drill, avoiding waste of land, seed, and fuel. Sensors, in conjunction with other electronic instruments, can now measure grain yield on a combine harvester, shaft speeds on the power takeoff, and grain moisture or flow quantity on a sprayer, and monitors can signal to a driver any malfunctions of a machine by visual or audio alarms. In the case of combine driving, where the operator must be aware of many simultaneous operations, these automatic monitoring systems are of considerable value. Electronic linkages are also replacing mechanical ones, as the old

▲ Riding high in a British orchard, this apple-picking machine is gentler than shaking the trees. Fingers along each side of the harvester probe the trees to pluck the fruit.

types are subject to wear and consequently imprecision, and in the cabs, consoles carrying switches, lights, and dials are outmoding levers.

The real breakthrough in electronic research and development is in the area of microprocessing. Small instruments can now store information on a circuit etched onto a tiny piece of silicon, and calculations can appear almost instantaneously on meters and dials. Because of the sensitivity of these instruments, electronics have not previously been well suited to the muddy and bumpy field environment, but new methods of protection are being devised to make them available to the modern farmer. As electronic devices become smaller, cheaper, and more robust, a demand for them will increase in the agricultural market.

Indeed computers and robots on the farm are already in the experimental stages. Australian researchers have built a sheep-shearing robot that takes 15 minutes to shear a single sheep, not as fast as its human counterpart—but of course, robots never get tired. In Japan, scientists have developed a computer-controlled, driverless combine for rice harvesting, and the French are developing robot designs for picking grapes and other fruit. Mobility and three-dimensional vision are the major stumbling blocks in robot design, but it is envisaged that robots will be used to plant, cultivate, and harvest a variety of crops.

FACT FILE

■ *The giant Rheinmetall trenching plow used in Germany in the early 20th century was capable of breaking up subterranean veins of iron ore, throwing up boulders of up to 1,650 lbs. (750 kg) in weight.*

■ *The Barrett, Exall, and Andrews rotary cultivator produced in 1855 consisted of a revolving frame attached to the back of a steam engine. Various tools could be attached, for cultivating or harrowing, and it was claimed to be able to cultivate 6 acres (14.5 ha) a day to a depth of 1 ft. (25 cm).*

■ *The Hebridean cas crom, or foot plow, was used until recently on remote islands and was ideal for stony ground. It consisted of a 6 ft. (1.8 m) curved wooden handle with an iron point set at an angle of 120 degrees to the handle and a footrest at the junction. The point was trodden into the ground and the turf levered up with the handle.*

SEE ALSO: Agricultural science • Agriculture, intensive • Agriculture, organic • Dairy industry • Elevator, grain • Fertilizer • Hydraulics • Irrigation techniques • Pest control • Soil research

Agricultural Science

The chief goals of agricultural research have always been to increase yields and reduce the farmer's costs. In the 1950s and 1960s, these goals were met by the introduction of hybrid seeds, mechanization, and chemical pesticides that deprived insects and disease organisms of their share of the crops. In the 1980s and 1990s, the new tools of biotechnology were brought to bear, creating plants and animals tailored to provide higher yields and resist disease. By the end of the 1990s, the first cloned animals had been produced, opening the way for herds of genetically identical livestock bred from superior animals and for a means of conserving the gene pool of rare breeds with useful characteristics.

Drugs manufactured by bioengineered bacteria are already in use to improve the health of domestic animals. Meanwhile, organisms that cause disease in insects are being bioengineered to do an even better job, so they can replace chemical pesticides. Growth hormones manufactured by biotechnology cause cows to give more milk and hogs to provide leaner meat.

One high-tech tool, artificial insemination, has been in widespread use since the 1950s, making it possible to spread the benefits of animal breeding programs quickly throughout the industry. About 75 percent of dairy cattle in the United States are produced by artificial insemination. In addition to improving the quality of herds, the technique has reduced costs for many farmers, who no longer have to keep their own bulls.

New technologies promise to increase the number of calves produced by the best cows as well as the best bulls. These cows are treated with hormones that stimulate the ovary to release up to six eggs per cycle, producing three or four embryos. The embryos are removed and implanted in "surrogate mothers," and the superior cow can be inseminated again in about three weeks.

The next step, still in the laboratory stage, is to allow the fertilized ovum to divide a few times, until the embryo consists of perhaps 32 cells, that is, after five divisions. The nucleus of each of these cells can be inserted into a donor egg from which the nucleus has been removed; that egg will develop into an embryo almost identical to the superior cow. After a very few divisions, this process no longer works, because cells in the embryo begin to differentiate to form specific parts of the animal. Researchers now are trying to learn more about how differentiation takes place, so they can forestall it and thus produce many offspring from one egg.

▲ An assortment of genetic varieties (hybrids) of corn produced for experimental cultivation. Different strains display variation in thickness, length, color, and number of grains. Crossbreeding such varieties can produce new strains with chosen features.

Modifying farm animals

Even the best animals can still be improved. Although terms like "genetic engineering" and "gene splicing" sound futuristic and, to some, even disturbing, the fact is that plant and animal breeders have been moving genes around for centuries, using conventional techniques of crossbreeding and selection. In some species, it has become an established practice to insert the genes for desirable characteristics, such as disease resistance or higher milk production.

One method of insertion is to remove an ovum from an animal just after fertilization and under a microscope, inject DNA-containing genes for the desired characteristics directly into the nucleus with a tiny needle. The egg is then reimplanted in a surrogate mother. This method is still unreliable: several hundred modified eggs may be needed to produce one animal in which the inserted gene is "expressed"—that is, manufactures the protein for which it codes—and not all of the animals in which the gene is expressed may pass the trait on to their offspring.

This technique has been widely used in laboratory animals such as mice and rats, but it is still very difficult and expensive to apply to larger farm animals. A few genetically modified, or "transgenic," farm animals have been created experimentally, although by 1992, none had yet been used in commercial farming. For example, pigs with an added gene for pig growth hormone grow faster and produce leaner meat. However, they are also subject to colds and arthritis, apparently resulting from the stress of rapid growth.

Before leaner pigs can be engineered for commercial use, further research is needed to understand the metabolic pathways by which fat is stored.

Green genes

The genetic makeup of plants lies at the heart of many modern developments in agronomy. Scientists have a growing understanding of the way genes work and how they interact to allow crops to fend off pests and diseases. This knowledge helps greatly in choosing the best combinations of parent plants and speeds up the complex crossings needed to obtain new varieties.

Genes also determine the nature of end products, whether it be flour from wheat or oils from brassica crops, such as cabbage. The prospects for bringing specific genes together in completely new ways are particularly exciting. By using methods that would rarely, if ever, occur in nature, breeders expect to produce "designer crops" to meet highly specific needs. Oilseeds in which the makeup of the extract has been adjusted to suit particular markets are well advanced. Farther off is the cereal that makes its own nitrogen fertilizer in the same way that legumes, such as beans and clover, do.

An animal's egg cell can be removed from the body and is large enough to manipulate under a microscope. The egg cell of a plant is often far smaller and is hidden inside the flower. Therefore, plant scientists often perform their genetic modifications on small pieces of plant tissue, such as a section of a leaf, or on plant cells growing in culture.

A favorite method for inserting genes into plant tissue uses a bacterium that causes a plant disease called crown gall. This bacterium infects a plant cell by inserting a ring of DNA called a plasmid into the cell. If the foreign DNA is linked into the plasmid, it may be taken up and expressed by the plant cell.

After the gene is inserted, a new plant must be grown from the bits of plant tissue or cells in culture. Regenerating plants in this way has been particularly difficult with important grains such as wheat and corn; a major goal of research over the past decade has been to develop reliable techniques for working with these plants. It is still more of an art than a science.

High-tech plant breeding

No gene-splicing technique is of any use unless the gene for a desirable characteristic has been identified; it is also more difficult when the trait is carried by multiple genes. Old-fashioned plant breeding, aided by by some high-tech innovations, therefore, is still of major importance.

▲ These potato chips were made from potatoes genetically engineered to improve their solids content. When fried, they absorb less oil, so they have fewer calories.

The basic tool of classic plant breeding is the cross and backcross. For example, a breed of corn that resists drought might be desired. The breeder might start by crossing a commercial variety of corn with a Mexican kind that grows in arid regions. The descendants of the cross that show drought resistance are backcrossed with the commercial variety. After many generations of selection and backcrossing, a plant that is almost identical to the original corn may be produced, but with drought resistance added.

Mapping of the plant genome using restriction fragment length polymorphisms (RFLPs) has provided plant breeders with a road map that greatly speeds their work. Genetic markers can be used to identify quickly the plants that carry desired traits and will show whether the trait is controlled by a single gene or by multiple genes on different chromosomes.

Mapping also narrows down the location of a desirable gene to a particular fragment of DNA

▶ Open field trials of genetically engineered plants—here, oilseed rape—have been taking place despite some fears that artificial genes may spread. While the technology has been accepted for some crops in the United States, there is widespread opposition in many European countries.

◀ This splash meter can help farmers control leaf blotch disease by showing when dye is splashed to leaf height. Fungicide can then be applied only when rain conditions require it, saving both spraying costs and environmental damage.

on a particular chromosome. That fragment of DNA can then be broken into smaller fragments that are spliced into plants; by testing the plants for the desired trait, it is eventually possible to narrow the search and find the gene, after which the protein for which it codes may be identified.

Sometimes no plant can be found with the characteristic a breeder would like to add. If the characteristic can be found in a plant that is not too distantly related, plant cells in culture can be fused. Like mules, many such interspecies fusions are sterile, but some can serve as breeding stock.

There is also a way for breeders to make their own genes: plant cells in culture are exposed to radiation or to a chemical that causes mutations then exposed to a stress such as a toxin produced by a disease organism. If a mutation exists in the culture that confers resistance to the toxin, cells with that mutation will survive and can be regenerated into plants that carry the resistance.

Agronomy is at the center of the debate over the use of genetic engineering. Many people maintain that the latest techniques for shifting genes from one plant to another are unnatural and should be avoided. Breeders usually counter that their processes merely hasten what might eventually occur anyway or simply involve using natural material in new ways. Whatever the rights and wrongs, most advanced countries have strict laws governing such work and the release of novel organisms into the environment.

Farmers as good neighbors

Other scientists are studying the larger systems by which farming relates to the world around it. Primitive farmers could move to a new field when the soil became exhausted, and their activities seldom had any effect on anyone outside their fields. As modern agriculture becomes more intense and specialized and space more limited, it becomes important to understand how chemicals interact with the soil and where they may go from there.

For instance, many intensive dairy farmers no longer grow all their own feed; they buy some of it from distant suppliers. As a result, they can no longer dispose of the manure produced by their cattle by spreading it on their grazing land as fertilizer, because they may not own enough land in proportion to the size of their herds. So they either overspread the manure, applying more than growing things can use, or dump it into holding ponds. Like chemical fertilizer, manure releases nitrates into groundwater. If these nitrates reach public water supplies, they can cause widespread disease; in lakes and streams, they may cause a blooming of water plants that interferes with, and ultimately kills, fish and other wildlife.

A more familiar example is the ongoing effort to reduce the use of chemical pesticides. Some growers have traditionally applied pesticides preventively, with the result that they sometimes applied chemicals that were not needed. Using methods such as integrated crop management, fields are carefully monitored and pesticides

▶ In an experiment to investigate the feeding patterns of natural predators of crop pests, biologists set these mini-tents to provide a controlled environment. The aim is to use natural controls in place of heavy chemical application.

applied only when insects appear in dangerous numbers (or ideally, just before that time).

Many diseases, pests, and weeds are now becoming resistant to the chemicals that are applied to control them. Until quite recently, weeds that had evolved resistance to herbicides were little more than curiosities, but now, about 100 species have strains able to shrug off our best weaponry against them. One way to overcome this problem is to vary the approach used frequently, as pests that have genetic resistance to one chemical may be susceptible to another or to biological controls. One such idea involves creating specially sown grass ridges within cereal fields. Scientists have found these so-called beetle banks form a warm over-winter habitat for the many insects that in spring and summer prey on aphids attacking the crop.

To till or not to till?

Soil tillage is an important topic in agronomy. Despite the advent of herbicides, the traditional moldboard or self-scouring plow remains the basic cultivation tool for many farming systems. However, in many parts of the world, growers, soil scientists, and machinery makers are exploring other ways of preparing the land for sowing crops.

Inverting large volumes of soil each season is expensive, and many soil scientists believe that it actually reduces soil quality. Much effort is put into checking the quantity of organic matter in the soil. If it is increasing, so is the soil quality.

A no-till, or direct-drilling, policy, in which seeds are sown straight into the land cleared of the previous crop, has attracted much attention in recent years. This technique requires specially designed machinery and relies heavily on good soil structure and pesticides for its success. But in the right area, it can improve the soil's water intake, improve its structure, and reduce erosion.

Computerized farming

The computer has become an essential tool in studying farming systems. Soil scientists are developing computer simulations to predict how nitrates, pesticides, and other materials will move through the soil, taking into account the structure and density of the soil and how rapidly it biodegrades chemicals.

More futuristic is the use of computers and orbiting satellites to help pinpoint precise field treatments. Grain harvesters fitted with global-positioning and yield-monitoring equipment can record crop output as it varies in each part of the field. The data can then be fed to computer-controlled fertilizer and spraying machines working over subsequent crops. This practice would allow nutrient deficiencies and weeds to be tackled only where strictly needed.

Eventually, scientists hope that a better understanding of the relationship between farming and the environment will lead to a sustainable agriculture that preserves soil and water quality while needing a lower input of fertilizer, pesticides, and other chemicals. Such a system would reduce the farmer's costs while protecting the environment.

FACT FILE

■ *Mexican researchers studying* Pseudomonas syringae, *a bacterium that causes a disease in beans, have discovered that it carries a gene that deactivates its own toxin. When they inserted that gene into tobacco plants, they found that the plants became resistant to the disease. (Tobacco, a much-studied plant, serves plant scientists as a sort of laboratory mouse.)*

■ *A major problem for produce marketers is the premature ripening and softening of fruits en route to market. Workers at the New York State Agricultural Experiment Station in Geneva traced this process to the action of an enzyme, polygalacturonase, which softens cell walls, and developed a method to block the action of the gene that codes for the enzyme. They are now studying the biochemical processes that cause the gene to be turned on in the first place.*

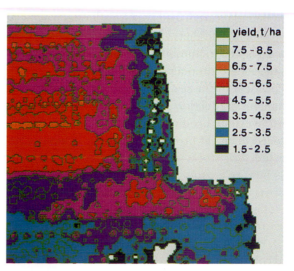

yield, t/ha
7.5 - 8.5
6.5 - 7.5
5.5 - 6.5
4.5 - 5.5
3.5 - 4.5
2.5 - 3.5
1.5 - 2.5

◄ In total crop management, fields are surveyed for weeds and herbicide use. Data recorded over time is used to control an automatic sprayer, so chemicals are applied only where needed. Sensors on the harvester provide a map of the yield from an area (left) so that the long-term effects of spraying and other inputs can be monitored.

SEE ALSO: AGRICULTURAL MACHINERY • AGRICULTURE, INTENSIVE • AGRICULTURE, ORGANIC • BIOTECHNOLOGY • BOTANY • DAIRY INDUSTRY • FERTILIZER • PEST CONTROL • SOIL RESEARCH

Agriculture, Intensive

Intensification in livestock farming improves productivity of meat, eggs, and milk by increasing the numbers of animals supported by available land, reducing the amount of labor required for management, and increasing the productivity of the individual animal.

However, when the numbers are increased, it creates problems: livestock can no longer support themselves by grazing or foraging and must have expensive supplements or manufactured feeds. Disease can be a potential problem, and diets and housing techniques are often adapted to minimize this problem. Housing has the added advantage of making the operation independent of the seasons and weather, allowing continuous production.

In all intensive systems, livestock producing eggs or milk or being fattened for meat production are separated from the breeding stock, which are usually kept under less intensive conditions. Maximum meat productivity is achieved by selective breeding to produce as many offspring as possible with rapid growth rates and good feed efficiency; that is, to put on the maximum possible bodyweight for the feed consumed.

Growth rates slow as animals near maturity, and livestock are usually slaughtered while still relatively young, because to raise them until they are fully grown would require a disproportionate quantity of feed. For example, a broiler chicken reaches a weight of 4 lbs. (2 kg) in seven weeks, when it is normally killed. For each 2¼ lbs. (1 kg) of feed it consumes, it gains 1 lb. (0.45 kg) in weight. If it is allowed to grow to a large capon, it will soon take 3 lbs. (1.4 kg) or more of feed to put on an extra pound or half kilogram of weight.

In animals growing at such a rapid rate, nutritional requirements vary as they grow, and very careful control of feed ingredients is necessary. Growth rates may be further stimulated by supplementing the diet with growth-promoting substances, such as animal antibiotics. Similarly, efficiency of production of eggs and milk is measured in terms of the quantity of feed consumed.

In most intensive farming systems, livestock are kept in sophisticated, controlled-environment housing. In traditional farming, solid and liquid waste are naturally dispersed over large areas of pasture, but with intensification, vastly increased quantities of waste are generated within a restricted area. When possible, automated disposal systems remove wastes, which are often stored in lagoons to be broken down by bacteria, dried and burned, or used as fertilizer.

Broiler chickens

Raising broiler chickens is the most highly specialized and efficient form of intensive farming; eight billion birds are produced annually in the

▲ Pigs being intensively raised in pens in a controlled environment. Lactating sows have to be prevented from rolling onto their piglets.

United States. Day-old chicks are raised in large houses with controlled ventilation, heating, and lighting. Feed is supplied automatically by a conveyor system, and water is piped in. A typical broiler unit consists of several adjacent poultry houses, each containing 15,000 birds in large pens.

The entire flock is supplied from the hatchery as day-old chicks, already vaccinated against some common diseases, and the birds may not be handled again until they are collected for slaughter. Because of extensive automation, the entire unit can be operated throughout the growing period by a manager and two assistants. To prevent disease, broilers are usually fed a medicated diet throughout their lives.

Battery chickens

The majority of eggs produced come from birds in battery houses. From three to six pullets are placed in each battery cage just as they begin to lay. Feed is supplied by conveyor or moving hopper and water by a nipple drinking system. Droppings pass through the wire cage floor, usually either into a droppings pit or onto a moving belt that removes them from the house. As eggs are laid, they roll through a gap at the cage front and are collected by hand or by conveyor. Light affects the hens' production of hormones involved in egg laying, so adequate house lighting is desirable. Medicated feed is not desirable for hens producing eggs, because drugs may collect in the eggs. The threat of disease is reduced by keeping the birds away from possible infection from their droppings. The wire floors minimize contamination of the eggs. There are 328 million laying hens in the United States producing 84.4 billion eggs each year.

Beef and veal production

In North and South America, intensive beef production is based on vast outdoor feedlots that may contain several thousand beasts. The cattle are beef breeds, such as the Hereford, or hybrids obtained by crossing milk cows—Holsteins—with beef breeds, such as Hereford or Angus. Feed based on corn is supplied from trucks fitted with hoppers, which discharge into feeding troughs as the vehicle drives along the feedlot. Alternatively, the corn may be fed as silage, discharged by augers from large silos directly to the feed troughs. Beef cattle grow to 900 to 1,100 lbs. (400–500 kg) in less than 12 months.

Intensive veal production is now predominantly based on large indoor pens. Surplus male calves born to dairy breeds such as Holsteins are fed on a liquid milk-replacer diet from multiple station feeders. Some veal calves are housed in individual pens on the smaller-scale production units. Three million veal calves per year are produced in the United States.

Other intensive systems are used with dairy herds where milking and feeding are partly automated in the zero-grazing system. There are nine million dairy cows in the United States, producing around 163 billion lbs. (74.4 billion kg) of milk each year.

Hog production

Hogs are usually raised intensively in small groups in pens. Production techniques vary according to the feed used. Lactating sows are frequently restrained—usually tethered—to prevent piglets from being crushed. Hogs grow to an average weight of 240 lbs. (about 110 kg).

Growth promoters

One of the main disagreements between the United States and Europe has been over the use of hormones as growth promoters and bovine somatotropin, which is used to increase milk yields in cows. The United States uses six scientifically approved hormones—estradiol, melengestrol acetate, progesterone, testosterone, trenbolone acetate, and zeranol—to increase meat yield. All six have been used without negative effects on public health in the United States and many other countries for decades, according to the USDA.

Bovine somatotropin (BST) is another hormone, secreted by the pituitary glands of cattle. It appears to play a complex role in regulating various bodily functions, including milk production. BST, which is sometimes called BGH, for "bovine growth hormone," is called sometribove by the U.S. Food and Drug Administration. Meat grown using these substances is currently banned by European regulatory organizations.

◀ An intensive veal-production unit with surplus male calves from dairy breeds. Three million veal calves are produced in the United States annually.

SEE ALSO: AGRICULTURAL SCIENCE • AGRICULTURE, ORGANIC • AQUACULTURE • BIOTECHNOLOGY • BOTANY • DAIRY INDUSTRY • FERTILIZER • HORMONE • VETERINARY SCIENCE AND MEDICINE

Agriculture, Organic

Everything ORGANICALLY GROWN
to recognised organic standards. We have at least four deliveries a week

Organic agriculture is an "earth friendly" farming technique that uses environmentally sound principles for raising crops and livestock to ensure they are free from synthetic pesticides, growth hormones, and antibiotics. Organic methods typically use pesticides and fertilizers derived from plants, animal waste, and minerals to ensure that crops remain healthy and grow well. Organic farming also incorporates the use of biological controls, such as the use of a natural predator to help keep pests at bay, or companion planting to either repel pests or encourage friendly insects. The methods used are claimed to increase soil fertility, balance insect populations, and reduce air, soil, and water pollution as well as make the resulting produce taste better.

Although it may appear that the rise of organic techniques is a recent phenomenon, in fact, it is intensive agriculture that is relatively new, particularly the use of chemicals such as petroleum-based fertilizers, herbicides, and pesticides. The use of such growth-promoting substances is a legacy of World War II, when they were introduced to reduce the need for scarce farm labor while increasing yields.

Biodynamics

One of the earliest modern examples of the organic movement is biodynamic agriculture, which was propounded by Rudolf Steiner, a clairvoyant and theosophist. He is recognized as one of the founding fathers of organic farming although his life work was diverse and included over 6,000 lectures, dozens of books, and radical approaches to education, the arts, and medicine. While a student at the Vienna Technical Institute, he became increasingly known as a pioneer of organic sciences.

Biodynamics has been described as a renewal of ancient peasant cultures and invokes a mystical connection with the soil and growing crops and with the inner spiritual life of human beings. Consciously rejecting the intensive-farming practices he saw as unnatural and the chemicals involved, Steiner preached a return to more natural methods. His theories envisaged human beings as part of a cosmic equilibrium that must be understood in order to live in harmony with the environment. The practice of biodynamic agriculture was developed at the end of the 1920s in Germany, Switzerland, Britain, Denmark, and the Netherlands.

History of organic farming

The use of the term *organic* to indicate a sustainable agriculture system appears to have been coined by Lord Northbourn in 1940 in his book *Look to the Land*. Lord Northbourn used the term to describe a system that focused on the farm as a dynamic, living, balanced, organic whole—or an organism—a clear parallel with the philosophy of Rudolf Steiner.

◀ Supermarket customers are finding a greater variety of organic products available on the shelves. The trend for more naturally produced food has arisen out of concerns for health, the environment, and the welfare of animals.

The term organic was first widely used in the United States by J. I. Rodale, the founder of the Rodale Press, in the 1950s. Rodale was the founder of *Organic Farming and Gardening Magazine* and a key popularizer of the term organic and associated ideas of sustainability. Unfortunately his claims for the benefits that organic farming could bring failed to convince the establishment that his approach bore scientific weight. Nevertheless, several scientists in the United States and Europe began investigating and promoting sustainability in agriculture at that time, notably Sir Albert Howard and William Albrecht.

Another important influence on the development of organic agriculture was clinical research, conducted by medical researchers in the United Kingdom in the first part of the 20th century, into the connection between soil condition, food quality, and human health. The conclusion of this work was that human health was measurably affected by poor soil management in agriculture and in particular poor management of organic matter.

The Soil Association

Organic agriculture in Britain began to flourish in the 1940s after World War II, when a movement, later known as The Soil Association, began to campaign to return soil fertility to its basic place in agriculture. It is founded on the theories propagated by the British agricultural scientist Sir Albert Howard in an agricultural testament published in 1940. The Soil Association is a charity that has been researching and promoting organic farming as the key to sustainable agriculture since 1946. It is the United Kingdom's leading campaigning organization and certification body for organic food and farming. It campaigns against issues such as the use of genetically modified organisms (GMOs) in food, the routine use of antibiotics in conventional farming, the exploitation of animals in intensive units, and the impact of large intensive-farming systems on the countryside and wildlife.

For the first 30 years, the association was primarily involved in basic research and building a membership base. The association bought a farm in Sussex to put its ideals into practice—it was divided into three units; one farmed using the new intensive techniques, one farmed traditionally, and one farmed using a mixed system. The trial's results were unfortunately unclear, but the attempt had enabled the association to develop a clearer understanding of both old and new traditions. The result was the compilation of the first organic standards.

Throughout the 1950s, organic farming began to take hold in France thanks to medical and consumer interest. Two separate movements came into existence: the first, Lemaire-Boucher, linked to commercial operators supplying inputs to producers, and an independent movement, the Nature and Progress Association.

In the 1970s, the pace at which organic methods were adopted began to increase as the modern ecological movement began to gain momentum. It was also the decade when the Soil Association introduced the idea of legally formulated specifications and quality controls for organic produce to give a legally binding guarantee for consumers. In France, organic farmers joined trade syndicates and organized into federations, such as the

◀ A wide variety of fruit crops are now being grown organically. Shoppers are once more becoming accustomed to less-than-perfect-looking produce—perfection can be achieved only by regular spraying with pesticides and growth promoters. When organic crops are sprayed to get rid of pests, more natural substances, such as diluted soap, pyrethrin, and copper sulfate, are used instead and less frequently than is the case with intensively grown crops.

Fédération Nationale d'Agriculteurs Biologiques. Major national organic farming organizations across the world joined to form IFOAM (International Federation of Organic Agriculture Movements).

In the 1980s, the northern European countries began to experience high demand for organically grown products, and with the accession of the Mediterranean states to the European Union, farmers and associations in southern Europe gained access to this fast-growing market. However, the numbers of organic farmers in the United Kingdom remained small until the government launched the Organic Aid Scheme in 1995. It was designed to help farmers during the difficult process of conversion to organic methods, which takes between two and five years.

Growth of the organic market

Organic farming is a small but rapidly growing agricultural sector in the United States, currently about 1.5 percent of production. Sales of organic foodstuffs increased from $1 billion in 1990 to more than $6 billion in 1999. Organic food sales are predicted to increase to over $13 billion by 2003 and are growing at a rate of 20 percent per year. The Organic Farming Research Foundation estimated that there were 6,600 certified organic farmers in the United States in 1999 and that a further 15,000 growers were farming organically but had not yet achieved certified organic status. Exports of organic products to Japan and Europe, where organic farming is more widespread, are also growing.

In Europe, from an average of less than 0.1 percent of the total agricultural area in 1985, certified organic production has increased to an average of over 2 percent. Figures from 1998 show that 4 percent of agricultural land in Germany, 5 percent in Denmark, and 11 percent

▲ A farmer stacking trays of onions grown on an organic farm. Organic farms use natural methods to fertilize crops and keep pests under control. Although these methods usually results in lower crop yields, there is no chemical residue on the produce. Onions are often coplanted with another crop, as their strong smell keeps some insects away.

in Austria were being farmed organically. The annual growth rate over ten years is 25 percent, which if continued, would lead to 10 percent of Western European agriculture being organic by 2005 and 30 percent by 2010. In the United Kingdom, the rate of adoption is also rapidly increasing: organically managed land grew from 0.5 percent in 1998 to 1.3 percent in 1999, corresponding to an area of over 600,000 acres (240,000 ha) of which 75 percent was classed as "in conversion." While the area of land being managed organically more than doubled in this short period, the number of organic producers also increased by 50 percent, equating to 500 new farmers, between April 1998 and April 1999.

The total 1998–1999 retail value of organic food sales in Britain was $390 million (£267 million). Around 70 percent of this total was imported. If the current growth rate of 40 percent per year continues, the value of the U.K. organic market will be worth over $1 billion (£667 million) within two years. In the United Kingdom, 210,000 acres (60,000 ha) of land at present have full organic status, and a further 450,000 acres (180,000 ha) are currently in conversion. The organic livestock sector is experiencing the greatest growth, and this trend looks set to continue.

In the United States, following the passage of the Organic Food Production Act in 1990, the U.S. Department of Agriculture began developing federal standards for organic foods. The USDA, working with the National Organic Standards Board, set out the national standards for the production of organic products in 2000, with the final rule becoming effective in February 2001. All certified organic foods must meet strict national organic criteria, and farmers and processors must be inspected annually by independent certification organizations. There are a number of other organic standards that predate the rule, including those established by the International Federation of Organic Agriculture Movements and federal bodies established by the Organic Food Production Act of 1990. Other bodies setting organic standards include state organizations established by individual state law and private bodies, established by private certification programs.

Allowable substances and practices that qualify as acceptable management strategies must have no negative impact on the land and help regenerate the environment. They include crop rotation, flame or electrical weeding, and mowing and grazing to manage weeds. In crop rotation, a field is used for one or two seasons to grow one type of crop, such as corn or wheat, followed by a season in which a legume, such as alfalfa or soybeans, is planted. Legume roots harbor beneficial bacteria that fix nitrogen from the air into the soil, enriching it and reducing the need for nitrogen-containing fertilizers. Crop rotation also conserves nutrients, since the roots of different crops vary in how far they reach into the soil, so nutrients are drawn from different depths.

Organic farmers also reduce soil erosion by using cover crops—short-lived plants, such as clovers—to protect the soil after one crop is harvested and until another is planted. Many organic farmers also practice no-till or low-till farming, which reduces the amount of nutrients washed out of the soil and reduces erosion.

Fertilizers such as dolomite lime, ground oyster shells, kelp meal, and rock powders are used for their micronutrients, and green manures, composted materials, and nitrogen-fixing organisms are added as sources of nitrogen. Refrigeration, freezing, and sealed containers are used to prevent pest infestations in processed foods, such as flour. Plant growth is promoted by using microbial inoculants or seaweed in either dry or liquid forms. Nontoxic seed treatments such as immersing them in hot water, adding legume inoculants or pelletization are used to help plants get a good start in the ground.

Pest avoidance

Intensive agriculture relies on a range of synthetic pesticides to kill weeds, disease-causing fungi, and harmful insects. These pesticides are made from chemically processed petroleum, natural gas, and ammonia, among other raw materials. The ingredients can be highly toxic and long lasting—one well known insecticide, DDT, was highlighted in Rachel Carson's 1962 book, *The Silent Spring*, for the devastating effect it had on all types of insects in the United States. Organic agriculture makes use of natural alternatives, such as repellent crops—plants that are known to ward off certain predators—planted among a vulnerable crop to help it resist attacks from pests. One example is the use of strong-smelling onions or garlic planted among carrots to ward off the destructive carrot root fly—this pest is able to locate tender carrot roots by smell. Crops can also be coplanted to encourage beneficial insects—for example, marigolds and other flowers such as sweet peas are planted among crops to attract pollinating insects.

Other natural methods of scaring off pests such as birds and insects include the use of water jets, insecticidal soaps, and microbial diseases, such as *Bacillus thuringiensis*. Organic farmers also use natural predators for pest control—for instance, nematode worms are watered into soil to

prevent infestations of vine weevil grubs, which destroy the roots of plants and cause them to die. The worms destroy the grubs, so they do not turn into the tough, adult beetle. Other natural predators include tiny *Encarsia* wasps, which are often released into enclosed spaces, such as greenhouses, where they prey on the "scales" that are the immature form of a whitefly.

The quality debate

Whether organic methods produce food that is in some way better than intensively produced equivalents is still open to debate, but adherents claim that both nutrition and taste are enhanced by organic cultivation. Organically produced foods must meet stricter regulations governing all these steps in the production process, and thus, organic farming is often more labor and management intensive and tends to be on a smaller scale. Organic produce is therefore more expensive compared with equivalent items that have been intensively farmed. However, proponents claim that if the indirect costs of conventional food production, such as the cost of cleaning up polluted water, replacement of eroded soils, and health care, were taken into account, organic foods would cost the same as conventional equivalents. However, there is no concrete evidence currently available to confirm this theory.

These restrictions mean that it is unlikely that organic agriculture will become the main method of food production for any country needing to produce crops or animals on a large scale and with minimal expense, such as the developing nations. Here, intensive agriculture is likely to continue to be the mainstay of food production.

▼ Pigs rooting and foraging for food in a large free-range area on an organic farm in Harburn, Scotland. Unlike intensively farmed livestock, these pigs are fed on organically grown foodstuffs that they would eat naturally, and they are treated with antibiotics, which are used routinely as growth promoters in intensive farming concerns, only if they become ill.

SEE ALSO: AGRICULTURAL SCIENCE • AGRICULTURE, INTENSIVE • BOTANY • HORTICULTURE • PEST CONTROL • SOIL RESEARCH

Air

Air is a mixture of gases enveloping Earth. It is mostly composed of nitrogen and oxygen—approximately 78 percent and 21 percent, respectively—along with several other gases found in much smaller quantities. They include argon, neon, helium, methane, krypton, hydrogen, nitrous oxide, and xenon. Air also contains several gases that are found in small, variable quantities. Among them are sulfur dioxide, ozone, carbon dioxide, nitrogen dioxide, and water vapor. The gases that are vital for life on Earth are oxygen, nitrogen, water vapor, and carbon dioxide, but the other gases are also important. Together, they form the atmosphere, which screens Earth from lethal radiation.

Although the atmosphere extends outward some 620 miles (1,000 km), it is really only the first few miles (normally measured in thousands of feet) that are significant, since three-quarters of the atmosphere's weight lies within 60,000 ft. (18,000 m). It is well within this layer, usually from around 15,000 ft. (4,500 m) down to the surface, that weather patterns occur, because at these levels, there are varying amounts of water vapor, which condense into cloud formations. This layer is called the troposphere, and meteorological conditions within it are affected by changes in temperature, because the air gets progressively colder and thinner the higher it is. These changes in temperature also lead to changes in pressure, which cause large bodies of air to move from one location to another to cause wind. The point at which temperature decline ceases is the tropopause, and the layer above it is the stratosphere. Ozone found in the upper part of this region, which extends to about 35 miles (56 km), protects Earth from harmful ultraviolet radiation from the Sun.

The mesosphere separates the stratosphere from the ionosphere, which begins at about 34 miles (55 km). In the ionosphere, there is no protective ozone layer to block solar radiation so that the atmospheric molecules are bombarded with ultraviolet rays, becoming electrically charged, or ionized. It is this ionized layer that reflects radio waves down to Earth and enables long distance signals and communications to be bounced around Earth instead of escaping into space.

Origins

When Earth formed, around 4.5 billion years ago, it was an extremely hot volcanic planet devoid of life. As it began to cool, the gases and steam that escaped from the cooling rock were prevented

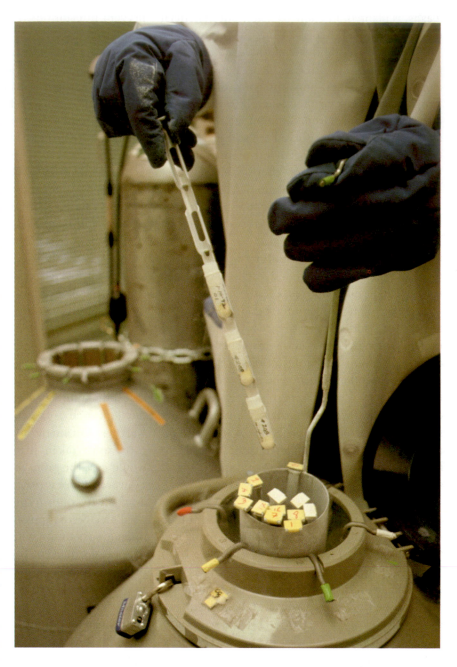

from escaping into space by Earth's gravity. Steam condensed to form the primordial oceans, and an atmosphere of nitrogen and carbon dioxide formed, providing the basis for life to develop.

This combination of gases enabled the development of the first simple forms of plant life around 3.5 billion years ago. Gradually, these plants caused the mixture of gases in the atmosphere to change as a result of photosynthesis. Photosynthesis is the manufacture of organic compounds (such as sugar and starch) from inorganic substances (like water and carbon dioxide) by living plant cells using the energy of sunlight absorbed by the plant pigment chlorophyll. One of the by-products of photosynthesis is oxygen, which plants then release into the atmosphere. With oxygen in the atmosphere, animal life, which uses oxygen as fuel, was able to develop and in turn produce carbon dioxide and nitrogen as

▲ Liquid nitrogen being used as a refrigerant in the rapid cooling of a biological sample.

waste for the plants to feed on, resulting in a state of equilibrium between these gases.

Today, however, the concentration of gases found in air is not only influenced by plants and animals. Automobile and airplane engines, industrial processes, and the large-scale clearance of oxygen-producing, nitrogen-consuming forests all have an effect on the ecological balance, putting an ever greater strain on green plants to keep the relative quantities of oxygen and carbon dioxide as well as nitrogen in the air constant.

Light

The composition of air has a noticeable effect on the way in which visible light reaches the surface of Earth. Like X rays or gamma rays, visible light is a form of electromagnetic radiation, which travels uninterrupted through space. While X rays and gamma rays are shielded from Earth by the upper atmosphere, visible light passes through easily. However, if there are particles of water vapor or dust in the atmosphere, the light can become scattered or absorbed, leading to a variety of optical effects, such as a rainbow or colorful sunsets, often seen in heavily industrial areas. In addition, volcanic activity may throw quantities of blue light-absorbing particles into the upper atmosphere, coloring the sun and sky red.

Similarly, sound is transmitted through air—it cannot travel in space. The source of a sound, such as a clapper striking the side of a bell, causes particles in the immediate vicinity to vibrate, pushing and pulling or compressing and decompressing the air outward from the source in a series of waves that can be detected by the eardrum, which echoes these vibrations, and perceived by the brain as sound. The speed of sound is affected by air temperature so that it moves more slowly through cold, heavier air.

Measurement

Wind speed is calculated from anemometer measurements, while the amount of water vapor in the atmosphere is measured with a hygrometer. Air temperature is measured in degrees Fahrenheit or Celsius, using a thermometer placed out of direct sunlight. Another important property of air is its pressure, which is directly related to relative humidity and temperature. Air pressure is measured using a barometer, and the measurement may be expressed in variety of different ways. The most common forms of measurement are in millimeters of mercury, millibars, or atmospheres. At sea level, atmospheric pressure is equal to 14.69 lbs. per sq. in. (1.01325×10^5 N/m^2), which is equivalent to 760 mm of mercury, 1.01325 bar, or one atmosphere.

Liquefaction

Any substances that are gases at normal temperatures and pressures, such as the gases found in air, can be converted to liquids by cooling and the application of pressure. Such liquefied gases have a number of industrial and scientific applications, and several techniques have been developed for their production.

Initial efforts involving the use of pressure alone proved successful with gases such as chlorine, ammonia, and hydrogen sulfide. Carbon dioxide was liquefied in a similar manner, and the process was taken a stage further by rapidly releasing the pressure so that some of the carbon dioxide changed back into a gas, producing a cooling effect that solidified the remaining carbon dioxide. Although it was possible to liquefy many gases by the application of pressure, this approach did not work with other gases, such as oxygen and hydrogen.

All gases have a critical temperature above which it is impossible to liquefy the gas. Cooling of the gas below the critical temperature allows it to be liquefied, and this approach was successful for the production of a number of important liquid gases, including oxygen and nitrogen (on their own or mixed together in air).

EARTH'S ATMOSPHERE

The gases that surround Earth create a many-layered system that includes the gases necessary for animal and plant respiration as well as those such as ozone that protect life from the harmful effects of high energy electromagnetic radiation. Most weather patterns occur relatively close to Earth's surface—below 2.8 miles (4.5 km) —where water vapor condenses into clouds.

Interplanetary space

Outer Van Allen belt begins

Exosphere

Inner Van Allen belt begins

Charged solar particles

Ionosphere

Thermosphere

F2 layer

Auroras

F1 layer

Noctilucent clouds

Mesosphere

E layer

D layer

Dust belt

Meteors

Stratosphere

Area of ozone concentration

Sulfate layer

Cirrus clouds

Mt Everest

Alto-stratus clouds

Cumulonimbus clouds

Cumulus clouds

Troposphere

Earth's surface

Height miles
10,130
9500
600
500
300
299
150
149
90
89
88
60
59
40
31
25
20
12
11
10
9
0

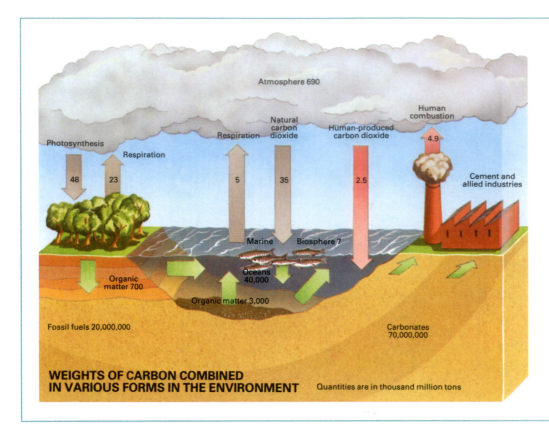

CARBON DIOXIDE CYCLE

The balance of the carbon dioxide cycle is being threatened by human activity. Excess CO_2 from animal respiration can be removed from the atmosphere by processes in the carbon cycle. However, carbon dioxide released through the burning of fossil fuels and chemical processing, especially of mineral carbonates—as in cement production—has increased the concentration of carbon dioxide in the atmosphere. Many climatologists believe this concentration is responsible for the slight increase in Earth's average temperature.

WEIGHTS OF CARBON COMBINED IN VARIOUS FORMS IN THE ENVIRONMENT

Quantities are in thousand million tons

Air liquefaction

A major commercial application of liquefaction is the liquefaction of air to allow separation of the constituents, such as oxygen, nitrogen, and the noble gases. In some cases, the expansion of a compressed gas through a valve results in a cooling of the gas—an effect that may be applied to liquefaction. This expansion and cooling is known as the Joule–Thomson Effect, named for the two British physicists, James Prescott Joule and William Thomson, who in 1853 described this process. The Linde process, invented in 1894 by the German chemist Carl von Linde, was the first commercial method to be used for air liquefaction, and the basic principles are still used in modern systems. The air to be liquefied is compressed and cooled, using water jackets to remove the heat of compression, and then allowed to expand through an expansion valve, resulting in a slight cooling. The cooled and expanded gas is passed through a heat exchanger to cool the compressed gas coming from the compressor, and then it is returned to the compressor inlet so that it can be recycled.

The cooling effect is cumulative, so the temperature of the compressed air supplied to the expansion valve gradually becomes lower until the expansion process results in liquefaction. The resulting liquid air is removed and additional air taken in at the compressor inlet to give a continuous process. Separation of oxygen and other gases from the liquid air is achieved by allowing them to boil off at successively higher and higher temperatures in a distillation system.

Attempts to liquefy hydrogen using Joule–Thomson expansion proved unsuccessful until it was realized that if the expansion was performed above a critical inversion temperature, the result was a heating of the gas rather than a cooling. The inversion temperatures for most common gases are well above ordinary ambient temperatures, so cooling occurs, but in the case of hydrogen (and helium), it is significantly lower—about –98°F (–72°C)—so liquefaction is possible only after the gas has been cooled sufficiently using other means, such as refrigeration.

The gases in air can be used for many different industrial processes and domestic applications. Nitrogen, for example, is fairly inert, making it useful in the chemical industry and as a refrigerant. Oxygen is used in steelmaking, in the chemical industry, and as a constituent of rocket fuel as well as in medicine for incubators, oxygen tents, and anesthetics. Liquid air is also used in cryogenics, the study of temperatures –148°F (–100°C) and lower. The results of this research may then be applied to science and industry.

SEE ALSO:

AERODYNAMICS • ANEMOMETER • ATOMIC STRUCTURE • BAROMETER • EARTH • ELECTROMAGNETIC RADIATION • GAS LAWS • GRAVITY • LIGHT AND OPTICS • METEOROLOGY • NITROGEN • NOBLE GAS • OXYGEN • PHOTOSYNTHESIS • REFRIGERATION

Aircraft-Control Engineering

Aircraft-control engineering is the technology that enables pilots to be aware of the status and position of the craft they control and to determine the behavior of those craft during takeoff, flight, and landing. The field encompasses the mechanisms that govern the power plants and control surfaces of aircraft as well as communication and navigation devices.

Thrust

One of the key parameters in takeoff and flight is the amount of forward thrust delivered by an aircraft's power plants—its engines. Some forward thrust is needed for landing, and reverse thrust may be deployed to reduce the stopping distance after an aircraft has touched down.

In the case of a propeller-driven aircraft, thrust control is achieved mainly by using control levers, or throttles, to adjust the amount of fuel delivered to the piston engines. The second factor is the pitch of the propeller blades, which is the angle from the plane of the propeller. Low pitch angles suit takeoff when airspeed is low; increased pitch is appropriate when the craft is moving rapidly through the air. Pitch may be under the pilot's direct control through mechanical linkages, or it may be under the control of an automatic system that selects the most efficient pitch for a given flight condition. Thrust reversal for braking is achieved by reversing the pitch of the propeller blades to blow air forward.

Throttles are the principal controls of turbofan engines—the most popular power plants for passenger airliners. For thrust reversal, the pilot operates a servomechanism that drops a cowling behind the jet outlet. Once the thrust reverser is in the lowered position, thrust is increased and the hot gases escaping from the rear of the engine are directed forward to slow the aircraft.

Turbojet engines—the power plants of high-speed military jets and the Concorde—are throttled in much the same way as turbofans. They may also be operated with thrust augmentation, for which there are two methods. In the first—afterburning—fuel is injected into the hot gases near the outlet of the combustion chamber. The fuel ignites and provides more thrust as the burning gases expand. In the second, a mixture of alcohol and water is injected into the combustion chamber with an increased amount of fuel. The evaporation of water prevents the combustion chamber from overheating and increases the expansion of gas in the engine, thereby increasing thrust. Both types of thrust augmentation have controls separate from the main fuel throttles.

In all types of engines, thermocouples monitor engine temperatures and activate alarms in the case of overheating, which could be a symptom of an engine fire. On noting such an alarm, a pilot would cut the fuel supply to the affected engine and trigger its extinguishers. Other sensors detect engine rotation speeds, fuel consumption rates, and the level of fuel in the tanks. The pilot uses these readings to monitor engine performance and avoid running out of fuel.

Control surfaces

Control surfaces are movable flaps mounted on the wings and tail of an aircraft. They modify the flow of air around the aircraft and provide a

▲ Highly Maneuverable Aircraft Technology (HiMAT) in the form of a U.S. aircraft. Pitot tubes (devices for measuring the pressure of moving air) are employed to provide signals for computing airspeed.

▶ A pilot's view of one of the most sophisticated fighter aircraft, the British Aerospace Sea Harrier, shows (1) radar controller, (2) nozzle lever, (3) flap selector, (4) radio, (5) HUD, (6) engine-speed and temperature gauges, (7) weapons control, (8) warning lights, (9) head-up display, (10) instruments, (11) missile-control panel, (12) radar screen, (13) fuel gauge, (14) radar warning receiver, (15) electronics panel, (16, 17, 18) target identification unit, and (19) navigation and communication computers and (20) associated switch gear.

means by which the pilot can control the lift, drag, and turning forces that act on a plane during flight. As such, they are the principal means of steering and braking aircraft at high speed.

The lift and drag of a large aircraft are modified by slats at the front and flaps at the rear of each wing. While the aircraft is cruising at high speed, flaps and slats remain fully retracted, the position that creates the least drag and provides just enough lift to keep the craft in level flight. During the approach for landing, the flaps and slats are extended. The increased drag in this configuration helps slow the aircraft while generating enough lift to prevent the aircraft from descending too rapidly. A similar configuration is adopted at takeoff to provide strong lift at low speeds. The flaps and slats are moved by hydraulic or electrical servomotors actuated by controls in the cockpit.

A plane is tilted nose up or nose down by moving hinged control surfaces, called elevators, mounted on either side of the tail. Tilting the free-moving trailing edge of the elevators downward lifts the tail and points the plane into a dive; the reverse maneuver points the plane upward.

Ailerons are flaps hinged to the trailing edge of each wing. The pilot turns the aircraft by tilting one aileron upward and the other one downward. The elevators must be raised to maintain height during turns, and some aircraft designs feature control surfaces called elevons, which combine the functions of elevators and ailerons.

The other principal control surface is the rudder. Unlike ships' rudders, aircraft rudders do not initiate turns; rather, they compensate for the differences in drag and lift between the two wings during a banked turn initiated by ailerons or

elevons. The rudder is necessary because the wing on the outside of the turn creates more drag, which would act against the turn.

In light aircraft, ailerons and elevators move in response to the pilot moving a joystick back and forth and from side to side; the rudder responds to pedal movements. Mechanical linkages connect the joystick and pedals to the control surfaces. In heavier aircraft, hydraulics or servomotors move the control surfaces in response to movements of a steering column. Where servomotors are used, force-feedback mechanisms produce a resistance to motion of the steering column that gives a more natural "feel" to column movements.

In the case of conventional aircraft, small flaps in the control surfaces, called trim tabs, are adjusted to compensate for the distribution of passenger and cargo loads and for flying conditions. Trim tabs have to be adjusted continually throughout the flight, but they maintain the aircraft aerodynamically neutral. That is, an aircraft with correctly adjusted trim tabs will stay in straight and level flight unless actively steered.

In fly-by-wire aircraft, a computer constantly monitors the requirement for trim and adjusts the control surfaces accordingly. When such an aircraft is steered, the fly-by-wire computer provides instructions for the control-surface servomotors that combine steering and trim requirements.

Navigational instruments

An aircraft usually starts a flight with a well-defined route to follow. The pilot—human or automatic—then follows that route using maps, altitude measurements, and positional information from navigational equipment.

The basic navigational tool is the compass. Magnetic compasses in aircraft measure the craft's orientation relative to Earth's magnetic field using detectors called fluxgates. The spinning axis of a gyrocompass, on the other hand, remains parallel to Earth's rotational axis and indicates the aircraft's orientation relative to true north.

Most aircraft carry automatic direction-finding (ADF) equipment, which helps navigation where there is poor coverage by more advanced systems. ADF uses loop antennas to detect low-frequency radio transmissions from beacons. When the axis of the loop points directly at a station, the signal from that station falls to zero. This is the null position. At all other angles, some signal is detected. ADF equipment works by keeping the loop in the null position and reporting the beacon's bearing relative to the aircraft's position. Two such bearings are sufficient to determine the position of an aircraft.

More sophisticated than ADF is VHF omnidirectional ranging (VOR). VOR transmitters radiate two VHF (very-high-frequency) radio signals: an omnidirectional broadcast and a beam that sweeps around a vertical axis 30 times a second. The sweep beam is modulated such that it is in phase with the omnidirectional signal only when detected from due north. From other directions, the phase difference between the two signals indicates the receiver's bearing from the beacon. VOR has a range of around 100 miles (160 km).

Busy air routes are equipped with distance-measuring equipment (DME), also called the Rebecca-Eureka system. Aircraft transmit radar pulses that trigger automatic responses from ground stations within a range of 200 miles (320 km). The time interval between the outgoing and received pulses is used to calculate the distance of the aircraft from the ground station. In a similar system, called Consolan, the ground station returns signals that contain information on the bearing from which it received the aircraft's pulse, thereby giving the bearing of the responding ground station relative to the aircraft. Tactical air navigation (TACAN) is a military development from DME that gives information on the distance and direction between suitably equipped aircraft.

Loran, the *long-range-navigation* system, uses pairs of master-and-slave systems that transmit at frequencies around 2 MHz. The slave stations transmit under radio instructions from the master stations, and the interval between receiving pulses from the two transmitters defines a parabola over Earth's surface in which the receiver must lie. Obtaining similar information from a second pair of transmitters defines the plane's position. Loran has a minimum range of 750 miles (1,200 km).

Autopilot

On a long flight, an autopilot system might control flight for the majority of the time between takeoff and landing. First, the pilot enters course details into the autopilot's controls. Thereafter, the autopilot detects any deviations from the intended course using information from an inertial guidance system or from a radio navigation

AVIONICS

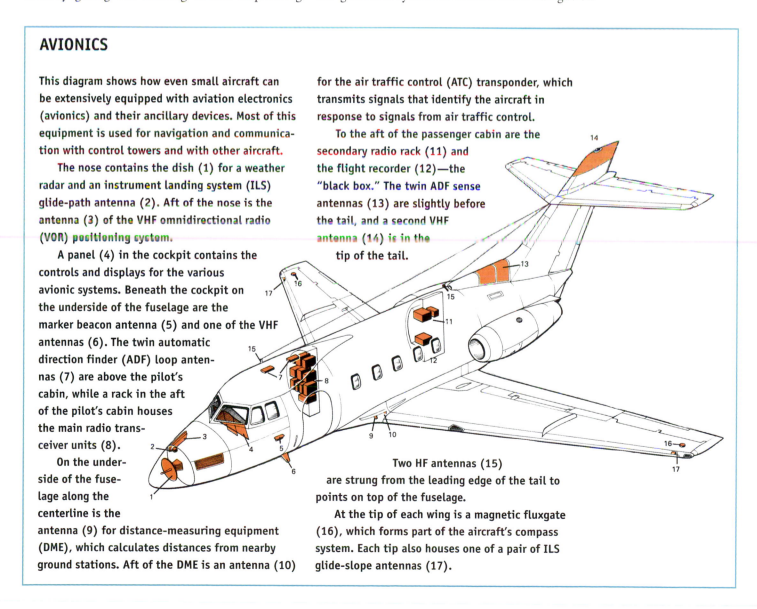

This diagram shows how even small aircraft can be extensively equipped with aviation electronics (avionics) and their ancillary devices. Most of this equipment is used for navigation and communication with control towers and with other aircraft.

The nose contains the dish (1) for a weather radar and an instrument landing system (ILS) glide-path antenna (2). Aft of the nose is the antenna (3) of the VHF omnidirectional radio (VOR) positioning system.

A panel (4) in the cockpit contains the controls and displays for the various avionic systems. Beneath the cockpit on the underside of the fuselage are the marker beacon antenna (5) and one of the VHF antennas (6). The twin automatic direction finder (ADF) loop antennas (7) are above the pilot's cabin, while a rack in the aft of the pilot's cabin houses the main radio transceiver units (8).

On the underside of the fuselage along the centerline is the antenna (9) for distance-measuring equipment (DME), which calculates distances from nearby ground stations. Aft of the DME is an antenna (10)

for the air traffic control (ATC) transponder, which transmits signals that identify the aircraft in response to signals from air traffic control.

To the aft of the passenger cabin are the secondary radio rack (11) and the flight recorder (12)—the "black box." The twin ADF sense antennas (13) are slightly before the tail, and a second VHF antenna (14) is in the tip of the tail.

Two HF antennas (15) are strung from the leading edge of the tail to points on top of the fuselage.

At the tip of each wing is a magnetic fluxgate (16), which forms part of the aircraft's compass system. Each tip also houses one of a pair of ILS glide-slope antennas (17).

system and altimeter. The autopilot then adjusts the settings of the control surfaces and engine throttles to correct the deviation from the intended course. Similarly, if the pilot changes the programmed course midflight, the autopilot takes action to put the aircraft on its new course.

Doppler radar

Doppler radar transmits radar pulses from an antenna at the front of the craft and detects frequency-shifted reflections from stationary or near-stationary objects, such as ground features and cloud formations. Doppler radar traces help detect and avoid storms and provide images of coastlines and mountains in the aircraft's path.

Landing

For the final leg of a flight—approach and landing—an aircraft is always under human control. Nevertheless, instrumentation helps ensure a smooth final approach and landing.

Most airports have an instrument landing system, or ILS. This system consists of vertical (glide-path) and horizontal (localizer) microwave radar beams that are directed along the approach slope from transmitters at the threshold of the runway. The flat glide-path and localizer beams cross along the ideal approach slope, which rises at around 3 to 4 degrees from horizontal along the projected center line of the runway.

Instruments in the cockpit produce a visual display of the aircraft's position relative to the ideal glide path and emit audible warnings if the actual approach deviates much from the ideal path. Vertical marker beacons along the approach give an indication of the aircraft's progress toward the runway. These devices are particularly useful in low clouds or fog, when the runway might become visible only in the final moments before touchdown. The pilot must activate the hydraulically operated landing-gear doors and await the indicator light that confirms that the landing gear is down and locked in place before landing.

Displays

While the information from instruments and sensors is vital for safe and efficient flight, its multiplicity could confuse rather than assist the crew if it were badly displayed. A great deal of thought goes into grouping the most critical displays and alarms in or near the forward view of the pilot.

In some aircraft, head-up displays project information onto semitransparent screens in the pilot's field of view. Data such as airspeed, altitude, bearing, and an artificial horizon appear on the screen without greatly obstructing the pilot's forward vision. Such displays help reduce fatigue.

ALTIMETRY

Altitude is a critical aspect of the flight of an aircraft. Altitude relative to mean sea level is relevant to air traffic control, which requires aircraft in the same geographical area to fly at separate altitudes. This altitude value is calculated from pressure measurements, since atmospheric pressure decreases with increasing altitude in a predictable way.

The vertical distance between the aircraft and the ground may differ from the altitude relative to sea level. This value is particularly relevant when making the final approach for landing or when flying in mountains. Height above ground is measured by use of a radar altimeter.

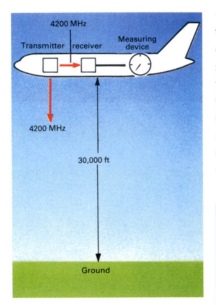

◀ A radar altimeter consists of a radar transmitter, a receiver, and a control computer. The transmitter repeatedly sweeps at a constant rate through a frequency range—4,000 to 4,400 MHz, for example. This upward sweep pattern is the basis for calculating the aircraft's altitude. The radar beam is directed toward the ground by an antenna in the underside of the aircraft's fuselage.

▶ The radar beam travels to the ground and bounces back at the speed of light. Its frequency is unchanged.

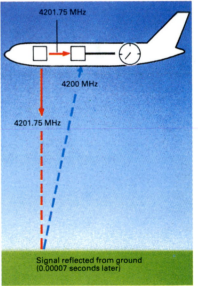

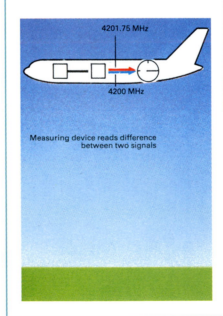

Measuring device reads difference between two signals

◀ An onboard computer compares the frequency reflected from the ground with the frequency being transmitted at the instant when the reflected beam is received. The difference indicates the time interval that has elapsed from transmission to reception of the reflected beam. This time interval, divided by the speed of light in air, is twice the distance to the ground.

SEE ALSO: AIRCRAFT ENGINE • AIRLINER • AIR-TRAFFIC CONTROL • HEAD-UP DISPLAY • HYDRAULICS • RADAR • SERVOMECHANISM

Aircraft Design

Aircraft design is an activity that produces plans for machines that can fly. In order to fly, the downward force of the weight of such machines must be approximately balanced by an upward force. For heavier-than-air craft this force, called lift, is usually generated by aerodynamic surfaces moving horizontally through air.

An aircraft must be designed with some means for maneuvering, which requires a torque to act around the center of mass of the craft. This torque can be generated by causing a temporary change in the aerodynamics of the craft or by applying thrust from rotors or jet engines with variable-geometry exhaust nozzles.

Apart from the basic requirements for flight, aircraft designers must take into account the intended use of the craft. Passenger aircraft have to be reasonably comfortable and economical,

▲ The designers of stealth aircraft such as this Northrop B-2 bomber had to take a fresh approach to aircraft design. The sharp angles and flat profile contribute to the minimal radar observability of the B-2. Also, its four General Electric F-118-GE-100 engines are concealed within the wing, which makes them less visible to heat-sensitive infrared cameras and muffles their noise. B-2s cruise at high altitudes at speeds just below that of sound.

whereas military aircraft must be efficient in combat and as close to invincible as possible; cost and comfort are minor considerations. Seaplanes must be able to land safely on water, and their center of buoyancy must match their center of mass, whereas conventional aircraft must have sturdy undercarriages for landing on relatively smooth but hard runways.

The flight speed and altitude of an airplane also influence its design. The source of thrust must be sufficient for the intended speed, and the aerodynamics of the craft must provide adequate lift throughout the speed range of the craft. The frame must also withstand the stresses of takeoff, landing, cruising, and thermal expansions and contractions caused by the temperature changes that occur during a flight.

Fuselage

The fuselage is the body of an aircraft; it is the section that carries the flying crew, instruments, passengers, and cargo. Most fuselages are made from aluminum or aluminum alloys, which combine low density with the necessary strength to bear the stresses of flight.

A typical airplane has a cigar-shaped fuselage, on either side of which is mounted a wing approximately midway from front to back. The front of the fuselage may be a protective radar-transparent dome, or radome, that houses weather radar and navigation antennas. The rear of the fuselage supports a tailplane and is tapered on its underside to allow the aircraft to tilt upward without catching on the ground at takeoff.

The tail may contain slugs of dense alloys or metals, such as depleted uranium, whose function is to make the center of gravity coincide with the center of lift—the point at which the lift appears to act, thus ensuring that the plane tends to fly level without requiring major trimming, or adjustment, of its elevator flaps.

The main portion of the fuselage, which is approximately cylindrical, is divided into pressurized compartments for passengers, crew, and cargo. The relative sizes of these compartments vary according to the function of the aircraft. Further compartments accommodate the undercarriage, when stowed during flight, and in the case of some military aircraft, bombs. Such compartments are not pressurized, since they are intended to open during flight.

Another type of aircraft is the flying wing. Unlike conventional aircraft, whose fuselages are streamlined to reduce drag but provide little or no

◀ The Rockwell B-1 bomber is a formidable combination of advanced design and complex avionics. A swing wing, or variable-geometry airplane, the wings rotate forward for greater stability at low speeds but sweep back for improved performance at high speeds and altitudes. Smooth lines and defensive avionics ensure a low radar profile.

lift, the whole of a flying-wing aircraft participates in generating lift. The squat profile of a flying wing is ideal for stealth aircraft, but its limited headroom is unsuitable for passenger craft.

Wings

Aircraft wings generate lift by two different mechanisms. First and foremost, they deflect air downward as they cut through air at speed. The force that increases the downward momentum of the air is matched, according to Newton's Third Law, by an upward force on the wings. This force contributes to the total lift. The strength of this effect increases with the downward slope of the wing from front to back, called the attack angle.

Second, wings generate lift through the Bernoulli effect, whereby the pressure of a fluid decreases with its increasing flow velocity. Wings that use this effect have a topside that is more convex than the underside. Air that passes over such an airfoil has a greater velocity—and lower pressure—than air that passes under the airfoil, and this pressure difference lifts the aircraft.

The amount of lift generated by an aircraft depends on its airspeed, and on the attack angle and shape of its wings. If airspeed falls, the wings can be tilted to increase the attack angle either by lifting the nose of the craft or by lowering wing flaps to increase the effective attack angle. At some point, however, the flow of air over the wing becomes turbulent and starts to beat down on the wing. Suddenly, all lift is lost, and the aircraft starts to drop like a stone—a dangerous occurrence that can be remedied only by turning the craft into a dive so as to increase the speed of the flow of air over the wing.

Jet aircraft must have thin wings with shallow attack angles in order to cruise at high speeds without incurring excessive lift and drag. However, the thinner the wing and the shallower

the attack angle, the greater is the speed at which an aircraft stalls. This is a potential problem at the low speeds desirable for landing and takeoff.

Subsonic jetliners fulfil the need for proportionately greater lift at low airspeeds near takeoff and landing by deploying leading-edge slats and trailing-edge flaps. When extended, the flaps and slats convert flat wings into strongly curved surfaces that provide greater lift—and increased drag—by scooping air downward. Gaps between the flaps and slats and the wing leak some air from the underside to the topside of the wing, having the effect of smoothing the airflow over the wing and reducing the critical speed for stalling. Nevertheless, jet aircraft take off and land at higher speeds than do propeller aircraft designed to cruise at lower airspeeds.

Supersonic aircraft must have extremely fine wings and shallow attack angles to be able to fly above the speed of sound without unacceptable disturbance from shock waves generated at such speeds. Such aircraft tend to have delta wings—so called for their resemblance to the Greek letter Δ (upper-case *delta*). When flying subsonically—

▼ This diagram shows the three axes of rotation of an aircraft—pitch, roll, and yaw. The control surfaces that produce motion of the aircraft around those axes are, respectively, the elevators, the ailerons, and the rudder. In a light aircraft, the ailerons and elevators are moved by moving a joystick, whereas the rudder is moved by pedals.

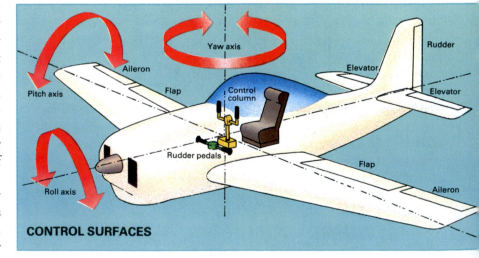

CONTROL SURFACES

Yaw axis · Aileron · Pitch axis · Flap · Control column · Rudder pedals · Roll axis · Rudder · Elevator · Elevator · Flap · Aileron

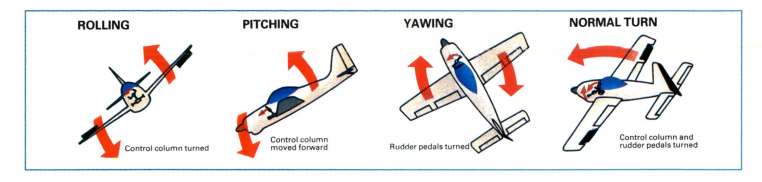

and particularly for takeoff and landing—pilots must raise the nose of such aircraft to increase the attack angle and achieve the necessary lift. Early designs for the projected Boeing Sonic Cruiser, which will fly close to the speed of sound, show a delta wing near the tail that widens to a more conventional wing at the rear. The design also shows smaller wings near the nose of the aircraft.

Some military aircraft meet the need to fly equally well at subsonic and supersonic speeds by modifying variable-geometry "swing wings." Such wings have a fixed rear section and a movable front section. In subsonic flight, the front section projects from the fuselage in a geometry similar to that of conventional aircraft wings. When passing through the sound barrier and in supersonic flight, the front portion sweeps back to join the rear portion. The combined wing that results resembles a diamond from which the rear point has been cut. In simpler designs, a swept-back fixed wing provides a compromise between the properties of delta and conventional wings.

Control surfaces

Once in the air, a pilot steers an aircraft by tilting it around three perpendicular axes that pass through the plane's center of mass: the pitch, roll, and yaw axes. These tilts are induced by adjusting control surfaces—essentially, hinged boards—that modify the aerodynamics of the craft.

Pitch is a measure of the nose-up or nose-down attitude of an aircraft. It is controlled by horizontal hinged surfaces on the trailing edge of the tailplane known as elevators. Moving these upward directs the airflow upward and results in a downward pressure on the tailplane, forcing the aircraft into a nose-up attitude. Turning the elevators downward has the opposite effect.

Yaw—nose-left and nose-right attitude—is controlled by a vertical rudder flap mounted at the rear of the tail fin. If the rudder is used alone, the aircraft slews sideways, but this way of turning is inexact and poorly controlled.

Roll is motion around the centerline of the fuselage. It is induced by tilting flaps on the wings—ailerons—in opposite directions at the same time. Lifting the right aileron while lowering the left aileron induces a clockwise roll viewed in the direction of flight, for example.

The ailerons seldom deploy alone: more usually, the ailerons and rudder are moved in combination to induce banked turns when the plane tilts toward the center of the turn. Some aircraft have control surfaces called elevons, which act as combined ailerons and elevators. Other aircraft have X-shaped tail planes that also incorporate the function of the rudder.

Vectored thrust

The wings and control surfaces of conventional aircraft require the craft to be moving forward in order to function. A few aircraft designs obviate the need for forward motion by using vectored thrust, whereby the air flow from their engines can be directed to the rear, vertically downward, or at any angle between at the will of the pilot.

Vectored-thrust aircraft are capable of vertical takeoff and landing (VTOL), where the thrust is first directed downward to gain height and then rearward to gain forward speed; the wings then start to provide lift. They are also capable of short takeoff and landing (STOL), where conventional lift at takeoff is augmented by downward-angled thrust. Such maneuvers are particularly useful in combat, when there might be insufficient space for conventional takeoff.

The British Aerospace Harrier, developed for the U.S. Navy as the AV8, is an example of a vectored-thrust aircraft. Powered by modified turbojet engines, Harriers have a front pair of movable nozzles that direct air from the fan, while a rear pair direct combustion. The Bell V-22 Tiltrotor aircraft has propeller engines mounted in wing sections that rotate from horizontal to vertical. Both aircraft can switch between the efficient forward flight of orthodox aircraft and the vertical maneuverability of helicopters.

▲ Roll is produced by the action of the ailerons, pitch by the action of the elevators, and yaw by the rudder. A normal (banked) turn is a combination of roll and yaw caused by moving the ailerons and rudder at the same time.

SEE ALSO: Aerodynamics • Aerospace industry • Aircraft-control engineering • Aircraft engine • Airliner • Aviation, history of • Supersonic flight • V/stol aircraft

Aircraft Engine

Aircraft engines, from the primitive original used by the Wright brothers in their first airplane onward, have sought to maximize the power-to-weight ratio that can be achieved. The term *aircraft engine* can, strictly speaking, be applied to any aircraft power unit, but it is normally applied to the specialized piston engines that were used in airplanes until they were largely superseded by the jet engine.

Aircraft engine development

The history of the development of the aircraft engine is of a struggle to combine high power, lightness, and reliability. These qualities were also required in the automobile engine, which was developed at much the same time, but even the earliest aircraft demanded more power than the early automobile industry could produce.

When the Wright brothers came to search for an engine to put into their latest glider in 1903, they thought they could manage to fly with one of only 8 horsepower, provided it was not too heavy. They approached, without success, half a dozen makers of car engines. Eventually, they built their own engine and got 12 horsepower from it, but it was still relatively heavy at 15 lbs. (7 kg) to the horsepower. Thirty years later, engine designers were aiming at a power-to-weight ratio of over 1 horsepower per lb. (2 horsepower/kg).

The Wrights' first engine had four cylinders set in line like those of a small car engine. The year after their first flight, a five-cylinder motor, designed by an American engineer, Charles Manly, developed 50 horsepower at a ratio of 4 lbs. (1.8 kg) to the horsepower.

In the years leading up to World War I, the French led the field in engine design, producing several 50 horsepower and two 100 horsepower engines by 1908. However, the best of these still had a power-to-weight ratio of only 3.7 lbs. (1.7 kg) to the horsepower.

Early engines were water cooled, and the cylinders were arranged in line or in a V-formation, as in an automobile. In 1907, a new and highly successful type was introduced; the rotary engine. In this engine, the crankcase and cylinders revolved in one piece around a stationary crankshaft. The pistons were connected to a single pivot mounted off-center so that they moved in and out as they revolved with their cylinders. The airscrew was connected directly to the front of the crankcase and turned with it.

This odd-sounding arrangement worked surprisingly well. It had fewer parts than a conventional engine, and since the cylinders moved rapidly around, they could be air cooled by fins mounted so as to take advantage of the draft. Both factors contributed to the lightness of the engine.

Rotary engines always had an odd number of cylinders, which reduced the amount of vibration that was created, since there were never two pistons moving in exactly the same direction at the same time. The original 1907 Gnome engine had seven, and later types, nine.

Other types of engine produced at the time included the Spanish Hispano-Suiza, a design well ahead of its time with eight steel cylinders arranged in a V and screwed into an aluminum block. In the later years of the war, this engine yielded, in successive versions, 150, 220, and 300 horsepower. The Rolls Royce Eagle, a V12 engine with a broadly similar layout adapted from an original Mercedes design, produced 360 horsepower in its Mark 8 version. This was the engine of the Vickers Vimy that carried Britons Alcock and Brown across the Atlantic in 1919.

The radial engine

Both the Rolls and Hispano engines had conventional water cooling. This system often gave trouble, since vibration and the shock of landing caused the plumbing to break. It was to overcome this problem that a third type of engine was introduced: the air-cooled radial engine, in which static cylinders were arranged in a circle and cooled by the backwash of the propeller.

This idea was not completely new, since the water-cooled Manly-Balzer engine of 1902, fitted

▼ Today's propeller-driven airliners, such as the British Aerospace 748, use turboprops instead of piston aero engines: they are not only lighter, quieter, and more free from vibration but also more fuel efficient. A turboprop burns fuel like a jet engine, but the gases are used to power a compressor, which drives the propeller. In a jet engine the gases are exhausted to provide thrust.

▲ Aircraft of the future, such as this high-maneuverability fighter model, will increasingly rely on lightweight, high-thrust jet engines.

to the unsuccessful Langley Aerodrome, had also been a radial. The air-cooled Anzani engine, which powered Louis Blériot's cross-Channel flight of 1909 was also a kind of half-radial, with three cylinders set in a fan shape. The first of the new generation of radials was the 14-cylinder Jaguar engine made by the RAF factory at Farnborough in England in 1918.

Problems with cooling

Proper cooling is one of the most critical points of aircraft engine design. Aircraft engines have always produced far more power for their size than automobile engines of the same date and have consequently run at much higher temperatures.

These problems led to great rivalry between the designers of air- and water-cooled engines. Their object was to produce completely reliable engines that were adequately cooled with the lightest possible system—thus improving the vital power-to-weight ratio.

As far as reliability went, the water-cooled engine seemed to have all the advantages. Any desired temperature could be maintained by altering the size of radiator fitted to the engine. The temperature of the engine was kept within safe limits by the boiling point of the cooling water, since the engine's temperature could rise no higher than this point until the cooling water had boiled away completely. Some engines used this feature in evaporative cooling systems, where the water was allowed to boil at the engine. The steam was ducted off, recondensed into water, and

then returned to the engine. This novel system had been in use as early as 1907 in the French Antoinette engine.

In some other aero engines, ethylene glycol (antifreeze) was used as a coolant, raising the boiling point to 285°F (140°C) to provide an additional safety margin.

The principal problem with this type of engine was the weight and complexity of the cooling system—it was one more thing to go wrong. Air-cooled engines did not suffer from this problem, since their system had no moving parts.

The cylinders were always arranged radially in one or more circular rows just behind the propeller, an ideal position for cooling. These cylinder rows were also spaced quite far apart so that their outside could be covered with large fins in order to increase the surface area and thus improve heat dissipation.

Early radial engines had their cylinders completely exposed to the air, but in the early 1930s, a shaped-ring cowling was added around the engine in order to improve the air flow around the cylinders and reduce the drag that was created by the wide, flat-fronted engine.

The main trouble with the air-cooled radial was that there was no fixed upper limit on its temperature, so it would overheat very quickly if it was overextended. This problem, however, led to a solution with considerable implications: the production of high-quality, heat-resistant alloys that made the development of the high-performance jet engine possible later on.

Advances in design

The aircraft engine designers of the 1920s and 1930s had little of today's complex testing equipment, such as ultrasonics and spectroscopes. They managed, however, to produce reliable engines with ingenious new features by means of good design and careful workmanship.

One of the best of these improvements was the sleeve valve, which replaced the valve gear of a conventional engine with a single tube sliding up and down between the piston and the cylinder—this completely encircles the piston and has ports, or holes, in its upper end. They slide past matching ports in the cylinder head, which are connected to the fuel supply and exhaust systems, thus opening and closing them at the correct time. This greatly reduces the number of moving parts in the engine, particularly as the sleeve can be moved by quite simple machinery set around the inner edge of the ring of cylinders instead of the conventional long train of rods and levers reaching to the outside.

The alloy of which the sleeve is made is vital. If it expands too much as it heats up, it jams against the cylinder; if it expands too little, it jams against the piston. The sleeve valve's designer, Roy Fedden, had to consult 60 firms before he found the right alloy.

Many engines had superchargers—compressors that force extra fuel and air into the cylinders and thus improve the engine's performance. They had been used as early as 1910 but were never entirely satisfactory, because the compressor needed power to drive it and thus wasted some of the extra power it provided. Several attempts were made to build a turbo-supercharger (turbocharger) powered by a turbine that was driven by the exhaust gases, but there was as yet no alloy that would withstand the high temperatures involved. The alloy was found later.

By the mid-1930s, engines were producing so much power that the propeller was being driven at an excessive speed. The tips of the blades broke the sound barrier and created shock waves that reduced the propeller's efficiency. The difficulty was overcome by gearing the propeller down. The more advanced American engines had variable gearing. By the end of the 1930s, most propellers also had variable pitch (blade angle) so that they could run efficiently at different speeds.

There was always an incentive for designers to produce more and more powerful engines. During the 1920s and 1930s, it was the glamorous (and lucrative) Schneider Trophy; later it was the desperate dash to build faster aircraft during World War II.

Among the most famous engines of this long period of rapid development were the British Jupiter in 1921, producing 485 horsepower,

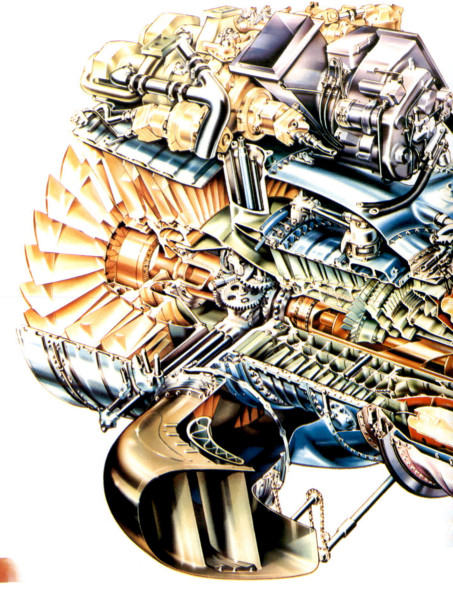

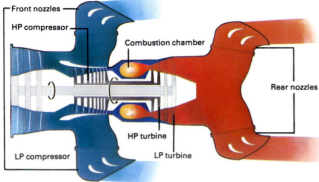

◀ The rearmost nozzles of a jet engine do most of the hard work. The front nozzles blow air drawn in by the low-pressure compressor, enabling a turbofan to move a large mass of air.

designed by Fedden; in 1926, the American Pratt and Whitney Wasp, producing 600 horsepower; and in 1929, the American Wright Cyclone, producing 1,525 horsepower—all nine-cylinder radials.

Meanwhile, Rolls Royce produced a V-12 water-cooled engine for the Schneider Trophy that gave 2,600 horsepower, though only for a few minutes at a time—all that was needed for two successful races. The basic design of the short-lived engine was used for the famous Rolls Royce Merlin, which powered the Spitfire, Hurricane, and Mustang in World War II. The original 1934 Merlin produced only 790 horsepower, but by the end of the war, this value had been considerably increased to well over 2,000 horsepower by successive modifications.

Radial engines included the British Bristol Hercules of 1936, a 14-cylinder, two-row radial that gave 1,980 horsepower, and a long series of American Pratt and Whitney Wasp engines, such as the 1937 Double Wasp (2,500 horsepower) and the 1945 Wasp Major, an amazing 28-cylinder, 4-row radial (3,800 horsepower). By this time, the piston aero engine had reached the end of its possibilities as an engine for large aircraft. It was used for years afterwards, and still is, for small aircraft, but leadership in design has passed to the jet engine and gas turbine.

▼ A Rolls Royce Pegasus Mk 104 engine of the British Royal Navy's Sea Harriers. The Pegasus is a two-stage turbofan engine with a low bypass ratio of 1.4:1 and 21,500 lbs. of thrust, all of which is divided between the Harrier's fuselage-mounted jet nozzles. The four nozzles swivel from an aft-facing direction to point downward 10 degrees forward of the vertical. On takeoff it uses a third of the fuel a jet with afterburners would require, while developing enough power to push the plane up. The Pegasus's thrust-to-weight ratio is nearly 6:1.

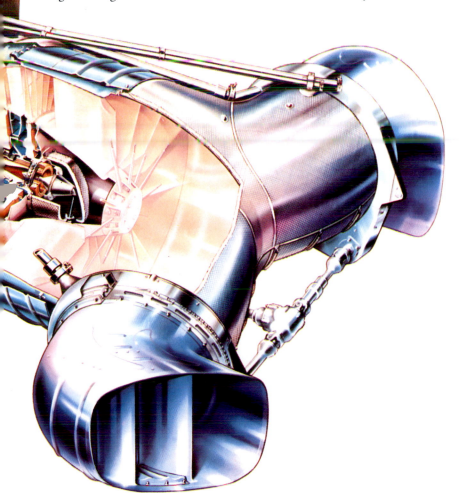

Jet engine and gas turbine

The gas turbine and its variant, the jet engine, are the latest developments of old principles. The word *turbine* comes from the Latin *turbo* which means a "whirl" or "top" and was originally used to describe submersed water wheels.

The gas turbine as we know it was patented by John Barber in 1791. His drawing showed the essential features of the modern engine: a compressor, from which air is passed to a continuous-flow combustion chamber in which fuel is burnt, and a turbine, through which the resultant hot gases pass. The hot gases turn the blades of the turbine, and this motion drives the compressor. There is more power than is needed to drive the compressor, because in a gas, the energy available from the expansion of a hot gas is greater than the energy required to compress it when it is cold.

The blades of a turbine, which experience a continuous flow of combustion, can withstand temperatures only up to about 1100 K (1520°F, 827°C) reliably over a useful period of time, even using complex modern nickel–cobalt alloys. The oxygen in the air can be only partly utilized to ensure a safe temperature of critical parts. This feature seriously limited the output and efficiency of the gas turbine and was a stumbling block for many years. The original Parsons steam turbine patent of 1844 referred to the use of a reversed turbine as an axial compressor for a gas turbine, and there were other proposals but no practical developments until early in the 20th century.

Turbochargers

The gas turbine principle was first successfully put to use in the turbocharger, a variant of the gas turbine that produces no power itself but increases the power output of the engine to which it is attached. A turbine is activated by the flow of hot exhaust gases from the engine. It in turn operates a compressor, which raises the density and thus the mass flow rate of the air charge to the combustion chamber of the engine. The first turbocharger was designed by Alfred Büchi and built by the Swiss corporation of Brown-Boveri in 1911. In 1916, turbochargers were first used in aircraft, and they were subsequently used in the most successful operative airplanes in World War II.

Jet engines

Frank Whittle, a pilot officer in the Royal Air Force who was later knighted for his achievement, patented a simple gas turbine and a nozzle to provide a jet-propulsion device, or turbojet, in 1930. In 1936, he formed Power Jets Limited to develop it, and in 1939, the company received a

contract for a flight engine. Various engines, American, German, and British, took the design forward over the next decade or so.

Since then, gas turbines have mainly been developed for airplanes, because they provide greater thrust with reduced weight and bulk. Also, the efficiency of the engine increases with increased speed and height. As a result, the gas turbine has now effectively replaced the piston engine and propeller for aircraft propulsion, except in light airplanes.

Efficiency

Early aircraft engines all used centrifugal compressors, which offered increased efficiency and greatly reduced engine frontal area compared with noncentrifugal designs, thus enabling improved aircraft aerodynamics.

Some 60 percent of the energy from burning fuel is absorbed by the turbine and used to drive the compressor. Significant efficiency gains can be made by improving the way energy is extracted by the turbine and used by the compressor.

Augmenting thrust

For supersonic flight, the simple jet engine is suitable, as the high speeds match more closely the aircraft's high forward speed. Jet speeds are sometimes increased by burning extra fuel between the turbine and the propelling nozzle using surplus oxygen left in the turbine gases. This phenomenon is called afterburning and increases thrust considerably. A characteristic of afterburning is that it increases the noise level of aircraft taking off. Another technique that is used to increase

▲ A Rolls Royce RB211 turbofan being checked with an X-ray camera mounted on a forklift truck. The large-diameter fan at the front of the engine produces a high bypass ratio and consequently a high propulsive efficiency. As the fan's diameter is much greater than the air intake, most of the air flows around the engine without going through its core.

thrust for takeoff is coolant injection, where a coolant is injected into the compressor or combustion chamber to cool the air.

Other types of jets

The turboprop engine, like the fanjet, makes use of extra turbine energy to save fuel but uses it to drive a conventional propeller rather than a fan inside the engine cowling. During the 1950s, turboprops were used on large jetliners, but they are used only on small aircraft nowadays. However, new turboprop designs are still being pursued, with one arrangement using multiblade fans mounted on the rear of the engine and directly driven from low-pressure turbines. Such engines are intended for mounting at the rear of the aircraft, with the fans acting as pusher propellers. The turboshaft is similar to a turboprop but used to drive a transmission shaft rather than a propeller shaft. Such engines are used to drive helicopter rotors.

Ramjets and pulse jets are also called athodyds, an acronym derived from aero thermodynamic duct. They have no rotating parts. In the ramjet, incoming air is compressed by a shaped inlet nozzle that slows its velocity and raises its temperature. After combustion, the hot gases expand and leave the rear nozzle at a velocity greater than that of the aircraft, providing the thrust. The ramjet operates only at forward speed, so a takeoff assist is necessary. Ramjets are most efficient in the 1,500 to 2,500 mph (2,400–4,000 km/h) range.

The pulse jet operates intermittently. The air enters through a valve that then closes; combustion takes place and thrust is produced. When the pressure on the combustion chamber drops, the valve opens and the cycle begins again. Pulse jets were used during World War II in the German V-1 flying bomb. They were unreliable and extremely noisy and had high fuel consumption but were simple and inexpensive to build. Since the war, they have been used for target drones.

The turboramjet is a hybrid jet engine in which the turbojet is closed off from the airflow when speed is attained, and the bypassed air used in a large afterburner.

Turbofan engine

The turbofan engine, which is used by many airliners, is an advanced form of jet engine. Ordinary jet engines work by sucking in cold air, mixing the air with fuel, and then igniting the fuel–air mixture. When the mixture is ignited, it expands and leaves the engine in the form of a jet of vapor that travels faster than the cold air coming into the engine. As it travels backward from the engine, this jetstream reacts against the engine with an equal and opposite force, and makes the engine move forward and in this way propels the airplane.

Jet engine operation

When a jet airplane is taking off or flying at low speeds, not much air is forced into the engine's air intake by the forward motion of the airplane, and so a compressor pumps air into the intake. The compressor rotates at the front of the engine and draws in large quantities of air, which it pressurizes and pumps to the combustion chamber. Here, fuel is added to the compressed air and ignited. The resulting high-speed jet of hot gas is made to flow through a turbine on its way out of the engine, making the turbine rotate. The turbine section of the engine is connected to the compressor section by a shaft that runs through the core of the engine.

Once the jet engine has been started and has been provided with a constant supply of fuel, the whole cycle is self-supporting, with the compressor forcing air into the combustion chamber and the jetstream turning the turbine, which in turn drives the compressor.

Jet engines are particularly suitable for use in high-speed aircraft such as military airplanes and supersonic airliners, but they can be uneconomical at the subsonic speeds used by most civilian airplanes. The fuel economy of a jet engine depends on two main factors. One is the thermal efficiency of the engine—that is, the efficiency with which the fuel is burned in terms of extracting as much useful energy as possible from each unit of fuel. The other factor used in assessing a jet airplane's performance is propulsive efficiency. This factor is a measure of the proportion of the power of the engine that is actually used to drive the airplane forward.

The propulsive efficiency of a jet engine is at its highest when the speed of the jet stream from the engine is as close as possible to the speed of

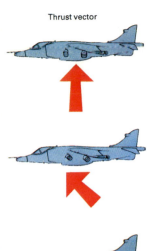

Thrust vector

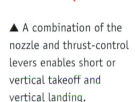

▲ A combination of the nozzle and thrust-control levers enables short or vertical takeoff and vertical landing.

◄ The Wright brothers built their original engine of 1903 themselves. It was a simple four-cylinder design weighing 180 lbs. (80 kg) and produced a maximum of 12 horsepower, which was rather poor even at the time.

the airplane through the air. Thus, an airplane with a cruising speed of 500 mph (805 km/h) will have a low propulsive efficiency if the jet stream from its engines is moving at 1,000 mph (1,609 km/h). Low propulsive efficiency is reflected in an unnecessarily high fuel consumption.

One way to achieve higher propulsive efficiency from a jet engine is to slow down the jet stream. This effect cannot be achieved, outside narrow limits, by increasing the size of the jet's exhaust nozzle, because the thermal efficiency of the engine depends partly on the relative sizes of the turbine and the exhaust.

The bypass principle

The method that has been used to slow down the jet stream is known as the bypass principle. In jet engines that use this method, not all of the air that enters the front of the engine is forced through the combustion chamber and turbine; instead, some of it flows around the sides of the engine and bypasses the combustion and turbine stages. The bypass air travels at a slower speed than the jet stream from the turbine and thus acts to lower the overall speed of the stream.

The proportion of the total airflow that passes around the outside of the jet engine is described by the bypass ratio. If twice as much air passes outside the engine as goes through it, the bypass ratio is 2:1. A high bypass ratio, and consequently high propulsive efficiency, can be achieved by mounting a large diameter fan on the front of the engine. It is this specific design of engine that is known as a turbofan engine, or fanjet, the type of engine that is most commonly found today in large commercial airliners.

Turbofan engines often have a bypass ratio of 5:1, because the diameter of the fan is much greater than that of the air intake to the compressor that feeds the combustion chamber, so most of the air drawn in by the fan flows around the engine without going through its core. Some turbofans use ducts to guide the air around the engine; these are known as ducted-fan engines.

Increased efficiency

The increase in propulsive efficiency of the turbofan can be around 25 percent, enabling airplanes powered by this system to travel much farther on the same amount of fuel. The other important advantage of the turbofan is its lower noise level. The slower jet stream from the engine creates less disturbance as it meets the atmosphere and therefore makes less noise. The fan itself is also a potential source of noise, but careful design of the blades can reduce this problem by a significant amount.

In a turbofan, with its high bypass ratio, air passing around the engine contributes approximately three-quarters of the total thrust. As a result, the engine will be lighter than nonbypass designs, because the size of the compressor, combustion, and turbine stages can be scaled down in proportion to the amount of air flowing through them. Any weight saving in the engine itself contributes to the overall fuel economy of the airplane, because the engine has less mass that it needs to propel.

New developments

Current developments in jet engine technology are taking the turbofan principle one stage further. A new breed of jets, with propellers mounted at the rear of the engine, are being developed for civil aircraft. The propellers of these propfan engines have fewer blades than the front-mounted turbofans and do not have an outer casing of the type that protects the blades of the turbofan. The propeller blades serve the same function as the turbofan, producing a stream of air at a relatively low speed compared with the exhaust from the jet engine. The effectiveness of the propfan depends on the aerodynamic efficiency of the propeller blades and the speed at which they rotate. Some propfan engines use gearing to make the propeller turn more slowly than the turbine in order to reduce the noise that a high propeller tip speed would cause.

Other developments are intended to enable the shape of the aircraft itself to be modified, enabling weight reductions and extra fuel efficiency. Boeing currently has a project at trial stage, the RS-2200 Linear Aerospike engine. This engine fills the base of the aircraft, reducing base drag. It is integral to the base, making installed weight less than that of a bell-shaped engine fitted on the wing. The Aerospike functions in the same fashion as a bell-shaped engine apart from its nozzle, which is left open to the atmosphere. The open plume compensates for decreasing atmospheric pressure as the vehicle ascends, ensuring that the engine's performance remains very high along the entire trajectory. With this altitude-compensating feature, a simple, low-risk gas generator cycle can be used.

Manufacturers are also developing engines using the latest computer-design technologies with a view to reducing fuel use and harmful emissions. For instance, the Pratt and Whitney PW300 family utilize fans designed by 3-D computer-modeling techniques to optimize fuel burn.

Engine parts are also being made from advanced titanium alloys to reduce weight and improve durability. A through-flow combustor ensures efficient and clean combustion to meet the latest nitrous oxide emission requirements. Noise-reduction requirements are addressed by a forced exhaust mixer that improves the fuel burn and thus reduces the resultant noise signatures.

Electronics are also helping to provide integrated engine thrust management; for instance, the Full Authority Digital Electronic Control (FADEC) concept enables enhanced control of engines and propellers.

Safety and reliability remain major drivers. The latest Rolls Royce engine, the Trent 500, has been tested to withstand a failed fan blade, bird strike, and tropical rain and hail and can start at –40°C and operate in severe crosswinds.

NASA has also begun serious testing of the scramjet, which sucks in oxygen directly from the atmosphere, powering the craft through the skies up to ten times faster than the speed of sound.

Two of the uncrewed research aircraft are planned to fly at Mach 7, with the third planned to reach Mach 10, about 6,700 mph (10,720 km/h). A scramjet is a duct with no moving parts through which airflow is permanently supersonic. Instead of turbines, it relies on high forward speed and efficient integration between its own profile and the underside of the aircraft to which it is attached to ensure that the incoming air is efficiently ingested and compressed before it is mixed with fuel and burned.

NASA calculates that 25 percent of the weight of such an air-breathing plane could be payload, replacing the stored oxygen. The acronym scramjet stands for super-combustion ramjet, and one of the main design features is that it avoids generating supersonic shock waves inside the engine. NASA's prototype, the X-43A, began its test flight stage in 2001 and is set to break new records as the fastest jet ever.

◄ A Rolls Royce Pegasus engine used in the V/STOL Harrier. This engine employs a turbofan design, which provides vectored thrust for vertical takeoff.

SEE ALSO: Aerospace industry • Airliner • Aviation, history of • Compressor and pump • Internal combustion engine • Propeller • Rocket and space propulsion • Supersonic flight • Turbine • V/stol aircraft

Air-Cushion Vehicle

Air-cushion vehicles (ACVs)—also known as hovercraft or ground-effect machines (GEMs)—are vehicles that, when in motion, are supported by a layer of air rather than by wheels or other direct means of contact with the passing surface.

This absence of contact with the surface has brought the advantages of both adaptability and speed: the latter is particularly well demonstrated when the ACV is compared with a conventional ship. For example, the large passenger ACV, the 300-ton (275 tonnes) SR.N4 Mk3 Super-4, is capable of speeds of 65 knots (120 km/h). The top speed for a crack liner is 35 knots (65 km/h). There are a number of reasons for this difference. First, in a conventional ship, that area of the hull which is normally submerged is subjected to drag as a result of the viscosity of the water through which it travels. Drag absorbs a good deal of engine power.

Second, wave formations are set up at the bow and stern of a ship when it is under way. Again, this wave-making process means a drain on the power supply. Although this factor is less important than drag at low speeds, as speed increases, it takes over as the major power-wastage problem.

Finally, there are natural phenomena of currents and also of wind effects on the exposed areas of hull and superstructure.

Considering the first two factors alone, it can be appreciated that the bigger and faster the ship, the larger the amount of energy wasted. There comes a point when the cost of deriving more speed from a ship outweighs the advantages—unless there are special military or research factors.

Since none of the ACV is immersed, it has none of these problems. At low speeds a wave-making process is set up, but at cruising speeds it disappears. So, though the ACV is affected by adverse winds, it is generally not only faster than a conventional vessel of the same size but also faster than larger ships.

In principle, the ACV works as follows. The hull can be thought of as being something like an upturned tea tray with raised edges. If such a structure were placed carefully on the surface of water, a quantity of air would be trapped beneath it, retained by the edges, which would now be jutting downward. If, however, you tried to propel the tray through the water, the air would escape and the tray would sink. Even if the tray did not sink, the submerged portions of the edges would be subjected to friction and would set up waves.

The pioneer designers were faced with two problems: how to raise the craft clear of the water, and how to keep the air cushion in place.

They overcame the first by ducting air into the cushion compartment at pressure a little higher than the atmospheric pressure, and the

▲ The biggest hovercraft are capable of carrying a number of cars and buses on two decks. The passengers leave their vehicles for the "flight" as such journeys are called, and sit in comfortable passenger compartments.

second by arranging a system of air jets around the edge to provide a curtain of air, thus slowing down the rate of leakage from the cushion. This system was improved by the addition of a flexible skirt around the vessel's edge.

It has been calculated that a pressure of only about 60 lbs. per sq. ft. (300 kg/m²) is required to raise an ACV of 100 tons (90 tonnes) or more to a height of 1 ft. (30 cm). The pressure required to inflate car tires is a good deal greater.

Types of ACV

Several variations of the basic ACV principle have evolved. The simplest is called the air-bearing system. Air is blown through a central orifice in the undersurface and leaks away outward in all directions from under the flexible retaining skirt.

The plenum chamber vessel has a concave under-surface, and the cavity forms the upper section of a cushion chamber, which is completed by the sea or ground surface. Again the air leaks away under the edges of the retaining skirt.

In the momentum curtain system, a ring of air jets is set around the circumference of the underside of the ACV. The air from these jets is

▲ An SR.N5 in service with the British Army in Malaysia, where vehicles of this type were well suited to jungle and swamp conditions. They carry a payload of 18 passengers or up to 2 tons (1.8 tonnes) of commercial freight.

directed downward and inward to retain the air cushion. This system has been further developed to include two rows of peripheral jets, one inside the other. The retaining air is blown out through one set, sucked up by the other after it has done its job, and recirculated, thus enabling greater efficiency because of a slower rate of air escape.

There are also several types of ACV propulsion systems. The most popular for large vessels has been the airscrew, or propeller, system. In the earliest machines, the fans that provided lift also drove air through a system of ducts to the stern where it was ejected for propulsion. In the SR.N4, the four engines that drive the lift fans

▲ The low-noise BHC AP.1-88 diesel engine hovercraft entered service on the Isle of Wight in 1983 and is much quieter than its gas-turbine-powered rivals.

▶ A Russian gas-turbine-powered hovercraft operating tourist passenger services along the Volga River to the Caspian Sea.

also drive external propellers for propulsion. In many other types, the lift and propulsion systems are separately powered. Some ACVs even have water propellers—these cannot go on land.

The problems of steering an ACV are very similar to those of steering an airplane. As the ACV has no contact with sea or land, there is a danger of drift during turns. The helmsman overcomes this problem by banking, or tilting, his machine like an aircraft. He does it by reducing pressure from the air jets on the side that he wants to dip. Directional control is exerted by varying the power of the propeller or by using the tail fins or both systems.

Development

The air-cushion principle has fascinated designers for many years. Pioneering attempts to use it were made, for example, as far back as the 1930s, in both the United States and Finland. However, it was not until after World War II that the real breakthrough came.

The inventor of the first successful ACV was Britain's Christopher Cockerell. Originally trained as an engineer and in electronics, he later turned his attention to the problems of boat and hovercraft design. He tried at first to retain an air cushion under a boat by fitting hinged flaps at the bow and stern of his craft between side keels.

Finding this technique to be ineffective, he replaced the flaps with sheets of water pumped vertically downward. Air containment was still not very efficient, and finally, he struck on the idea of using peripheral air jets for the purpose.

The world's first hovercraft, the SR.N1, was unveiled in 1959 when it traveled from the Isle of Wight to mainland England. Only a few weeks later, it crossed the English Channel in two hours, and in 1965, the world's first regular passenger service was set up between the Isle of

Wight and the mainland. For many years, a fleet of SR.N4s carried passengers and cars regularly between Britain and France and in 1982 captured 20 percent of the total traffic. This service was discontinued in 2000, and hovercrafts are increasingly being replaced in commercial service by the modern, maneuverable hydrofoil.

However, several services remain, and large numbers of enthusiasts own small craft. In 1983, an entirely new type of hovercraft, the BHC AP.1-88, went into service between Ryde on the Isle of Wight and Southsea in England. Instead of having a hull that is riveted together, like an air-craft fuselage, it has a welded aluminum hull, and in place of the more usual gas-turbine engines, it is powered by four Deutz 428-horsepower air-cooled marine diesel engines. Two of them drive the lift fans, and two drive the two ducted propellers at the rear of the craft via toothed rubber belts. The AP.1-88 is much quieter and cheaper to run than a gas-turbine-powered hovercraft of equivalent size.

The AP.1-88 is 77 ft. (23.55 m) long and 33 ft. (10.1 m) wide and is capable of carrying up to 101 passengers (depending on seating arrangements) at speeds of up to 58 knots (107 km/h). It can be adapted to carry freight or vehicles for either civil or military purposes. A second AP.1-88 service, linking Malmo in southern Sweden with Copenhagen's Kastrup airport, began in 1984.

Uses of ACVs

Because the air cushion acts as a form of support and also as an effective spring, the modern ACV can cope with waves of up to 10 ft. (3 m) and can operate over rough ground. It has been used for military purposes by the U.S. armed forces in Vietnam and elsewhere in the Far East.

There is also the whole area of ACV application on dry land. The concept has been used in the design of several devices, including a type of lawn mower, a hover pallet for transporting heavy loads around the factory, and enormous craft like the U.S. ACT 375, designed to carry a 375-ton (340-tonne) payload.

There is also a hybrid system, the Bertin Hovertruck, which has conventional wheels for travel over highways and solid ground, but to travel over marshland, a built-in air-cushion system supports three-quarters of its weight.

▲ This air-cushion transporter (above and left) spreads the load of heavy weights evenly across a cushion of air. The load is placed on top of the uninflated cushion, which then has air pumped into it. These devices are capable of moving over 200 tons (180 tonnes).

FACT FILE

- *Probably the world's biggest user and developer of hovercraft is Russia, which services the communities along the 5,000 miles (8,000 km) of coast between Murmansk and Vladivostock with an estimated 10,000 surface-effect ships.*

- *The U.S. Navy, needing large, fast combat and support ships, experimented with diesel and gas-turbine powered hovercraft capable of 80 knots (135 km/h) and weighing up to 13,000 tons (11,700 tonnes). These hovercraft were exceeded in size by the planned, but never built, East German Atlant nuclear-powered ferry, which was designed to carry 4,000 passengers and 2,000 vehicles across the Atlantic in two days.*

- *In Canada, an air-cushion-assisted golf cart has been developed. The hover mechanism reduces the weight on the wheels in wet conditions, enabling the cart to be used throughout the year.*

SEE ALSO: AERODYNAMICS • AMPHIBIOUS VEHICLE • HYDRODYNAMICS • HYDROFOIL • MARINE PROPULSION • SEAPLANE AND AMPHIBIAN

Airliner

An airliner is an aircraft used for the commercial transportation of passengers and cargo. Most airliners carry passengers with some amount of cargo apart from the passengers' baggage; some airliners are customized to carry only cargo.

Early passenger airplanes

The first scheduled passenger service to use an airplane started on January 1, 1914—little more than 10 years after Orville and Wilbur Wright's first motor-powered airplane flights toward the end of 1903. During its four months of operation, the two-seater seaplane of the Saint Petersburg–Tampa Air Boat Line took some 1,200 passengers on a 20-minute crossing of Tampa Bay, Florida.

In Europe, the four years of World War I caused major disruption of the ground infrastructure, thus stimulating the use of airplanes for passenger traffic. In North America, mail companies used airplanes for rapid deliveries, thereby establishing a network of air carriers.

In 1927, the introduction of the Ford Trimotor—the first all-metal aircraft—enabled mail carriers to develop as passenger carriers. Nicknamed the Tin Goose, the Trimotor was the first airplane designed primarily for passengers rather than cargo. It had 12 passenger seats, and its cabin had enough headroom for passengers and attendants to walk upright.

The year 1933 saw the introduction of the Boeing 247—an insulated 10-seater passenger craft with retractable landing gear, wing flaps, and variable-pitch propeller engines. Soon after, the Donald Douglas company introduced three types of airliner: the DC-1, DC-2, and DC-3. The DC-3s seated up to 21 passengers,

and their 1,000-horsepower (750 kW) propeller engines enabled them to fly from coast to coast across the United States in less than 16 hours. Such performance led the DC-3 to dominate the passenger airline market in the late 1930s. The Douglas aircraft were the first to have stress-bearing bodies that eliminated the need for internal supports and that are now a universal feature.

Pressurization

While many early airliners were insulated against the low temperatures encountered at high altitude, they operated at ambient pressure. Consequently, they could fly at altitudes only where the air was sufficiently dense for the passengers to breathe and remain conscious. This imposed a flight ceiling of 8,000 ft. (2,400 m), which is where altitude sickness sets in.

The Boeing Stratoliner of 1940 was the first airliner to eliminate this altitude restriction by

---

THE BOEING 767-200

Launched in 1978, the medium-range, wide-body Boeing 767-200 can carry a maximum of 290 passengers, eight abreast, in its passenger cabin, and up to 22 standard-sized cargo containers in its underfloor cargo hold. In a typical equipment configuration, the 767 has two Pratt & Whitney JT9D-7R4D turbofan engines, each delivering up to 48,000 lbs. (213.5 kN) of thrust. The maximum cruising speed of this airliner is 571 mph (914km/h), but a more economical cruising speed of 534 mph (854km/h) is usually adopted. The layout and equipment of the 767-200 are typical for passenger jet airliners of this size and range. The 767 was designed concurrently with the narrower 757, with which it shares a cockpit design and many other features.

(1) Radar dish (2) Radome (3) Captain's seat (4) 1st officer's seat (5) Engineer's seat (6) Engineer's panel (7) Folding seat (8) Entry doors (both sides) (9) Forward toilet (10) First-class cabin (18 seats) (11) Forward freight door (12) Electronics bay (13) Air conditioning riser ducts (14) Leading edge slat (extended) (15) Vent surge tank (16) Integral fuel tank (17) Spoiler (deployed) (18) Toilets (19) Inboard double-slotted flap (20) Rear spar fuselage frame (21) Tourist cabin (193 seats) (22) Cargo door (rear, open) (23) 10 cargo containers in rear hold (24) High-frequency (HF) antenna (25) TV antenna (26) Tail VOR (VHF-omnidirectional-ranging antenna) (27) Auxiliary power unit (APU) (28) Honeycomb construction (29) Static dischargers (30) Tail logo light (31) Aft galley (32) Aft toilet (33) Pressurization unit (34) Undercarriage mounting beam (35) Wheel bay (36) Hinge link fairing (37) Inner aileron (38) Flap hinge fairings (39) Outer aileron (40) Stringers (41) Main undercarriage (42) Turbofan engine (43) Engine-mounting pylon (44) Slat drive motor (45) Air conditioning distribution ducts and manifolds (46) Landing and taxiing lights (47) Cargo containers (48) Electronics cooling plant (49) Nosewheels (50) Nosewheel bay (51) Glide-slope antennas

▶ A mock-up image of Airbus Industrie's A380, which is due to enter service around 2005. In its highest-density seating configuration, the A380 will be able to carry 990 economy-class passengers.

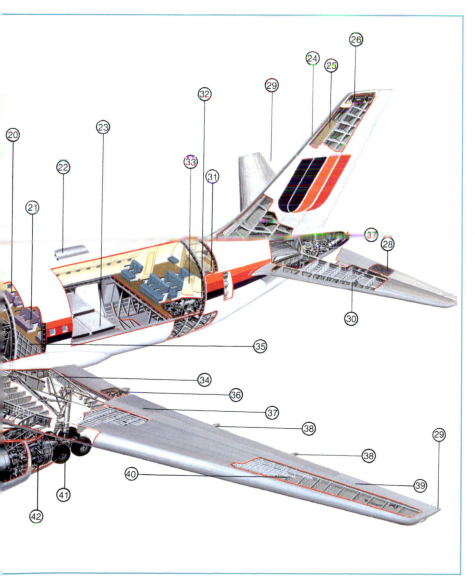

use of a pressurized cabin. The Stratoliner, derived from the B-17 bomber, carried 33 passengers at altitudes up to 20,000 ft. (6,100 m). Higher altitude limits allowed the Stratoliners to fly above the turbulence of storm clouds, which had been a major cause of airsickness in the early days of passenger flight. The reduced air resistance at higher altitudes also permitted faster flying speeds, and the Stratoliner was capable of cruising speeds of around 200 mph (320 km/h).

Jetliners

The passenger airliners of the 1940s featured many of the design elements of modern airliners: they had monocoque (load-bearing) aluminum or aluminum-alloy bodies; pressurized, insulated, and heated cabins for crew and passengers; a single wing on either side of the fuselage; and an underfloor hold. The next great advance was the introduction of jet propulsion, which had been patented in 1930 and developed for military aircraft during World War II.

The first commercial jetliner was the British DeHavilland Comet, which entered service in 1952. The four-engine Comet cruised at 550 mph (885 km/h), a speed that drastically reduced journey times taken by propeller aircraft. The square windows of the first Comets were prone to break at high altitude, causing a series of depressurization accidents and two fatal crashes. They were replaced by stronger round windows in the later models.

The faster flight times of the Comets stimulated the market for long-distance air travel.

Their teething troubles created an opportunity for U.S. manufacturers to launch two models that would become the workhorses of the 1960s' jet age: the Boeing 707 and the Douglas DC-8.

The four-engine Boeing 707, launched in 1958, could carry 110 to 120 passengers at cruising speeds around 625 mph (1,000 km/h) over ranges greater than 4,200 miles (6,700 km) between refuelling stops. A total of 878 Boeing 707s were built by the end of production in 1978, and most of the 120 or so still in service have now been converted for cargo use.

The Douglas DC-8—also a four-engine craft—was launched in 1959. Somewhat larger than the 707s, DC-8s were designed to carry between 132 and 179 passengers over ranges up to 7,000 miles (11,200 km). A total of 295 Douglas DC-8s were built in around a decade of production; around 80 units are still in service.

The Boeing 707s and Douglas DC-8s offered unprecedented speed and comfort for passengers and improved reliability for airline operators. As competition between operators became fierce during the 1960s, the quality of in-flight meals and refreshments, served from onboard galleys, and the amount of legroom between seats became critical factors in winning custom.

Size of aircraft

In the 1960s, the developing passenger air travel market demanded new sizes of jetliner. Short-range shuttle journeys required smaller aircraft than the 707s and DC-8s. This demand was met by aircraft such as Boeing's trijet 727 (94 seats; entered service 1964) and twin-jet 737 (100 seats; entered service 1968) and the McDonnell Douglas DC-9 (70 seats; entered service 1965).

▲ Launched in March 1970, the Lockheed L-1011 TriStar was the second "jumbo" jet to enter service. The TriStar is powered by three Rolls Royce RB211-22B turbofans, each capable of delivering 42,000 lbs. (187 kN) of thrust at 625 mph (1,000 km/h). The TriStar can carry up to 400 passengers and 16 standard LD3 underfloor cargo containers over ranges greater than 4,250 miles (6,800 km).

Another market sector required much larger wide-body "jumbo" jets for the economical transport of customers on long-haul routes. The first and largest of these jets was the Boeing 747, which entered service in 1970 and can seat from 397 to 500 passengers, depending on the seating configuration. The most prominent characteristic of the 747, apart from its size, is the bulge in its top slightly aft of the nose. This bulge houses an upper deck of first-class seating.

The first version of the Boeing 747, the 747-100, was fitted with four Pratt & Whitney JT9D-7A turbofans with a maximum thrust of 46,950 lbs. (208.9 kN) each and had a maximum speed of just over 600 mph (960 km/h). The more powerful 747-200B was typically fitted with four 53,110 lb. (236.2 kN) Rolls Royce RB211-524D4s and had a top speed of 613 mph (981 km/h).

Depending on load, the ranges of these models were from 5,680 to 7,990 miles (9,080–12,780 km). The maximum takeoff weight of the 747-100 was 750,000 lbs. (340,195 kg). Its wingspan was 195 ft. 8 in. (59.6 m), its length 231 ft. 10 in. (70.7 m), and its maximum height 63 ft. 5 in. (19.3 m). The wing area was 5,500 sq. ft. (511 m²).

The diversity of jetliner capacities has continued to grow and currently covers the range from corporate jets, which carry small teams or even individuals, to the "megatop" Boeing 747-400, which can hold up to 568 passengers. The next great advance will be the Airbus A380, due to enter service around 2005. The A380 will carry up to 990 passengers in two full-length decks.

Speed

The fastest passenger airliner in service is the Anglo-French Concorde, which cruises at 1,362 mph (2,179 km/h)—Mach 2.02 (2.02 times the speed of sound)—at an altitude of 51,300 ft. (15,600 m). After almost two decades of development, the 128-seater Concorde was launched in 1976. The revenue from Concorde has not justified its development costs, and it is unlikely to be replaced by another supersonic airliner. Boeing currently plans to build a "sonic cruiser" that will carry up to 300 passengers at speeds of Mach 0.95 (641 mph, 1,025 km/h) or more.

SEE ALSO: AIRCRAFT DESIGN • AIRCRAFT ENGINE • AIRPORT • AIR-TRAFFIC CONTROL • ALLOY • SUPERSONIC FLIGHT

Air Lock

The air lock is a chamber designed to allow movement between compartments containing air at different pressures or between a pressurized or vacuum compartment and outside atmosphere with a higher or lower pressure.

A very common application, and one which demonstrates the principle involved, is its use in the caisson. This device is used for carrying out work on submerged bridge foundations, harbor structures, and so on. It consists of a wide vertical tube that reaches from the surface to the work site. To keep the tube free of water for the workers, the pressure of the air inside must be maintained at the same level as that of the water around its lower end—inevitably greater than the surface air pressure.

This end could be achieved by simply sealing the top of the caisson with an airtight trap door and pumping air inside to the necessary pressure. However, as soon as anyone attempted to open the trap in order to enter or exit, the pressurized air inside would rush out. Water would then flood the caisson. The problem is overcome by having two airtight trap doors with a space between—the air lock. If a worker wishes to leave, valves between the work area and air lock are opened, equalizing the air pressure on each side. The worker can then climb the ladder to the lock and enter, closing the trap door and valves behind to seal the work chamber again.

If workers do not need to undergo decompression, they can open the upper door and let themselves out. In this case, some of the high-pressure air will rush out, but that in the work chamber will be unaffected in any way. If decompression is needed, then the pressure level in the lock is gradually reduced to atmospheric level by venting it through a set of valves in the upper door.

The journey is accomplished in reverse in very much the same way, except that the air in the lock will be at surface pressure when the workers enter. So, after the door is closed behind them, the air pressure in the lock is pumped up until it is equal in pressure with the work chamber, allowing them to take the next step.

Tunnel air locks

Similar air locks are employed in the construction of tunnels that run under the seabed or under rivers. High-pressure air is pumped into the work area to keep the water out, and pressure is maintained by a bulkhead. This air lock is the walk-through type, with an airtight door at each end on either side of the bulkhead.

A further version of the air lock is used in submarines, either to allow the crew to escape in emergencies or to allow divers to work outside the hull. The difference here, though, is that the air pressure inside the submarine is always lower than that of the water outside. Hence, if an exit were attempted simply by opening a hatch, the vessel would be rapidly flooded.

An air lock allows the departing diver to seal the first hatch behind him or herself, thus rendering the submarine safe, and then to open the valves on the outer door to let the seawater in. When the lock is filled with water, the diver can open the outer door and leave the vessel.

On reentry, the diver shuts the outer door, blows out the seawater with compressed air, and closes the outer valves. Then the pressure is equalized with that inside the submarine at a speed necessary to prevent decompression sickness, and the diver enters the main hull.

Air locks are also used in spacecraft as a means of allowing astronauts to leave the craft—the internal pressure of the module must be maintained against the vacuum of space. Air locks are also employed in clean-room environments, the manufacture of electronics equipment, for example, which is extremely sensitive to dust. Materials necessary for these manufacturing processes may pass through an air lock in order to avoid contaminating the internal clean air with dust and particles from outside.

▲ The air lock connecting the mid-deck crew area of a space shuttle with its cargo hold.

▼ Astronaut Thomas D. Jones in the airlock of the space shuttle *Atlantis*.

SEE ALSO: AIR • PRESSURE • ROCKET AND SPACE PROPULSION • SPACE SHUTTLE • SUBMARINE • VACUUM • VALVE, MECHANICAL

Airport

Air travel is among the safest and most popular means of transport. In the United States, for example, the number of passenger miles flown annually on scheduled domestic and local routes is measured in hundreds of billions.

Surprisingly, in all but a few instances, passengers board their intended plane at the expected location and takeoff and land on schedule. Such an outstanding success rate is the result of meticulous organization and careful planning aided by the latest in high technology.

It would have been difficult in the early days of the airplane to envisage the growth potential of civil aviation and the complexity of air services and airports that is now routinely provided. Today, the spread of cities and the greater impor-

tance of air travel means that airports have to be planned to meet a careful balance between aviation and environmental needs.

A major airport requires good highway and rail links with the city center. Passengers should be able to park their cars within a short walk of the terminal in which their airliner is docked.

In between the car and the aircraft, the airport, airlines and control authorities, like immigration and customs, must provide the embarking passenger with ticket and check-in counters, passport checkpoints for international flights, concourses with lounge and general consumer services such as duty-free shops, and a pier connecting the terminal with the door of the aircraft. The disembarking passenger wants to get out of

the aircraft as quickly as possible and either leave the airport or catch a connecting flight. Passengers that are catching connecting flights want to get to the appropriate gate—though it might be some distance away—without a long walk and without bothering about baggage. All this trafficking has to be accomplished without mixing the inward- and outward-bound passengers. Those who choose to go to and from the airport by rail have similar needs. Ideally, one train should serve all the terminals of the airport without making passengers change. Another track should be used for automated shuttle services between all the gates.

Security systems are also important: space must be allotted for X-ray baggage-screening systems, and metal-detector portals, and the passageways must be wide enough to allow sniffer dogs searching for illegal substances to have unrestricted access to passenger and baggage areas.

To these requirements, the airport designer must add those of the airlines. The largest airports, such as London Heathrow, employ up to 100,000 people whose jobs include dealing with passengers and their baggage, servicing and refueling aircraft, air traffic control, and so on. Nearly as many workers may go into and out of an airport each day as passengers. They need to have parking spaces and offices and separate access for service vehicles to the aircraft.

The aircraft themselves make great demands on space. Runways two-miles (3.7 km) long and 150 ft. (45 m) wide are required for modern commercial jets. Most airports have at least two runways and turn-offs and taxiways to enable the shortest taxiing time to and from the terminals.

A modern aircraft requires a terminal apron of at least 100 yds. (90 m). During rush hours at big airports, there may be as many as 50 aircraft in

◀ An aerial view of Schipol Airport in the Netherlands. Arrivals to and departures from the airport itself are centered around the parking lots and railroad terminus (mostly underground here) to the right of the picture. The main airport building with its customer services and flight facilities is in the middle; down from there the long arms of the flight terminals themselves stretch out to the airplanes clustered around them on the ramp. Taxiways are designated by a white or yellow unbroken line down the middle and lead out to the runways. All airports are designed to similar specifications so that aircrews are not forced to adjust to differing national practices.

hop flights, have found they can save time in refueling by using high-pressure refuelling tankers that use powerful pumps to push aviation fuel into the airplane at an accelerated rate.

Landings

The aircraft approaches its runway by ILS (instrument landing system). ILS equipment on the ground provides approaching aircraft with heading (directional) and glide-path information. Aircraft normally join the center line (align with the runway) 5 to 6 miles (8–10 km) from the runway and follow the guidance beams until they have landed. Procedures are becoming increasingly automated, and many aircraft can carry out the complete approach and landing without any manual pilot control at all. ILS was originally designed for use in bad weather but is now regularly used at major airports to keep traffic flowing smoothly. Radar is a valuable partner for ILS. Surveillance radar normally covers several hundred square miles of airspace around each airport. An incoming aircraft is seen as a blip on the radar screen, which is used by the air traffic controller to steer the pilot on to the ILS beam.

Less busy airports use VOR (VHF omnidirectional range) beacons, which are also used as en route radio beacons. VOR is less satisfactory than ILS because it gives heading guidance only.

Visual landing aids are still important. The visual approach slope indicator, or VASI, which operates day and night, is not a substitute for ILS, an airfield-in-sight aid. Bars of red and white lights on either side of the runway are angled to show the pilot all red lights when he is below the glide path, red and white lights when he is on the correct glide path, and all white if he is too high. The runway itself has white centerline lights and bars to mark the touchdown area. At the end of the runway, the centerline is red. The edges of the runway are marked with white lights. Taxiways have green centerline lighting with blue lights along the edges.

The lights set into the runway and designed to withstand the 300 tons (270 tonnes) exerted by a landing aircraft, are nearly flush with the ground, so they are not an obstacle. The light from a 200 W tungsten-halogen bulb shines through an aperture no more than 0.5 in. (13 mm) above the runway.

Runways have to be kept clear of obstacles—stones, parts of aircraft, and so on—which can easily burst a tire. To ensure runways are clean, vacuum cleaners and sweepers are used 24 hours a day. Snow clearance can be such a problem that plow blades, brushes, and blowers are required. Birds may also pose a problem—birds sucked into

dock, representing a frontage of some 3 miles (5 km). If each airliner has 350 seats, it may generate a hundred cars; half a dozen aircraft a day may dock at one gate, so parking for 600 cars has to be found for each gate.

Aircraft also need parking and maintenance space. Planes are designed for on-condition or on-wing maintenance, in which replacements for faulty units are fitted while the plane is parked. Such systems enable routine maintenance to be performed speedily and accurately, but aircraft still have to undergo scheduled intensive maintenance at regular intervals.

Airliners have to be turned around as quickly as possible between flights to reduce costly time spent on the ground, when they are not actively earning money. The time between flights may be as little as 20 minutes, during which passengers have to be disembarked and the aircraft refueled, checked, cleaned, and reprovisioned and the next group of passengers embarked. Some airlines, particularly those specializing in low-cost, short-

▲ Check-in area at London's Gatwick Airport. Most international airports use computerized systems that can link passengers and their baggage to a particular flight, a vital service in big airports handling a large number of different carriers.

a jet engine can cause considerable damage so most airports go to considerable lengths to scare them away. London's Heathrow airport uses a falconer, who flies birds of prey at regular intervals to scare wild birds away.

Without doubt, the airport's least-used equipment is its fire, crash, and rescue vehicles. The introduction of larger aircraft has required big increases in the quantities of fire-extinguishing materials, such as foam. The trend is toward a knock-out punch—that is, a large quantity of fire-damping material applied in one minute so that the passengers and crew can be disembarked as quickly and as safely as possible. A fleet of "quick dash" trucks carrying cutting devices, breathing apparatus, ladders, axes, and other emergency rescue equipment is on constant alert in the event of an accident.

More commonly seen on the ground are aircraft tugs, capable of pulling the heaviest aircraft, and also fuel tankers, which carry up to 24,000 gallons (90,000 l). A Boeing 747 has twice this capacity, so large airports use hydrants linked by underground piping to a fuel-farm storage center. With this system, flow rates of thousands of gallons per minute are possible.

Cargo handling

The airport provides the space and the airline supplies the equipment for cargo handling. The standard international pallets and containers are today common to all airports. The transfer between aircraft hold and surface vehicle is dealt with by equipment ranging from the simple roller-slide or forklift truck to the more complex automatic power conveyors. The scissor-lift platform lends itself well to big and heavy loads and also high holds and is standard equipment—truck or trailer mounted—wherever cargo has to be offered up to aircraft of different hold heights.

Baggage handling

Baggage handling is recognized as one of the major sources of problems in airline operations. Worldwide, ten million travellers, each with a number of individual items, are handled each day, and compensation must be paid for any bags that get lost. To improve the system, suitable baggage-handling equipment has been developed that largely uses conveyors. Passenger baggage comes in an infinite variety of shapes and sizes—not only suitcases made of varied materials but also backpacks, duffel bags, folding strollers, skis, golf clubs, and boxes.

Three factors have compounded the difficulties of baggage-conveyor manufacturers: the advent of wide-bodied jet airliners, capable of carrying 300 to 500 passengers, which utilize mini-containers holding about 1,000 individual units that must be quickly and accurately handled; increasing air traffic, which has led to departure and arrival gates far removed from the main building and check-in points and from long and often complicated conveyor systems; and multi-level terminals, which may require baggage to be lifted or lowered vertically 40 ft. (12 m) or more without dominating expensive floor space or destroying the building's visual appeal.

Handling methods

Any arrangement for conveying baggage must carry individual items, without damaging them or removing or damaging their destination labels, and guide each unit efficiently to its destination.

A modern conveying system handling outbound baggage will accept items from dozens of check-in points and deliver them to any of several aircraft loading points. Terminal 4 at Britain's Heathrow Airport has 64 check-in desks with eight primary conveyors to four automatic tilt tray sorters. There are separate conveyors for nonstandard baggage. The terminal capacity is 2,000 passengers an hour in each direction, using 22 aircraft stands on a continuous basis.

▼ International terrorism and smuggling of contraband have increased the need for airport security. All major airports now have X-ray equipment for checking a passenger's luggage for weapons and other illegal items.

◀ Cargo-only Boeing 747. These aircraft are specifically designed for commercial freight loads and have articulating nose cones for easy loading.

The curve of this chute is designed to allow the baggage to slide quickly between floors without being damaged by impact.

Airport baggage handling can be divided into three phases: arrival and acceptance; conveyance within the building; and delivery to the aircraft or the passenger. Outbound, the first phase involves identification of the flight and destination of the bag, which could be going to any one of several stops on the aircraft's route.

At larger international airports, passengers place their bags on short conveyors mounted on electronic weigh scales. Check-in personnel read the weight, then the bags are moved to short addressing conveyors and given a destination tag. Transfer of bags to dispatch conveyors is initiated by programmable controllers that ensure bags from check-in desks can be conveyed with equal priority, without causing jams, in the shortest possible time. Bags are then either sorted manually by flight number and destination or, if automatic sorting systems are used, guided through the system to the correct aircraft loading stand.

Baggage from incoming flights is loaded on to a conveyor, which takes it to a point in the main terminal where baggage in transit is taken from the incoming plane to join the connecting flight.

Automatic systems are used at big, busy airports because they help to reduce high labor costs and speed the flow of baggage. A relatively simple method of controlling a bag from a check-in point to its aircraft loading position is to attach a bar code sticker. Controlling scanners in the conveyor system read the code and route each bag to its destination. The latest systems use photocells, which carry the same information as labels: the bag's owner, flight number, final destination, and intermediate connections and airlines. Using bar codes or photocells enables the destination data to be logged on a computer, so bags can be tracked throughout their journey simply by scanning the bar code at transfer points.

Conveyors

Three main forms of conveyor are used at airports for moving baggage. An airport baggage complex may use one or more methods in a complete system, as each has advantages and disadvantages. Belts made of heavy-duty rubber or multilayer flexible materials provide good, non-slip surfaces for straight runs, but modified belt units have to be provided at corners and bends.

A second method involves the use of pallets or plates linked together to form a continuous moving flat surface. Pallet conveying systems can follow very complicated routes. Each pallet is formed from molded rubber or plastic and will withstand the considerable shock from loads of weights dropped onto them—75 lbs. (34 kg) released from 18 in. (46 cm) is typical.

The third method is to provide individual trays, each carrying one bag. The trays, which move in a continuous chain, can be programmed to tip their contents when they reach a predetermined point in the system.

Tipping trays provide one method of changing the path of a bag, for example, from the main conveyor to a collecting point. Other commonly used methods include arms or plows, which on demand, move across the conveyor to intercept a bag and divert it. Another method is to tilt a conveyor belt, causing the bags to run along a fence. Parts of the fence can be opened to allow individual bags to fall through onto a chute. Powered or gravity roller conveyors, used in warehouse systems, have a very limited use with airport baggage because items may stick on them.

Some international airports have gate room check-in at piers, which are built from the terminal onto the airport apron. Late passengers take their bags to the gate room, where they are placed on a spiral chute that conveys them to apron level. These stainless steel chutes are profiled to control the rate of baggage descent.

Future baggage-handling systems may be even more sophisticated: Las Vegas airport already has an unusual baggage check-in system that allows passengers using certain airlines to check their bags at their hotel or at car rental outlets.

SEE ALSO: AEROSPACE INDUSTRY • AIRLINER • AIR-TRAFFIC CONTROL • AVIATION, HISTORY OF • HELICOPTER • RADAR • RADIO • SECURITY SYSTEM • X-RAY IMAGING

Airship

An airplane obtains its lift from its speed through the air and the airfoil wing shape, whereas an airship, or dirigible (meaning it can be steered or directed), uses a gas that is lighter than air. The motion is provided by motor-driven propellers.

The gas in the gasbag is considerably lighter than the air it displaces, thus making the airship as a whole slightly lighter than its own volume of air. It therefore rises until it has reached a height where the air is thinner—and thus light enough to balance the weight of the airship.

This lift has to be controlled to make an airship workable. Early airships used to achieve lift by releasing gas and replacing it with air, a wasteful method that caused gradual reduction of lift as more and more gas was lost. This loss could be compensated for by carrying water as ballast, which could be released to lighten the airship. Later airships replaced the system with ballonets, collapsible air bags inside the gasbag but connected to the outside air. By varying the amount of air in the ballonets with pumps, the volume of the gas in the rest of the bag can be changed. There are usually two ballonets, to the forward and rear of the gasbag, so that the balance of the ship can be adjusted.

The tail fins operate just like those on an aircraft and are the control surfaces by which the ship is steered. Conventional elevators are used to change the altitude of the craft when it is moving; the change of atmospheric pressure with altitude is compensated for automatically by varying the amount of air in the ballonets.

The lightest gas is hydrogen, which is also fairly inexpensive to manufacture. However, its extreme flammability has resulted in the much more costly, slightly less effective, but completely safe helium being used in all modern airships. Helium is found in small amounts with natural gas in the United States but is otherwise very expensive to produce.

Types of airships

There are, or have been, three categories of airships, rigid, semirigid, and nonrigid. The rigid types consisted of a light metal framework containing several gasbags slung inside under nets and with a separate outer cover. The German zeppelins and most airships of the 1920s and 1930s were of this type. The metals used were lightweight aluminum alloys, the outer skin was cotton, and the gasbags were cotton lined with goldbeater's skin, a thin membrane taken from the intestines of cows.

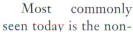

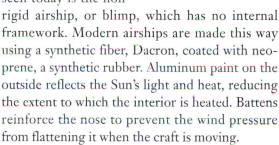

◄ Inflating a blimp. The flexible envelope of the airship is laid out and filled with helium. Ballast weights attached to the blimp prevent it from becoming airborne (below). Finally, a passenger gondola and motors are attached prior to flight.

The other types, semirigid and nonrigid, are known together as pressure airships, since their shape is maintained mostly by the internal pressure. The semirigid types had a metal keel along the length of the envelope.

Most commonly seen today is the nonrigid airship, or blimp, which has no internal framework. Modern airships are made this way using a synthetic fiber, Dacron, coated with neoprene, a synthetic rubber. Aluminum paint on the outside reflects the Sun's light and heat, reducing the extent to which the interior is heated. Battens reinforce the nose to prevent the wind pressure from flattening it when the craft is moving.

Development

The early development of the airship occurred in France. After the invention of the balloon in 1783, ways were sought to make its movement independent of the direction of the wind. The problem was to produce a suitable light, yet powerful means of propulsion, and it was a Frenchman, Henri Giffard, who first produced a 3-horsepower engine weighing about 350 lbs. (160 kg). His 75,000 cu. ft. (2,124 m³) hydrogen-filled craft ascended from the Hippodrome in Paris in 1852 and flew at 5 to 6 mph (9 km/h) over the city.

The first rigid airship was built in Germany in 1895 by a Croatian wood merchant, David Schwarz. It was braced internally by a system of steel wires. Five years later, the German inventor Count Ferdinand von Zeppelin carried Schwarz's idea further in his much bigger airship built at Friedrichshafen. It had an aluminum frame consisting of 16 hoops connected and kept rigid by diagonal and longitudinal wire stays. The design

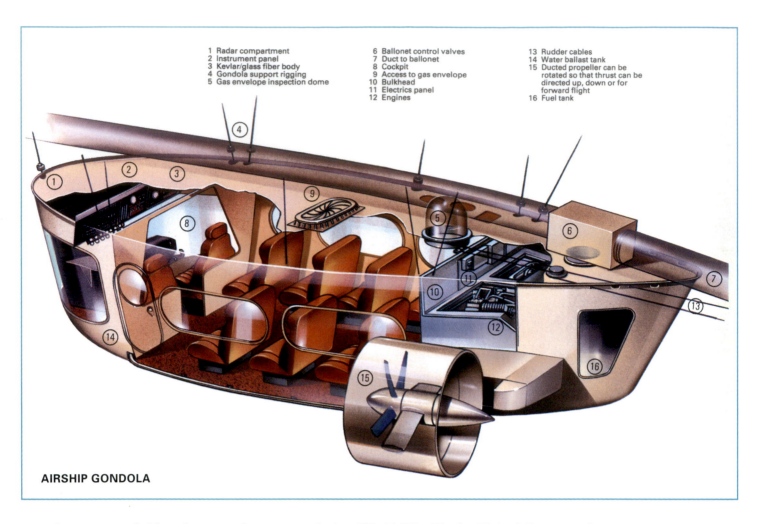

1 Radar compartment
2 Instrument panel
3 Kevlar/glass fiber body
4 Gondola support rigging
5 Gas envelope inspection dome

6 Ballonet control valves
7 Duct to ballonet
8 Cockpit
9 Access to gas envelope
10 Bulkhead
11 Electrics panel
12 Engines

13 Rudder cables
14 Water ballast tank
15 Ducted propeller can be
   rotated so that thrust can be
   directed up, down or for
   forward flight
16 Fuel tank

AIRSHIP GONDOLA

proved a success, and although one was lost, more than 20 airships of the same type were built.

In contrast, the British had given only occasional attention to the development of the airship. Consequently, at the Battle of Jutland, the British fleet had no airborne observers, whereas the German fleet had the help of 29 airships. Soon zeppelins were making raids on English targets. The Royal Navy reacted quickly. They arranged for the construction of some small, nonrigid airships, which proved excellent at detecting and attacking enemy submarines. The British finished the war in 1918 with a fleet of 103; Germany had 68 rigid airships.

The heyday of the giant rigid airship was in the late 1920s and 1930s. The United States decided to use only helium in its airships and also banned the export of helium. Therefore, the large British and German craft had to rely upon hydrogen. The flammability of the gas and the lack of maneuverability of the ships often had appalling consequences. Many of the largest airships met with disaster, notably the British *R101* in 1930, the American *Akron* and *Macon* in 1933 and 1935, and the zeppelin *Hindenburg* in 1937.

The heavy loss of life in these crashes swung opinion against the use of airships, and they were no longer used for carrying passengers. However,

during World War II, the United States used large numbers of nonrigid airships without a single loss for sea patroling. Their ability to operate for long periods of time at low speed and low altitude made them invaluable for minesweeping and escorting convoys.

Postwar revival

In recent years, advances in aeronautical engineering and technology have led to a resurgence of interest in airships, especially of the nonrigid kind, as a safe means of transport for passengers and particularly cargoes. New materials, such as carbon fibers and titanium alloys, polyamide-based synthetic fabrics, Mylar, and neoprene-coated Dacron, together with computer-aided trim and ballast controls, gas turbines, and diesel engines have increased the potential of airships as a transport medium. The Goodyear company, for example, continues to operate a small number of commercial blimps that are used for aerial advertising and as vibration-free television camera platforms for sporting events.

▲ The 7-passenger gondola of *Skyship 500*. Airships have not been used as a commercial form of passenger transport since the disasters of the 1930s.

SEE ALSO: AERIAL PHOTOGRAPHY • AERODYNAMICS • AVIATION, HISTORY OF • BALLOON • FIBER, SYNTHETIC • GAS LAWS • HYDROGEN • NAVIGATION • PRESSURE

Air-Traffic Control

Air-traffic control (ATC) is one of the crucial factors in air safety. It is a system for preventing collisions between aircraft, particularly in congested areas in the neighborhood of airports, where the air is full of aircraft of different sizes traveling in various directions at various speeds and heights. ATC also monitors the progress of aircraft along a flight path and the position of aircraft when moving on the ground prior to takeoff and after landing at airports.

Established routes called airways are used for the majority of flights. Airways are corridors in space and are defined by a fixed width (usually around 32 miles, or 50 km) and fixed altitudes, which allow aircraft to fly in opposite directions along the airway. These vertical separations in space are divided into upper, middle, lower, and controlled airspace, with 1,000 ft. (305 m) intervals between them. Areas around airports or places where a number of airways intersect are included in controlled airspace to minimize risk of collision. There may also be restrictions on aircraft movement around military installations.

Flight plans

With certain exceptions, each flight requires a flight plan that includes aircraft identification, airport of departure and destination, route plan, desired cruising level, departure time, and elapsed time of the flight. These plans are checked before takeoff, and emergency exit corridors are decided.

The data is transmitted, generally by land line or computer link rather than radio, to the air-traffic control center from airports within the controller's zone or from adjacent zones. The information is always to a standard format to minimize the risk of omission and to simplify its communication.

Above 25,000 ft. (7,500 m), the pilot may be allowed to alter his route provided that he has filed an agreed flight plan. On those parts of long-distance routes that are uncongested, the pilot uses the built-in navigational aids of the aircraft, and sometimes electronic aids on the ground, to navigate and avoid collisions by flying predetermined routes at specified heights. However, as soon as a flight approaches a much flown-over

▲ A crewman monitoring air-traffic control radar consoles in the combat information center aboard the aircraft carrier USS *Constellation*. The military have their own mobile ATC centers for operations overseas, but must conform to international air-safety traffic standards to avoid collisions with civilian aircraft.

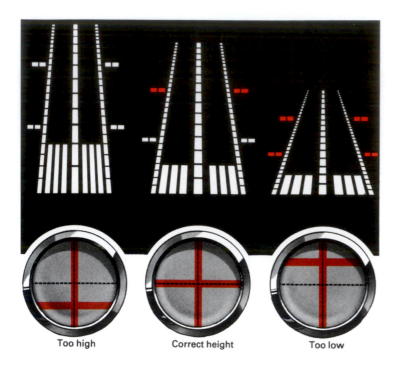

Too high   Correct height   Too low

area or nears an airport, it enters a control zone, where it is obliged to follow a specific course at a given speed and height prescribed by the air-traffic controller.

The air-traffic controller is the decision maker, who alone has complete information on all aircraft movements within the control zone. The controller exercises discretion on the minimum safe spacing between aircraft, both vertically and horizontally, and determines priority in takeoff and landing within the framework of flight schedules.

The minimum information required by a controller is the current height and position of all aircraft under his or her control, the intentions of all aircraft under or soon to be under control, and the identity of each aircraft. The controller gets this information from a flight progress board, which informs on intention, identification, vertical position, and timing, and from a plan-position radar that gives the exact position and distance of all aircraft within the control zone.

The controller's work involves continuous updating of information as new situations develop and earlier ones pass from his or her control. Controllers receive advance information of traffic about to enter each control zone from adjacent zones and inform adjacent zones of traffic leaving each zone. They also monitor and control all traffic within a zone.

The controller communicates with the aircraft normally by VHF (very high frequency) radio-telephone with a range of up to 200 miles (300 km) when the aircraft is at high altitude, although the range decreases as the aircraft descends. A radio direction finder (RDF) system is frequently employed with the VHF radio link to supply the

▲ Runway approach lights, with visual approach slope indicator (VASI) lights on each side. Each light has two narrow beams—one red, one white. If the airplane is too low, the pilot sees both sets of VASI lights as red, if too high, they appear white. For a correct alignment, red should be seen over white.

compass bearing of any call received. All communications between pilots and controllers are spoken in English and use standard phrases and terms to avoid the possibility of confusion.

Wind speed and direction, visibility, cloud base, air temperature, and barometric pressure data are fed to the controller from local sources and from meteorological centers, though a wind sock and anemometer may be placed within view of the airport control tower to indicate the strength and direction of any crosswinds on the ground. Runway visibility can now be accurately measured by electronic means so that aircraft can takeoff and land in difficult weather more safely.

Radar control systems

The basic radar system gives a continuous plan, as seen from above, of all aircraft within radar range. The plan position indicator (PPI) radar display shows an aircraft target as a bright spot, with the range (distance) of the aircraft indicated by its distance from the center of the screen and its bearing by the angle to the center. An electronic means, known as video mapping, makes it possible permanently to superimpose fixed features, such as defined airways, on the screen. It is also possible to eliminate all unwanted permanent radar echoes from stationary objects and display only those that are actually moving (with moving-target indicators).

In yet another refinement, the radar echo from a particular aircraft can be tagged with its identity or other information as a code of letters and numbers. The identity tag of each aircraft slowly moves across the screen in synchronization with the movement of the aircraft.

PPI radars are in three broad categories: long-range surveillance, airfield control, and airfield surface movement. Long-range surveillance radars typically have a range up to 300 nautical miles (550 km) from approximately 2 MW peak power. Airfield control radars operating at less power have typically a range of 50 to 150 nautical miles (95–280 km). Airfield surface-movement radars are designed for very high definition, and range is normally confined to runways, taxiways, and aprons of the immediate airfield. Modern surface-movement radars have sufficient picture resolution to identify individual aircraft.

These radars are all of the primary type, which obtain information from a reflection of the radar beam from the aircraft or other target and require no cooperation from the aircraft. Another important type of radar system is known as secondary surveillance radar (SSR), in which equipment carried on the aircraft receives the transmitted ground signal and transmits a reply. The reply is

entirely automatic and generally includes a coded message giving identity of the aircraft and present altitude, both of which can be integrated into the main PPI display and tagged to the appropriate aircraft on the display.

Instrument landing system

The controller normally controls aircraft up to the final approach to the airfield, when the pilots can lock on to the instrument landing system (ILS). This system provides a fixed radio beam so that an aircraft can align itself with the runway and adopt the correct descent path. The equipment comprises two ground transmitters, one emitting a beam to guide the aircraft in azimuth or compass bearing, the other a beam to guide the aircraft in altitude. The beams are known as the localizer and glide path, respectively. Both beams

▲ A VHF omnidirectional radio range/distance measuring equipment array, which provides aircraft with course data.

▼ ILS uses narrow beams to guide aircraft. The stacking beam marks where they line up, marker beams indicate distance, and localizer and glide path beams mark the correct line of approach. A clearance antenna wipes out unwanted parts of the beam.

are modulated with tones at audio frequency (at a pitch that enables them to be heard), which are used to activate instruments in the aircraft flight deck or indicate audibly to the pilot whether the plane is deviating to the left or right of the center-line and above or below the glide path.

Along the approach centerline are three vertically transmitted fan-shaped beams known as the outer, middle, and inner marker beacons. Once brought to the position for final approach, the marker beacons indicate the distance to go, and ILS proper shows any deviation from the center-line and glide path. If the pilot keeps to the centerline and glide path, the aircraft will be brought to the threshold of the runway at about 200 ft. (60 m) altitude and can then complete the landing visually. The controller directs the aircraft to the appropriate runway exit.

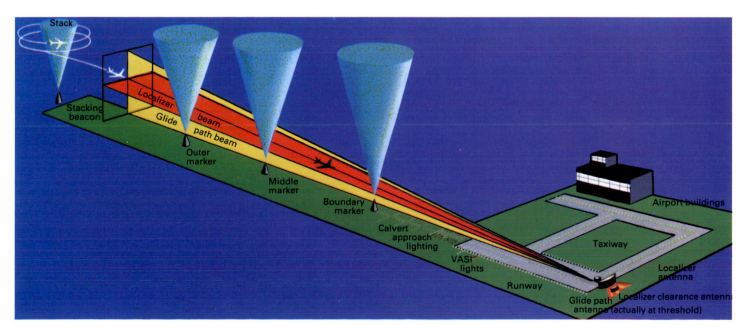

Blind landing

Suitably equipped aircraft can use ground-based ILS (provided it is exceptionally accurate) combined with the autopilot and additional airborne electronic aids (principally highly accurate radar altimeters) to land in near-zero visibility. The main complexity in such a system is the duplication and even triplication of airborne equipment to secure acceptable reliability. Blind landing has been achieved thousands of times in commercial practice. The pilot monitors the landing throughout and can take manual control at any instant.

Microwave landing system

The microwave landing system (MLS) was devised in the 1970s but is only just beginning to replace ILS in a phased replacement plan at most major international airports that began in 1998. MLS has a number of advantages over the conventional system in that it can be used to position the aircraft three-dimensionally in space, a useful feature in the crowded conditions around airports. MLS comprises four signal transmitters, one located at each end of the runway to provide the approach and back azimuth transmitter and the remaining two to transmit elevation and distance data. This extra data can be coupled with precision area navigation (RNAV) to enable courses to be flown through congested airways and a number of approach patterns to be flown at the same time. It also has a further benefit in that smaller aircraft can make their final approaches closer to the runway without the bigger jets having to reduce their airspeed to let them in.

The antennas used in MLS are smaller because of the higher frequencies used, and a mobile system can be set up by a small team in a matter of hours. This feature is useful for remote airfields that are not permanently staffed or in situations where the landing capability has been interrupted. Because MLS has an azimuthal coverage region of ± 62 degrees rather than ILS's ± 40 degrees, pilots can approach at much steeper or even curved angles.

Modern aids

The electronic computer plays a central role in ATC. It processes and stores information and supplies data to individual controllers in a large complex. The computer's main function is to reduce what would otherwise be a very demanding workload on controllers so that they can concentrate on supervision of aircraft movements and the all-important decision making.

Each country has its own ATC, but in some regions, for example, Europe, where aircraft can pass through countries very quickly, there is often

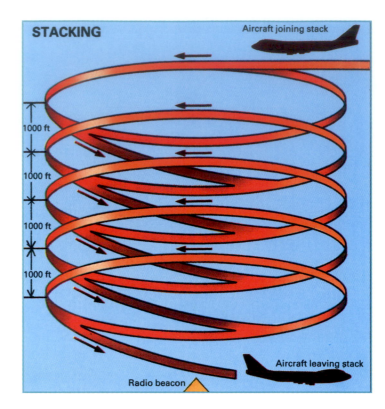

STACKING
Aircraft joining stack
1000 ft
1000 ft
1000 ft
1000 ft
Aircraft leaving stack
Radio beacon

▲ When an airport is too busy for incoming aircraft to land immediately, they have to circle in stacks until a runway is free. A vertical distance of 1,000 ft. (305 m) separates the levels between airplanes. U.S. airports prefer to use flow controls—rather than stacking—which holds an airplane at its departure point until a landing opportunity at its destination is confirmed. This method reduces the stress on air-traffic controllers to monitor large numbers of aircraft circling the crowded airspace around airports. Delaying flights on the ground rather than in the air allows passengers to disembark if necessary.

a coordinating body that is responsible for establishing a coherent strategy for flights throughout the region. The Eurocontrol Air-Traffic Management Program has 30 member countries and is part of a plan to put a uniform shared air-traffic management system in place by 2015. This program will enable a "gate to gate" system to be set up, in which each flight is managed and treated as a continuum thoughout its journey between member states. In the case of scheduled flights, all the data can be pooled in advance so that all the partners in the system are aware of the impact any change to the flight plan would have.

Another improvement in technology could allow airplanes to fly at smaller vertical separations at higher levels in future. In 1966, the vertical separations above flight level 290 (29,000 ft.) were increased to 2,000 ft. (610 m), because barometric altimeters were found to be less accurate at increasing altitudes. Evaluations of altimetry systems that can maintain accurate height keeping have been underway in flights over the North Atlantic since 1997, and it is expected that an extra six flight levels between levels 290 and 410, which will cut the vertical separation to 1,000 ft. (305 m), will become operational over Europe from 2002. Benefits of these extra levels will include additional airspace capacity for more flights, a reduction in in-flight delays, and fuel economies for the airlines.

SEE ALSO: Aircraft-control engineering • Airport • Inertial guidance • Navigation • Radar

Alcohol

Alcohol is most familiar as an ingredient of alcoholic drinks, but drinkable alcohol is only one of many different kinds. Drinking alcohol is properly known as ethyl alcohol or ethanol, and it can be fatal in large doses. Small amounts of other alcohols can cause brain damage and death.

Industrial alcohol is used as a solvent and in the manufacture of acetic acid, ether, chloroform, plastics such as polyethylene (polythene), and the tetraethyl lead added to gasoline as an antiknock compound—though this additive is gradually being banned in many countries, including the United States, because it is poisonous.

Methyl alcohol, or methanol (wood alcohol, so-called because it was originally made from the destructive distillation of wood), is used as a solvent in the manufacture of formaldehyde and in antifreeze. It is also used in methylated spirit, which is ethanol made undrinkable by adding about 9 percent methanol and very small amounts of benzene, pyridine, and dye, which by their taste, smell and color, considerably reduce the danger of accidental poisoning. Methanol may also be used in in antifreeze and is also useful as an alternative to gasoline-producing low pollution emissions and a high octane rating.

Ethanediol, or ethylene glycol (sometimes referred to simply as glycol), is also used in antifreeze to make various plastics and synthetic resins, such as polyurethane, and many modern adhesives. Glycerol (also known as glycerine) is used to make other plastics, explosives (nitroglycerine), cosmetics, inks, and antifreeze. It is a by-product in soap making.

Structure of alcohols

When one or more of the hydrogen atoms in a hydrocarbon is replaced by the hydroxyl group, –OH, the result is an alcohol. Ethane, C_2H_6, for example, becomes ethanol, C_2H_5OH. Hence the names for alcohols: methanol, ethanol, propanol, butanol, and so on, corresponding to the related hydrocarbon gases, methane, ethane, propane, and butane. These alcohols, which contain a

▼ Distilling equipment in a typical Scottish distillery making malt whiskey, which has to be distilled twice to give it its characteristic flavor.

single hydroxyl group, range from volatile liquids to waxy solids. Those with 12 or more carbon atoms are solid, while those with fewer than 12 carbon atoms are liquid.

Isomerism

Structurally, from propanol onward, the alcohols show isomerism—that is, there is more than one position where the –OH group can go, although the overall number of carbon, hydrogen, and oxygen atoms remains the same. This structural difference can give molecules different characteristics, that is, the molecules undergo different types of chemical reactions. For example, primary alcohols (where the –OH group is attached to the end of a carbon chain) can be oxidized to aldehydes and to carboxylic acids, while secondary alcohols are oxidized to ketones. In secondary alcohols, such as isopropyl alcohol or propan-2-ol, the hydroxyl group is attached to a carbon atom that is in the middle of a carbon chain. A tertiary alcohol has a hydroxyl group attached to a carbon that is bonded to three other carbons. Alcohols with more than one hydroxyl group are known as polyols. Both ethanediol and glycerol belong to this class. These alcohols usually have a syrupy consistency.

Reactions of alcohols

Alcohols (for example, methylated spirit) can be burned to give carbon dioxide and water vapor. They react with both inorganic and organic acids to give esters. This reaction is the equivalent of an inorganic reaction between an acid and an alkali to give a chemical salt. For example, hydrochloric acid reacts with caustic soda to give sodium chloride. Similarly, methanol will react with salicylic acid to give methyl salicylate, or oil of wintergreen, as it is commonly known. Alcohols can be dehydrated (water can be removed from them) to give ethers or olefins (alkenes), depending on the reaction conditions.

Production of alcohols

Most of the ethyl alcohol for industrial purposes is produced by the hydration of ethylene using a high temperature and a suitable catalyst.

$$C_2H_4 \quad + \quad H_2O \quad \rightarrow \quad CH_3CH_2OH$$
ethylene   water   ethanol

Methanol is made by the action of hydrogen on oxides of carbon using high pressure, a moderately high temperature, and a catalyst.

Ethanol for drinking purposes is made by the fermentation of sugars. Hexose sugars ($C_6H_{12}O_6$) are needed for the fermentation action in which yeast cells produce an enzyme that splits the sugar into alcohol and carbon dioxide. This gas causes the liquid to froth, giving the process its name, fermentation, from the Latin *fervere*, meaning "to boil." The amount of alcohol produced will depend on the strain or type of yeast used and the temperature. Sometimes in the fermentation of grapes in wine making, the yeast used is that present naturally as a bloom on the skin of the grape. In most wine making, however, and in the brewing of beer, where barley is used as a source of starch and ultimately of sugar, the yeast is added.

Usually, starch in the form of barley, rice, potatoes, or maize is hydrolyzed, or broken down, into a sugar, maltose, by the action of an organic catalyst that occurs naturally and is known as an enzyme. In brewing, the germination of the grain produces the enzyme. A sweet liquid, or wort, results, and this is turned into glucose by another enzyme, maltase, which is found in yeast. The glucose is turned into alcohol by a third enzyme, zymase, also found in yeast. Dilute acid or alkali may be used instead of enzymes for converting starch to sugars.

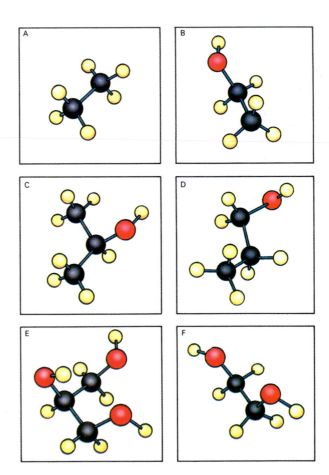

▼ Molecular models of (A) ethane, (B) ethanol, (C) isopropanol, (D) propanol, (E) glycerol, (F) ethylene glucol. The black spheres represent carbon atoms, red spheres, oxygen, and white, hydrogen.

SEE ALSO: BEER AND BREWING • CHEMICAL BONDING AND VALENCY • CHEMISTRY, ORGANIC • DISTILLATION AND SUBLIMATION • FERMENTATION • POISON • SOAP MANUFACTURE • SPIRIT • WINEMAKING • YEAST

Alkali Metals

The alkali metals are a group of elements that are classified together in the periodic table, where they form group 1A. In order of increasing weight of their atoms, the alkali metals are lithium (Li), sodium (Na), potassium (K), rubidium (Rb), cesium (Cs), and francium (Fr). Sodium and potassium are the most important members of the group. All are extremely light, silver-white metals—lithium, with a density half that of water, is the lightest solid element. Cesium, the heaviest of the group, has a relative density of 1.87.

Alkali metals are all soft enough to be cut easily with a knife. They conduct heat and electricity well and are easy to melt and vaporize at comparatively low temperatures, forming gases with molecules consisting of two atoms.

These metals are never found in a pure form in nature, since they are extremely reactive and even react violently with water, forming hydroxides and releasing hydrogen. For this reason and because of their softness, they are useless as structural metals in spite of their lightness. Cesium bursts into flames even in moist air. Alkali metals therefore must be isolated from moisture, so they are stored under paraffin or in sealed evacuated containers.

Their reactivity is due to the fact that the lone outer electron of each of their atoms is unusually easy to detach, transforming the atom into an ion with a single positive charge and thus giving it a strong tendency to combine with the negative ions of other elements. These ionic bonds are very strong, making it difficult to split these compounds to obtain pure alkali elements. Alkali metals cannot be isolated by normal electrolysis since this process involves the use of water, with which the extracted pure metal would immediately react. Instead, it is done by the electrolysis of the compound after it has been melted to make it liquid.

The tendency of the metals to give off electrons makes them useful in photoelectric cells and television camera tubes, usually in the form of a thin film deposited on glass.

Lithium

Lithium, the lightest element of the group, is in some ways more like the elements of the next group in the periodic table, the alkaline earth metals. In particular, its carbonate and phosphate are only sparingly soluble in water. Lithium carbonate is the most widely used lithium compound. It is incorporated in glass ceramics such as cooking ware and modern flat-top stoves because it imparts resistance to thermal cracking and is

◄ Caustic potash (KOH) is recovered electrolytically from Dead Sea potassium chloride deposits at this Israeli plant.

used as a flux to lower operating temperatures in aluminum reduction cells.

Lithium soaps, such as lithium stearate, are used as gelling agents to solidify greases. Lithium hydride is used as a source of hydrogen, such as that used in meteorological balloons:

$$LiH + H_2O \rightarrow LiOH + H_2$$

lithium hydride   water   lithium hydroxide   hydrogen

Lithium salts are used in fireworks to give red colors. In medicine, the salts have been used for the treatment of rheumatism.

Important future uses are in the manufacture of lightweight, rechargeable batteries, which may be used in electric vehicles, and in the longer term, lithium has a potential role in thermonuclear fusion, a vast future energy source. The fusion system—a reaction between deuterium and tritium (heavy isotopes of hydrogen)—appears feasible, and tritium is obtainable from lithium.

Lithium is found in naturally occurring complex silicate minerals such as spodumene, $Li_2O \cdot Al_2O_3 \cdot 4SiO_2$—written $LiAl(SiO_3)_2$—and in brines. Lithium is recovered from spodumene by first roasting the mineral and then bleaching it with acid. The sparingly soluble carbonate can be precipitated (solidified) and dissolved in acids to form other salts. Metallic lithium is obtained by electrolysis of the chloride, LiCl, fused with potassium chloride, KCl, to lower the melting

◀ When lithium is heated it gives off a bright red light, and this effect is used in the manufacture of domestic fireworks.

point. The molten lithium rises to the surface and is collected under a bell to prevent it from coming into contact with the air.

Sodium

Sodium is a silvery white alkali metal that tarnishes rapidly in air, emitting a green phosphorescence visible in the dark. The origin of its chemical symbol, Na, is the Arabic word *natrun*, from the Greek word *nitron*, "soda ash" (sodium carbonate). The name sodium is simply a latinization of the word soda. Sodium metal was not isolated until 1807, when the British chemist Sir Humphry Davy succeeded in electrolyzing molten caustic soda. Two of its compounds, however, have been used since ancient times. Sodium chloride (common salt), in addition to being necessary to sustain life, has always been employed both to preserve and flavor food. The other important compound is sodium carbonate, or soda; it occurs as the mineral natron and has also been prepared by leaching (treating with water)

the ashes of plants that grow on the seashore. The treatment of land plants or sea kelp in the same way yields a similar compound, potassium carbonate, K_2CO_3, which was originally known as mild vegetable alkali, or potash.

In addition to deposits of common salt (NaCl), soda (Na_2CO_3), borax (sodium borate, Na_3BO_3), and Chile saltpeter (sodium nitrate, $NaNO_3$), sodium is a constituent of many rocks, usually in the form of an aluminosilicate, such as a plagioclase feldspar.

Production

In spite of the fact that Davy had first produced sodium by electrolysis, early commercial production of the metal did not take advantage of this technique, because large quantities of electric power were not economically available. Instead, sodium was prepared by a process, devised in the 1880s by Castner, an American working in Britain, in which caustic soda and carbon in the form of pitch were heated to 1832°F (1000°C) in the presence of spongy iron. The caustic soda was reduced by the carbon to metallic sodium. By the 1890s, the technology of electricity generation had advanced sufficiently to encourage Castner to revert to Davy's original method. He designed a cell in which the caustic soda electrolyte was kept at about 50°F (10°C) above its melting point, which was reduced from 604°F (318°C) to less than 572°F (300°C) by adding sodium chloride and sodium carbonate.

Today, sodium is normally produced from sodium chloride in a Downs cell, which is similar to the Castner cell except that the anode is made of carbon and placed centrally, and the sodium is formed at an annular iron cathode. Although the current efficiency is twice that of the Castner cell, the Downs cell operates at about twice the voltage, so the overall energy efficiency of the process is no higher. Nevertheless, the ready availability of sodium chloride and the chlorine by-products still weigh in favor of the Downs process, and it is almost universally used.

Uses

One of the uses of sodium is in the production of sodium compounds. Sodium peroxide, Na_2O_2, is made by passing dry air over sodium metal at 572°F (300°C). It is used as a bleach, for textiles and also for the production of other bleaches such as benzoyl peroxide ($C_6H_5COO)_2$, which is used to whiten flour. Sodium cyanide, NaCN, is used in huge amounts for the extraction of gold, for case hardening steels, and in electroplating baths. It is prepared in two stages. First, sodium metal is heated in ammonia at 662°F (350°C) to form sodamide, $NaNH_2$, a compound that finds application in the dyestuffs industry and in the production of lead azide, $Pb(N_3)_2$, an explosive. Next, sodium cyanide is formed by reacting the sodamide with red-hot charcoal. Sodium also plays an important part in the manufacture of sodium alkyl sulfates for detergents. In the past, the major use of sodium was in the production of tetraethyl lead, $Pb(C_2H_5)_4$, the antiknock constituent of motor fuel. However, the lead present in this compound causes pollution, and so today it is less commonly used. Pure sodium metal is added in concentrations of less than 0.1 percent to effect the modification of aluminum-silicon alloys.

The high thermal conductivity and thermal capacity of liquid sodium is utilized in the production of valves for high-performance internal combustion engines. The valve stems are filled with sodium, which greatly enhances the removal of heat from the valve head. This property combined with a low neutron-capture cross section has led to its use as a heat-transfer medium in fast neutron nuclear reactors, where a large amount of heat must be removed from a small reactor core in the shortest possible time. If desired, the melting point of sodium can be greatly reduced by adding potassium: an alloy of 23 percent sodium and 77 percent potassium has a melting point of 10°F (–12°C); in other words, like mercury, it is a liquid at room temperature. Such alloys find applications in high-temperature thermometers.

Sodium, suitably contained, has also been considered as a conductor for electric power transmission. Its conductivity on a volume basis is only one-third that of copper, but in terms of weight, it is nearly three times as good. It is also much cheaper.

The familiar yellow sodium street lights have discharge tubes filled with sodium vapor. Electrons are continually raised to excited energy states in the atom by the high operating voltage, and they emit monochromatic (one-colored) light as they drop back to the ground state. The red color emitted as the light warms up is due to the neon gas with which the tube is filled—the effect is similar to that of a neon light.

Potassium

Potassium, K, is generally similar to sodium, although it is slightly more reactive. Like sodium, it reacts vigorously with water, releasing hydrogen, but in the case of potassium, it sets the hydrogen alight and burns brilliantly.

Potassium salts are essential for the cells of all plants and animals—plants take them from the soil. Over 90 percent of world potash (potassium-bearing minerals) consumption is for fertilizer use. The carbonate, K_2CO_3, was first obtained by washing wood ash and evaporating the washings in pots, hence the name potash and the latinized name potassium. Potassium chloride, KCl, is used as a fertilizer, the carbonate is used in glass manufacture, and potassium hydroxide, or caustic potash, KOH, is used in production of soft soap. Black gunpowder is a mixture of saltpeter, KNO_3, with charcoal and sulfur. Potassium bromide and potassium iodide are used in photography.

Rubidium, cesium, and francium

Rubidium was formerly recovered from processing lithium ores but now is obtained as a by-product of cesium recovery from pollucite, a complex cesium-bearing hydrated aluminosilicate. Cesium and rubidium are used in photoelectric cells, while cesium is also used in atomic clocks and in television cameras. Being heavy and easy to vaporize and ionize, it has been suggested that both rubidium and cesium could be useful as fuels in ion propulsion for space travel. Francium is a very short-lived radioactive alkali metal that rapidly decays into other elements and so can be studied only using trace amounts.

▼ A piece of sodium placed on a wet surface bursts into flame spontaneously. Sodium weighs less than water and decomposes it to produce sodium hydroxide and hydrogen gas in an extremely violent reaction that generates so much heat that the hydrogen often ignites. Because sodium is so reactive, it must be stored under oil to exclude air, which would rapidly oxidize it to sodium oxide.

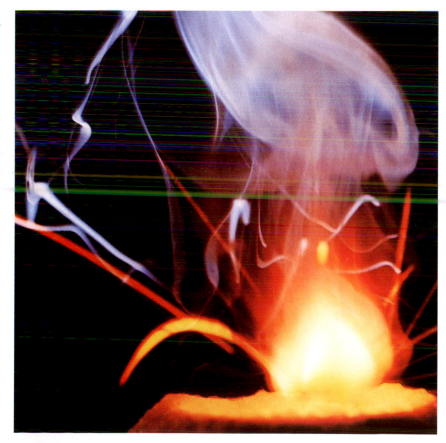

SEE ALSO: ACID AND ALKALI • ATOMIC STRUCTURE • ELECTROLYSIS • ELEMENT, CHEMICAL • ION AND IONIZATION • METAL • OXIDATION AND REDUCTION • PERIODIC TABLE • SALT, CHEMICAL • SALT PRODUCTION

Alloy

An alloy is a substance composed of two or more elements, at least one of which is a metal. Since metals are seldom 100 percent pure, the term *alloy* is usually reserved for metallic mixtures that are formulated as such rather than those that are mixtures as a consequence of impurities. When formulating an alloy, the chief aim is often to retain or reinforce the desirable properties of an element while eliminating undesirable properties. Copper, for example, is an excellent conductor of electricity, but it is too soft for many applications. Additions of small quantities of other elements to copper produce alloys that are good conductors and that are hard enough to withstand mechanical machining processes. In addition to mechanical strength, properties such as conductivity, temperature, and corrosion resistance can be modified by alloying.

Making alloys

In the simplest alloy-making technique, the components of an alloy are melted together in the appropriate proportions. However, this is possible only when there is an overlap between the temperature ranges for which the constituent elements are liquid. In other cases, one component might boil at a temperature lower than the melting point of another component, and much of the low-boiling component would be lost by evaporation if all components were heated together.

There is a great difference between the melting and boiling points of the components of brass, for example, which are copper and zinc. To overcome the loss of zinc by evaporation, brass is made by first melting copper—melting point 1983°F (1084°C)—in a heat-resistant pot, called a crucible. Zinc—melting point 786°F (419°C), boiling point 1665°F (907°C)—is then added. The alloy forms without the zinc evaporating to a great extent. If the metals were simply heated together, much of the zinc would boil away before the copper even started to melt.

Another technique for blending metals that have widely differing melting points uses master alloys. Consider the example of an alloy that consists of 5 percent metal A, which, when pure, melts at 2000°F (1093°C), and 95 percent of metal B, which melts at 842°F (450°C). The alloy may be made by first melting metal A and adding an equal amount of low-melting metal B. The resulting blend—the master alloy—melts at a lower temperature than does metal A. Therefore, the master alloy can be diluted with metal B to the required final composition at lower tempera-

tures than would be necessary if using pure A. The use of a master alloy therefore reduces the amount of heat energy required for blending.

Structure and hardness

Many properties of alloys are best understood by examining the changes that occur in metallic structures when different types of atoms mix together in one substance. More precisely, changes in properties such as hardness and corrosion resistance can be understood by considering the defects that occur in the structures of pure metals and how such defects are "healed" by the inclusion of atoms of other elements.

The atoms in solid metals form crystalline lattices, in which a simple geometric arrangement of atoms repeats countless times in a regular manner. Such structures are mechanically soft, since their atoms are arranged in flat planes that slip over one another if sufficient external stress is applied. When the stress is removed, the atoms fall into the closest lattice positions without returning to their original positions. Hence, the shape of the metal changes permanently—a phenomenon called plastic flow.

In reality, the ease with which atomic planes slide over each other is increased by the presence of defects, called dislocations, in the crystal structure. The movement of dislocations in a metal can be compared to the movement of rucks in a carpet. A ruck can be pushed from one end of a

▲ Producing powder for alloying by the atomization method—molten steel is being poured into jetted water.

carpet to the other without great effort, and the whole carpet moves as a result. To move the carpet through the same distance by pulling one edge would require much more effort. Similarly, when stress is applied to a metal that has dislocations, the dislocations shift through the metal and allow adjacent crystalline regions to move relative to one another so as to relieve the stress.

When stress is applied to a metal that contains impurities, any dislocations in the structure move until they strike impurity atoms, which stop their progress. Hence, the presence of different types of atoms, whether introduced intentionally to make an alloy or present as impurities, increases the hardness of a metal. Also, since dislocations at the surface of a metal are prone to chemical attack, the elimination of dislocations by the inclusion of appropriate impurities increases the resistance to chemical attack and corrosion.

Solid solutions

Many alloys are prepared in their molten state, then cooled. Most combinations of metals are miscible (able to mix) in all proportions in their molten states, and such blends of metals can be regarded as solutions of one or more elements in the major component of the alloy. Metals that are immiscible when molten cannot be alloyed in this way, since they separate like oil and water.

In some cases, a blend of metals solidifies to form an alloy whose composition is uniform and identical to the composition of the liquid blend.

Such alloys are called solid solutions; they have granular crystalline structures where each grain has the same composition as the molten mixture. Only a few pairs of metals—copper and nickel, for example—can form solid solutions through the complete range of possible relative proportions.

Solid solutions have two different types of structures: substitutional and interstitial. These terms refer to how the atoms of the minor component—the additive element—fit into the lattice of the major component—the base metal.

In a substitutional solid solution, atoms of the additive element occupy lattice positions that would be occupied by base metal atoms in a pure sample of that metal. Such structures form when the atoms of both elements are similar in size, as is the case with copper and nickel, for example. The slight difference in atom sizes hinders lattice movements and hardens the material, although the effect is not often very marked.

In interstitial solid solutions, atoms of the additive element are much smaller than those of the base metal, so they fit into interstices (gaps) between lattice positions. The additive element is usually a nonmetal, such as carbon or nitrogen, and the presence of such atoms in interstices is highly effective in blocking the movement of dislocations. Hence, tiny amounts of additive element can cause dramatic increases in hardness, so adding 0.1 percent carbon to pure iron produces a tenfold increase in the strength of the metal, turning soft iron into hard steel.

Multiphase alloys

In many cases, the composition of a liquid mixture exceeds the solubility limits of its components in the solid state. Cooling such a mixture causes two or more types of solids to crystallize, each within the solubility limits of its components. Each of these substances is a separate phase, since its composition is uniform but distinct from the other phases that solidify with it.

When liquid mixtures of lead and tin solidify, for example, they form two distinct phases, called α and β (Greek letters *alpha* and *beta*). The α phase consists of 95 percent lead with 5 percent tin dissolved in it; the β phase consists of 99 percent tin with 1 percent lead. The relative amounts of the two phases depend on the total quantities of the two metals in the system.

When a multiphase alloy is polished and viewed under a microscope, the different phases can be distinguished one from the other. In some cases, grains of different compositions alternate throughout the solid; in other systems, granules of one phase are dispersed in a continuous matrix of another phase, like nuts in some candy bars.

▶ The idealized crystal structure of a pure metal consists of stacked layers of metal atoms (top). Applying a force to part of a metal block causes these layers to slip past one another, resulting in a permanent change of shape. In reality, solid metals consist of small regions of crystallinity separated by dislocations (middle). Applying a force to a metal block causes such dislocations to travel through the metal, resulting in deformation. In an alloy (bottom), one type of atom (red) fills the dislocations in the structure, making the alloy harder to deform.

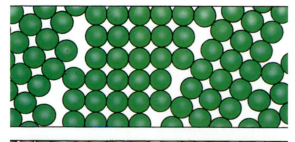
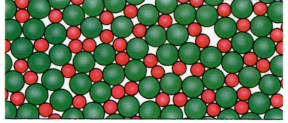

Intermetallic compounds

Some alloy phases have weight compositions that correspond to exact and simple number ratios of one type of metal atom to another—1:1, 1:2, or 2:3, for example. Such combinations are called intermetallic compounds, since their formulas resemble those of conventional compounds.

Intermetallic compounds tend to have regular lattice structures, which make them extremely hard and brittle when pure. Nevertheless, such compounds contribute hardness to a flexible alloy when dispersed as grains in a solid-solution matrix. Lead–tin–antimony alloys, for example, have a microstructure of comparatively large crystals of tin–antimony intermetallic compound set in a softer matrix of lead, tin, and antimony. They are well suited for use in bearings, since the intermetallic compound provides wear resistance and the softer matrix enables the bearing to mold to the profile of the rotating shaft.

Precipitation hardening

Intermetallic compounds play an important part in a process called precipitation hardening. This process starts with a hot or molten alloy whose composition would imply the presence of a compound that is intermetallic at room temperature but a solid solution at high temperature.

If such a solution is cooled rapidly, the lattice becomes rigid and prevents the migration of atoms necessary to form the intermetallic compound. Consequently, the components of the alloy are frozen as a supersaturated solution. If such a substance is then heated in a controlled manner, atoms become able to migrate, and the intermetallic compound starts to form crystals within the alloy, which therefore gets harder. The small particles of precipitated intermetallic compound are effective barriers to the movement of dislocations, so their presence hardens the alloy.

Precipitation hardening is useful for parts that must be machined into shape. The supersaturated alloy is machined while still relatively soft, then the hardness is developed by reheating. This approach reduces the wear on machine tools.

Heat treatment of steel

One type of supersaturated solid solution plays an important part in the heat treatment of steel. When steel is heated to more than 1500°F (800°C), it forms a solid solution of carbon in iron called austenite. If it is then cooled gently, regions of ferrite and pearlite start to form when the temperature falls below around 1300°F (700°C). Ferrite is a soft, solid solution of carbon in iron; pearlite consists of layers of ferrite and cementite—a hard and brittle iron carbide with formula Fe_3C. If steel is cooled rapidly from more than 1500°F (800°C) by quenching with cold oil, the austenite transforms just above room temperature into martensite—a hard, solid solution of carbon in iron. The martensitic lattice is highly distorted, and the movement of dislocations is exceedingly difficult, accounting for its hardness.

While martensite is extremely hard, it is also very brittle, thus limiting its usefulness in applications where some flexibility is required. Brittleness can be overcome by tempering—reheating to between 1000°F (500°C) and 1300°F (700°C)—followed by slow cooling. The period of reheating allows some of the martensite to transform into ferrite and pearlite, restoring toughness without too great a loss in strength.

Powder metallurgy

Powder metallurgy is a technique for producing alloys and manufacturing alloy parts from their powdered components. The component powders are blended, pressed into shape, and then sintered—heated until they unite without melting.

Powder metallurgy has numerous advantages over alloying by mixing in the liquid state. One advantage is that alloys can be prepared with compositions that would be immiscible in the liquid state; another is that refractory metals—those with extremely high melting points, such as tungsten—can be alloyed below their melting points.

The first stage is powder preparation, for which there are at least five methods. Tungsten and molybdenum powders are most conveniently

► These tungsten-based components are powder metallurgy products that would be impossible to make by any other method. They can be made to close tolerances and with uniform quality. Segregation of large particles (a problem with traditional casting) is minimized.

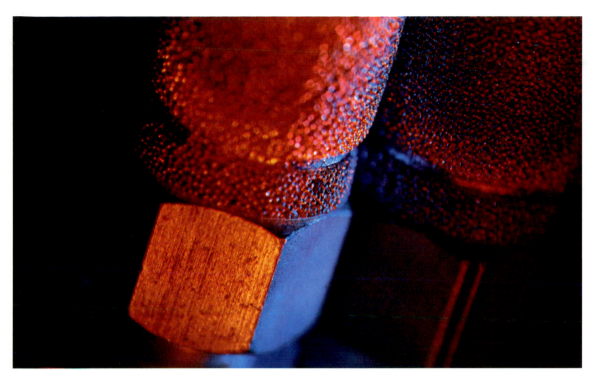

◄ Alloying from powders is a unique method of making components, such as these air filters, which have a porous structure but can withstand high pressures. Because of the possibilities it offers, powder metallurgy is becoming increasingly popular for working many different types of engineering materials.

produced by chemical reduction of the metals' compounds to produce the elemental metals as fine precipitates. Copper, iron, and chromium can be produced as finely divided powders by electrolytic reduction of their compounds. Nickel powder is produced by vapor-phase thermal decomposition of its carbonyl, $Ni(CO)_4$, a volatile liquid. Low-melting metals are conveniently powdered by running streams of molten metal through jets of fluids, such as air, water, steam, or an inert or reducing gas; the jets break the stream into fine droplets that solidify as fine powder. Alternatively, molten metals can be spun to form fine filaments that can then be powdered by chopping and grinding processes.

Once the component powders of an alloy have been prepared, they must be blended in the required proportions. Blending can be done in a ball mill, a rotating horizontal cylinder that contains heavy balls that tumble and grind the powders together as the cylinder turns. The blended powders are then packed into a mold, sometimes with a wax binder, and compacted by hydraulic or mechanical punches. This process determines the shape of the finished object and confers enough mechanical strength for the "green" molded object to be manipulated before sintering.

Sintering is the process that fuses the compacted alloy together without melting. The sintering temperature depends on the alloy composition but is generally not less than two-thirds of the melting point of the alloy. During sintering, atoms diffuse between solid particles, eliminating most of the voids between them and binding them into a solid mass. Heat for sintering can be provided by electric or gas-fired furnaces, or it can be generated by the passage of an electrical current through the molded object.

Sintering furnaces are generally flushed by reducing gases—hydrogen, hydrocarbons, or cracked ammonia, for example—or evacuated for highly reactive metals, such as titanium, chromium, and niobium. Sintering times vary from around 30 minutes to several hours, depending on the composition of the alloy.

Powder metallurgy produces homogenous alloys without the formation of large particles of intermetallic compounds, which can be a problem with alloys produced from molten metals. Sintering uses less energy than melting, and molding produces less waste alloy than casting and subsequent machining of parts.

Some 10 to 15 percent of the volume of sintered parts is accounted for by residual porosity. Porosity can be a bonus for some applications, such as metallic filters, but is generally considered a drawback for the reduction in mechanical strength that it causes. Porosity can be reduced by repressing and resintering components.

Some shrinkage occurs as voids are eliminated during sintering, and it must be anticipated by using oversized molds. Powders do not flow like fluids, so molds must be designed carefully to help ensure uniform packing throughout.

Powder metallurgy is well suited to making high-volume items, such as drill bits and parts for sewing machines. In such cases, mold designs and dimensions are optimized for packing and shrinkage and may then be used many millions of times over. The technique is also useful for fabricating

refractory items, such as blades for gas turbines, where sintering eliminates the need to heat the alloy to an extremely high melting point.

Common alloys

Bronze—the oldest manufactured alloy—is a blend of copper and tin in a ratio of around 10:1 by weight. Brass—another copper alloy—contains between 10 percent and 45 percent zinc by weight. Cast iron (pig iron) is an impure form of iron that contains between 2 percent and 4.5 percent carbon and traces of manganese, phosphorus, silicon, and sulfur. Other alloys of cast iron may also contain elements such as nickel, chromium, and molybdenum.

Steel is an alloy of iron that contains less than 2 percent carbon by weight, less than 1 percent manganese, and even smaller amounts of silicon, phosphorus, sulfur, and oxygen. Alloy steels typically also contain the following elements in these approximate proportions by weight: chromium or nickel, 0.4 percent or more; molybdenum, tungsten, or vanadium, 0.1 percent or more; manganese, 10 percent or more. Stainless steel—more precisely, 18-8 stainless steel—contains 18 percent chromium, which forms a tough chromium oxide surface film that inhibits rusting.

Specialized alloys

Nimonic alloys are nickel-based alloys that also contain aluminum, titanium, and molybdenum. They are particularly good at resisting deformation at high temperatures and find an important application in gas-turbine blades.

Aluminum alloys are designed for a range of specialized tasks where a strong, low-weight material is essential. Silicon, copper, and magnesium are used to alloy aluminum, usually with small amounts of other elements such as manganese, zinc, titanium, and nickel. One of the first synthetic aluminum alloys was Duralumin, a tough, light, and strong material used in the construction of zeppelin airships and—in modified form—in modern aircraft parts. Duralumin con-

◀ In making sand-cast alloy wheels, the alloy is heated to about 1330°F (720°C) so that it becomes molten enough to be poured.

▲ The molten metal is poured into molds made of sand negatives, sealed with wet sand and located with dowels through a funnel made of the same sand, and left to cool.

▶ The inside and outside of a wheel rim is machined to close tolerances, and to improve its appearance. The inside of the rim must be completely smooth to reduce the possibility of repeated punctures. After machining, the wheel undergoes crack testing.

tains around 4 percent copper and small amounts of magnesium, manganese, and silicon.

Invar is an alloy that consists of 63.5 percent iron, 36 percent nickel, 0.4 percent manganese, and 0.1 percent carbon. Its most notable property is that its dimensions remain constant over a wide range of temperatures, and thus it is a useful material for making high-precision measuring rules. The inventor of Invar—the French physicist Charles Guillaume—also developed Elinvar, a nickel–chromium–iron alloy that has invariable elasticity over a wide range of temperatures.

Fusible alloys are alloys that melt at lower temperatures than the melting point of tin, which is 449°F (232°C). They include solders, which are usually alloys of some 60 percent tin with lead.

Wood's metal is an alloy of equal parts of bismuth, cadmium, lead, and tin that melts at 158°F (70°C). It finds use as a seal in fire sprinklers: when heat from a fire reaches the sprinkler, the seal melts and releases a flow of water to quench the flames.

Amalgams are mercury-based alloys that tend to be liquids or pastes, depending on the amount of mercury present. The formation of amalgams is used to extract metals in the metallurgical industry and to make cements for dental fillings.

Nitinol and shape memory

Nitinol—a simple alloy of nickel and titanium—is one of the most extraordinary alloys to have been developed. Nitinol possesses properties that have perplexed materials scientists for more than thirty years, in particular, an unusual phenomenon called the shape-memory effect.

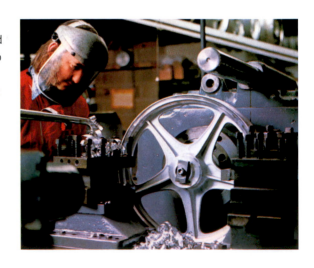

If a piece of Nitinol wire is bent into a circle, for example, then heated and quenched, it will "remember" its circular shape. It may then be bent or crumpled, but subsequent reheating will cause it to return to its original shape. This is the shape-memory effect, or SME. The effect is not exclusive to Nitinol: other alloys, including brasses, also exhibit SME to some degree.

Nitinol is not only capable of remembering, it also has the ability to "learn." If the heating-cooling-crumpling-reheating process is carried out sufficiently often and the metal is always crumpled in exactly the same way, the Nitinol will not only remember its original shape, but gradually it will learn to remember its alternative crumpled form as well and begin to return to it every time it is cooled. Eventually, the metal will crumple and uncrumple, totally unaided, in response to changes in temperature and without any sign of metal fatigue.

Engineers have produced prototype heat engines driven by the force of Nitinol springing from one shape to another in response to alternate high and low temperatures. One of the first of these engines was produced by Ridgway Banks in 1973 and was found to be able to produce about half a watt of mechanical energy. Since then, many others have been designed with significantly greater energy outputs.

The energy from these engines is not entirely free, since heat energy is required to produce the temperature differences needed to run the engine. However, the optimum temperatures at which the metal responds can be controlled by

◀ A mold for producing timing-case covers by the process of powder metallurgy. This technique is useful for making large quantities of small components cheaply and to a high-standard finish.

altering the relative proportions of nickel and titanium—some alloys respond at room temperature. Furthermore, the necessary temperature range between the warm phase and the cold can be as little as 21°F (12°C). Thus, a Nitinol engine could exploit a variety of low-grade heat sources, from geothermal springs to the hot coolant water produced by many industrial processes.

Nitinol also holds great promise in the field of medicine. Lightweight and resistant to corrosion, Nitinol could prove invaluable as an implant material. Its shape-changing property could aid the delicate positioning of artificial implants such as those used to treat spinal disorders. A slightly bent Nitinol rod could be inserted into the back close to the spine, where body heat would straighten the rod with great accuracy and control, ensuring perfect alignment and support of the spine. Nitinol has also been used for artificial limb joints and bone plates and to close bone fractures. The metal is even being considered as an engineering material for artificial hearts.

Not all Nitinol's applications are confined to research and development: the aerospace industry has been using the alloy for some years in latch-and-release mechanisms for the instrument booms of artificial satellites. The speed and reliability of Nitinol's shape-memory response, the alloy's low density, and its total immunity to metal fatigue make it an invaluable material for use in a variety of aerospace applications.

FACT FILE

- Continuous-wave, pulsed, and Q-wave lasers can all be used to produce surface-alloy coatings. High laser power melts coatings and the main body of material so quickly that most of the workpiece stays cool. A minimum of materials is used, and the resulting interface between the main body and its coating is strong.

- Amorphous alloys are noncrystalline steels made by cooling the molten metal on a spinning drum at a rate of a million degrees a second. Also known as metallic glasses, amorphous alloys are very easily magnetized and demagnetized, making them ideal for use in devices such as transformers and tape-cassette recording heads.

SEE ALSO: Aluminum • Atomic structure • Brass • Bronze • Carbon • Casting • Dentistry • Electrolysis • Element, chemical • Gas turbine • Iron and steel • Machine tool • Magnetism • Mercury • Metal • Metal cutting and joining • Nickel • Sheet metal • Zinc

Aluminum

▲ A geodesic dome structure, constructed of aluminum-alloy tubing. Such buildings are both light and structurally strong.

Aluminum, chemical symbol Al, is the most important element of group 3 of the periodic table. It is a light, silver-white metal 2.7 times as heavy as water, soft but with good tensile strength and an excellent conductor of heat and electricity. Aluminum melts at 1220°F (660°C) and is easily cast and pressed.

Aluminum's other advantages are that it is also ductile—suitable for drawing into wire—and malleable, that is, easy to roll into sheets and foil. A structure fabricated from aluminum weighs approximately half as much as a similar steel structure of comparable strength.

Apart from its strength combined with its light weight, aluminum has another useful property—resistance to corrosion, because of a thin, hard oxide film that forms on its surface, protecting the metal from further oxidation. The oxide film can be thickened by anodizing, that is, oxidizing by an electrolysis process. The anodized film can be dyed, making aluminum ideal for architectural panels and household utensils.

Powdered aluminum is used in aluminum paint. In the powdered form, it is considerably more reactive than a solid block of metal and therefore is useful as a strong reducing agent for removing oxygen in chemical processes. When a mixture of aluminum powder and iron oxide is ignited, as in the thermite process, a large amount of heat is produced, and the iron oxide is reduced to molten iron. This technique is used in welding steel and iron and in incendiary bombs.

Occurrence of aluminum

Aluminum is the third most abundant element in Earth's crust after oxygen and silicon, making up about 8 percent of the total. Iron, the next most abundant element, is only 5 percent of the total. Like so many of the metals, aluminum is not found in its pure form but associated with other elements in igneous rocks, and minerals. An aluminosilicate such as feldspar, $KAlSi_3O_8$, is the main constituent of many rocks such as granite, which is quartz and mica cemented together with feldspar. These rocks are gradually weathered and broken down by the action of carbon dioxide from the air dissolved in rainwater, resulting in the formation of kaolin, china clay, $Al_2Si_2O_5(OH)_4$. Further weathering ultimately gives bauxite, $Al_2O_3 \cdot H_2O$ or $Al_2O_3 \cdot 3H_2O$, which is a hydrated form of aluminum oxide occurring widely and used for commercial aluminum extraction and refining.

Pure aluminum oxide, also known as alumina, Al_2O_3, is found as corundum, a crystalline, extremely hard mineral. It also occurs combined with magnetite (iron oxide), a form known as emery. Both are used as abrasives. Traces of other metal oxides present in aluminum oxide tint it to form precious stones. Chromium gives a red coloration to ruby, whereas cobalt accounts for the blue color of sapphire.

Uses of aluminum compounds

Crystalline alumina is used as an abrasive and, in powdered form, for column chromatography, an analysis technique in which a liquid mixture of compounds is allowed to trickle down through a glass column packed with powdered alumina, causing the various compounds to separate at different levels. Aluminum hydroxide, $Al(OH)_3$, is used as a mordant in dyeing. A fabric that will not accept a dye is impregnated with the mordant. The dye reacts chemically with the mordant to form an insoluble "lake," or pigment, thus dyeing the fabric. Aluminum hydroxide dissolves in acids to form salts and in alkalis to form aluminates—few substances do both. Sodium aluminate, $NaAlO_2$, is used as a flocculating agent during water- and sewage-treatment processes, coagulating impurities. It is also used in papermaking.

Aluminum sulfate, $Al_2(SO_4)_3 \cdot 18H_2O$, is widely used as a source of aluminum hydroxide. It is also used together with sodium carbonate in foam fire extinguishers. It forms double sulfates with other metals. These substances are known as alums, for instance potassium alum, $K_2SO_4 \cdot Al_2(SO_4)_3 \cdot 24H_2O$. Alums are used in manufacturing processes (such as dyeing), during the papermaking process, and in the production of medicines, textiles, and paints.

When chlorine gas is passed over aluminum foil, a white solid, aluminum chloride, Al_2Cl_6, is formed, an important catalyst in the synthesis of aromatic compounds.

Uses of aluminum

Aluminum is now the second most widely used metal after iron. Aluminum and its alloys, such as duralumin, are used as structural metals for a wide variety of products from aircraft to cooking utensils. Aluminum foil is made by hot rolling followed by cold rolling and is used in food packaging. Foil is also being used to replace copper wire in electric windings. Other electric applications for aluminum foil include use in capacitors. Cross-country electric cables consist of a steel core surrounded by pure aluminum. Pure polished aluminum is an excellent reflector and does not tarnish. Aluminum mirror reflectors are used on large astronomical telescopes.

Aluminum alloys have been used in buildings for cladding panels, door and window frames, roofs, and Venetian blinds. Die-cast aluminum cylinder blocks are used in a number of cars. Other forms of transportation where these alloys have been successfully incorporated are in the superstructure of large ships, such as the *QE II*—

◄ Mining bauxite by the opencast method. Before alumina can be used in the electrolytic process, it must be extracted from the other oxides that make up bauxite.

and on a much smaller scale, but where weight saving is equally important, in air-cushion vehicles (hovercraft). Aluminum is also used in domestic appliances such as refrigerators, in air conditioners, and in cooking utensils and food processing equipment. Alumina (corundum) is used commercially in large quantities in the manufacture of insulators and spark plugs.

Hydrated aluminum chloride, otherwise known as aluminum chlorohydrate, $AlCl_3 \cdot H_2O$, is the active ingredient in antiperspirants and deodorants, acting by making the pores constrict. A number of other aluminum salts are used by the cosmetics industry.

Aluminum extraction

Pure metallic aluminum does not occur naturally. Being a highly reactive element, it is always found tightly combined with other elements, and it must be separated from them chemically during the process of extraction.

Large-scale aluminum production depends on the reduction of aluminum oxide, alumina, to aluminum metal by the process of electrolysis. Alumina can be easily obtained from bauxite, the main ore of aluminum. Bauxite is a claylike, amorphous material formed by the weathering of silicate rocks and often contains other metallic oxides, mostly of iron. Although bauxite is the only practical source of aluminum, the element is also found in small quantities in other substances as diverse as pottery, clay, and emeralds. The alumina content of bauxite varies widely and only high-grade ores with more than 45 percent alumina are worth mining.

Before alumina can be used in the electrolytic process, it has to be separated from the other oxides that make up bauxite. Crushed bauxite is digested in a strong caustic soda solution at high temperature. The alumina reacts with the hot hydroxide solution and forms soluble sodium aluminate in the caustic soda. All the impurities remain undissolved and can be filtered off. The aluminum is recovered from the solution as an oxide strongly combined with three molecules of water. So strong is the bond between the aluminum oxide and the water molecules that it must be heated to 2372°F (1300°C) to drive off the combined water, finally giving anhydrous alumina, Al_2O_3.

Aluminum from alumina

To break the strong bond between the oxygen and the aluminum molecule requires a large input of energy, and this is provided by a low voltage, high amperage current of electricity passed through a bath containing molten alumina.

Pure alumina melts at 3632°F (2000°C), a very high and impractical temperature to maintain in an industrial plant. However, by dissolving the alumina in cryolite (Na_3AlF_6), a double salt of sodium and aluminum, the working temperature of the process can be brought down to a far more manageable 1830°F. Even so, about two-thirds of the electricity used in the process goes to maintain the solution in a molten state.

The alumina-cryolite solution is contained in a heavy metal cell or pot with massive carbon cathodes in the base connected to the negative side of the direct current power supply. Carbon anodes, connected to the positive side of the supply and normally made in blocks about 2 ft. (0.6 m) square by about 4 ft. (1.2 m) long, are suspended above the pot and lowered into the electrolyte during extraction. The voltage across the solution is only about five volts, but since its resistance is low, the current is very high. Heavy conducting leads provide the power to each pot and supply the rows in which scores of pots are arranged. A typical modern aluminum smelter will have several hundred pots in total, each one holding perhaps 20 tons (18 tonnes).

When the current is turned on, the carbon in the electrodes reacts with the alumina to produce free aluminum and carbon dioxide:

$$2Al_2O_3 \quad + \quad 3C \quad \rightarrow \quad 4Al \quad + \quad 3CO_2$$

alumina   carbon   aluminum   carbon dioxide

Molten aluminum sinks to the bottom of the pot and collects over the cathode. It is periodically siphoned off into insulated containers and

▼ Massive conductors carry the enormous current needed for the electrolysis of alumina. Nevertheless, the voltage across the cell is only about 5 volts. Because of their huge requirements, aluminum smelters are always located near cheap sources of electricity, which in the past have often been hydroelectric plants. Smelters are now increasingly drawing on nuclear-generated power.

◀ Paper coated with aluminum oxide is a powerful industrial abrasive used in many industries. Such high-speed belts are used for shaping and finishing.

taken to holding furnaces, where it may be alloyed to give it special properties. From there, it is normally cast into billets, slabs, or ingots for further processing.

The carbon comes from the anode, which is consumed by the process. As it turns into carbon dioxide, the anode is slowly lowered into the cryolite solution until it is exhausted. Large amounts of electricity are used in this process; the power used by a typical family household in a year would not supply much more than a quarter of a ton of the metal. For this reason, aluminum smelters are always near cheap sources of power. In the past, this power has frequently been hydroelectric, but some smelters now draw heavily on nuclear power as well as coal or oil-generated electricity. With the cost of power increasing, there has been recent interest in developing other methods of extraction that are viable on a commercial scale. A chloride method has been tried in the United States, and a process using lime is also being developed. However, these and other new methods have not been as successful as hoped, and they account for only a small fraction of the total global production. To date, hydroelectricity remains the most common method of obtaining the massive amounts of power that the industry needs.

The aluminum from the electrolytic process is 99.0 percent to 99.8 percent pure, the main impurities being traces of iron and silicon. Even purer aluminum, 99.99 percent pure, can be obtained for special purposes by further refining, although it is by its nature quite soft and weak.

Aluminum welding

The hard, persistent oxide film always present on the surface of aluminum offers excellent protection against corrosion and other damage. The film, however, prevents proper welding of aluminum if it is not first removed or broken up.

In general, the techniques employed in welding aluminum and its alloys are similar to those used for welding steel but with modifications to overcome the difficulties caused by the oxide film.

These difficulties occur because of the properties of the film. It has a melting point above 3600°F (2000°C); it is insoluble in solid or in molten aluminum; it resists ordinary welding fluxes; and it reforms as soon as it is removed. Less important difficulties arise because aluminum conducts heat about five times better than steel does. More heat is conducted away, so more heat must be applied. In addition, aluminum has a higher electric conductivity than steel, and so arc welding demands higher currents.

The basic methods of welding aluminum are gas, arc, resistance, and to a limited extent, electron-beam welding. Arc and resistance welding account for about 90 percent of welds made.

Welding aluminum

Electron-beam welding of aluminum is practical for both tiny integrated circuits and quite thick material and has been widely used in the aerospace industry. Another technique, ultrasonic welding, is limited to very thin materials and is used principally for joining aluminum foil. Arc welding, which is the most widely used technique, works by striking an electric arc between an electrode and the workpiece, using the workpiece as part of the electric circuit. The heat thus generated is used to form the weld.

▶ Arc welding is the most common method used to hold aluminum structures together. An AC power supply strikes an arc between the welding electrode and the workpiece, the high temperature generated by the arc melting the surfaces to be joined.

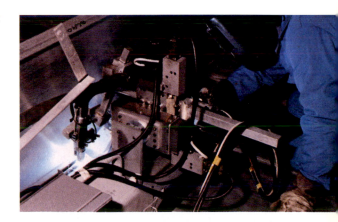

SEE ALSO: ALLOY • CHEMICAL BONDING AND VALENCY • CONDUCTION, ELECTRICAL • ELECTROLYSIS • ELEMENT, CHEMICAL • METAL • METAL CUTTING AND JOINING • OXIDATION AND REDUCTION • SHEET METAL

Ambulance

An ambulance is a vehicle designed for the rapid transportation of sick or injured people to a place where they can receive full medical attention. Most ambulances are road vehicles, but they may also be helicopters or airplanes. Ambulances are rarely custom-built but are converted from a standard-design vehicle. For example, in the United States, the Cadillac hearse chassis provides great passenger comfort though little space for essential equipment.

It is vital to have space and equipment in the ambulance to provide emergency first care for patients, but it has been found in practice that emergency mobile operating rooms are inefficient. Performing a delicate operation at the scene of a road accident with nearby heavy traffic and the lack of full hospital facilities is too hazardous to be worthwhile. Consequently, ambulances are designed simply to transport their patients rapidly in the greatest possible comfort, while carrying enough equipment to deal with the most common causes of ambulance fatalities. Ambulance crews are trained to perform necessary emergency treatments as well as make diagnoses and monitor the patients while in their care. In addition, the advent of new computerized diagnostic machines has made it possible to provide doctors at the hospital with a complete patient profile on arrival at an emergency room, saving much valuable time—and, in some cases, lives—in the operating room.

Ambulance layout

Any ambulance needs plenty of interior space. It must carry bulky gear, such as suction apparatus to clear blocked airways and oxygen equipment to aid respiration, and still have enough space to enable full first aid procedures to be carried out. Other necessary medical aids include stretchers, equipment for administering blood transfusions, defibrillators for giving electric shock treatment to cardiac patients, and supports and immobilizers for people with spinal or neck injuries. Some ambulances may even carry incubators for premature babies. Because ambulances must contain such a diverse range of medical aids, large cus-

▼ Paramedics helping a patient with an injured neck. The patient is strapped down onto a cot and has a brace to hold his neck in place. The male paramedic is measuring the patient's vital signs using a monitor attached to the patient's finger.

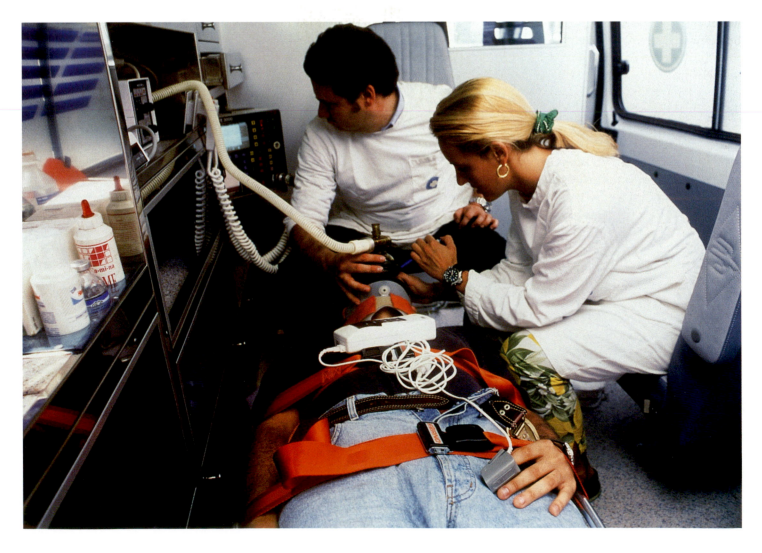

tom designed vehicles are of more use than converted automobiles, though the latter is more common and may well give greater comfort.

Using a commercial vehicle as a basis usually results in a harsh ride. To improve this situation, a well-designed ambulance needs a long wheelbase so that the patient does not have to lie over the rear axle; a low center of gravity, to prevent the body of the vehicle from rolling when cornering at speed; and a low floor, to make loading of stretchers easier. These considerations mean that front-wheel drive is necessary, since it does not require a bulky transmission shaft leading to the rear wheels. By using automatic transmission, jerky and awkward gear shifts are avoided, making the ride more comfortable for the patient and easier for the driver, who may need to drive at speed through dense traffic.

When adapting a chassis to an ambulance, an entire body is often fabricated from glass-reinforced plastics or glass fiber, which is light and nonrusting and can be molded to any desired shape. Storage cupboards and the bottle holders for saline or blood drips can also be made from this material. Despite being adapted from commercial vehicles, ambulances are required to exhibit high performance and reliability. The wheels in particular take a great strain and have to be inspected regularly for signs of cracking.

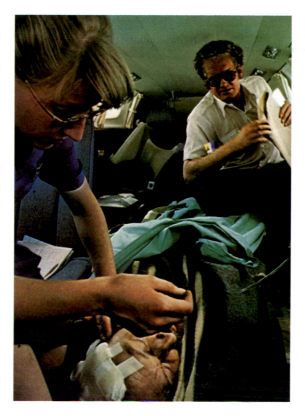

◄ Many people in remote, sparsely populated or inaccessible areas rely on light aircraft flying ambulances as their only efficient means of transport, particularly in an emergency situation.

FACT FILE

■ *In the course of the Korean and Vietnam Wars, the helicopter came into its own as an ambulance. The Air Rescue Service evacuated over 10,000 wounded, often from the front line, in Korea. Casevac choppers had external stretcher pods and could get a casualty onto the operating table within an hour of his being wounded. In-flight techniques included blood transfusion, which could be completed before landing at a MASH (Mobile Army Surgical Hospital) unit. In Vietnam in 1968 alone, helicopters flew 42,000 medevac missions.*

■ *The first ambulances with defibrillators were pioneered by Dr. F. Pantridge in 1966 in Belfast, Northern Ireland. This system has led to a much improved chance of survival for people who have suffered heart attacks. The first such system in the United States was instigated in 1968 at St Vincent's Hospital in New York City.*

Electric equipment

Ambulances must have a comprehensive system for warning of their approach, including flashing lights and sirens. To run these systems, and to provide power for the suction unit, premature baby unit, and bright internal lighting, a heavy-duty alternator is needed.

Flashing lights are also needed at the level of a car's rear windows so that automobile drivers realize what sort of vehicle has suddenly appeared in their rear-view mirror.

In addition to the standard first-care equipment, ambulances may be provided with electronic monitoring recorders. Ambulances are also equipped with two-way radios to enable them to be deployed more efficiently.

Air ambulance

Air ambulances contain much the same kinds of equipment as conventional ambulances but are used in different circumstances. Helicopter ambulances, for example, may be used when the patient is in an area inaccessible by other means, such as on a mountain or at sea. Airplane ambulances can be used to carry patients even longer distances, such as in the case of repatriation from a country that lacks advanced medical skills and in disaster-relief situations.

SEE ALSO:	AUTOMOBILE • BATTERY • ELECTRONICS IN MEDICINE • HEART SURGERY • OPERATING ROOM • RADIO • SURGERY • SUSPENSION SYSTEM • X-RAY IMAGING

Amino Acid

Amino acids are the building blocks of which protein molecules are made and thus are the basic structural material of all living matter.

Although there are many millions of different kinds of proteins, only 20 amino acids are commonly used in protein synthesis. To form proteins, amino acid molecules are linked together in a large number of different ways and often in huge numbers. For example, hemoglobin consists of the protein globin, which is formed of 574 amino acid molecules, and a complex organic compound, hem, which gives blood its characteristic red color. The information necessary for the correct sequencing of amino acids is contained in deoxyribonucleic acid (DNA).

Animals constantly use up protein through processes such as muscle growth and enzyme production. As a result, they need a constant supply of amino acids that can be used where required for energy and for building into protein. They get this supply by taking in protein, hydrolyzing it (breaking it down) into separate amino acids through the action of enzymes in the digestive tract, and rebuilding them into the proteins that are needed. Enzymes are themselves proteins and function like catalysts in the body, speeding up the various biochemical reactions.

The 20 amino acids are valine, leucine, isoleucine, threonine, methionine, phenylalanine, tryptophan, lysine, histidine, glycine, alanine, serine, cysteine, tyrosine, aspartic acid, asparagine, glutamic acid, glutamine, arginine, and proline. Of these 20 amino acids, only the first 9 are essential in the human diet; the rest are synthesized from other sources. A lack of any of them in the diet causes malnutrition.

The general amino acid formula is $NH_2 \cdot CHR \cdot COOH$, with R standing for either a hydrogen atom (in the case of the simplest amino acid, glycine) or a more complex organic radical or group of atoms. The formula contains both the acidic or carboxyl group, $-COOH$, and the alkaline or amino group, $-NH_2$. When an amino acid molecule dissolves in water, it ionizes, but because the carboxyl group has a negative charge and the amino group a positive charge, the resulting ion is electrically neutral and called a zwitterion.

If a positively charged ion, such as a hydrogen ion (H^+) from an acid, is introduced into an amino acid solution, it is attracted to the negatively charged portion of the amino acid zwitterion, neutralizing it and leaving it with only its positive charge. Similarly, a negative ion, such as a hydroxyl ion (OH^-) from an alkali, is attracted to the positively charged portion of the amino acid molecule.

This ability of amino acids to collect any stray positive and negative (and therefore acidic or alkaline) ions allows them to act as buffers in living cells, maintaining the delicately balanced pH (a measure of acidity or alkalinity) that the cells must have in order to function.

▲ Magnified crystals of asparagine, an amino acid found in asparagus, beets, and other vegetables. Although the human body needs asparagine for the synthesis of certain proteins, it is termed a nonessential protein because it can be readily synthesized in the body.

SEE ALSO: ACID AND ALKALI • ATOMIC STRUCTURE • CATALYST • CELL BIOLOGY • ENZYME • GENETICS • ION AND IONIZATION • MOLECULAR BIOLOGY • PROTEIN

Ammonia Manufacture

One of the most important industrial processes is the manufacture of ammonia, which is needed for fertilizers, for the manufacture of nitric acid and for use as a refrigerant and as a cleaning agent.

Ammonia is manufactured from the gases nitrogen and hydrogen by the Haber–Bosch process. In most modern plants, the nitrogen is obtained from air, of which it makes up 78 percent by volume, and the hydrogen from natural gas.

$$N_2 \quad + \quad 3H_2 \quad \rightarrow \quad 2NH_3$$
nitrogen $\qquad$ hydrogen $\qquad$ ammonia

The impetus to make ammonia came after a prediction from a British scientist, Sir William Crookes, in 1898 that the world's supplies of nitrogen compounds, which were in the form of Chile saltpeter, were being used up and unless an alternative source was found, the world would starve for lack of fertilizer. In 1909, a German chemist, Fritz Haber, managed successfully to synthesize ammonia under high pressure using a catalyst. Karl Bosch, a German chemical engineer, later developed the laboratory technique into a full-scale commercial process.

Theoretically, a low temperature combined with high pressure is required to produce ammonia, but in practice, temperatures of about 900°F (500°C) and pressures from 150 to 1,000 times atmospheric pressure are used with good results. Below 900°F (500°C) the yield of ammonia is high, but the rate of reaction is too slow. At higher temperatures, the reaction is faster, but the yield of ammonia is lower. Higher pressures improve the yield, around 20 percent at 250 atmospheres and around 50 percent at 800 atmospheres. In addition, by using a catalyst the rate of reaction can be speeded up.

The catalyst is usually iron oxide, which is often mixed with a small quantity of a promoter such as aluminum sesquioxide to increase its effectiveness. The iron oxide is reduced by the hydrogen to spongy pure iron when the process is started up. Over a period, the catalyst gradually loses its effectiveness as it becomes poisoned by traces of carbon dioxide, carbon monoxide, and sulfur compounds.

In the process itself, the catalyst is packed into catalyst beds inside the steel reaction vessel, which is designed to withstand very high pressure. The steel must also be resistant to attack from hydrogen, especially under the high temperature and pressure conditions. The nitrogen and hydrogen gases are purified, compressed, and passed

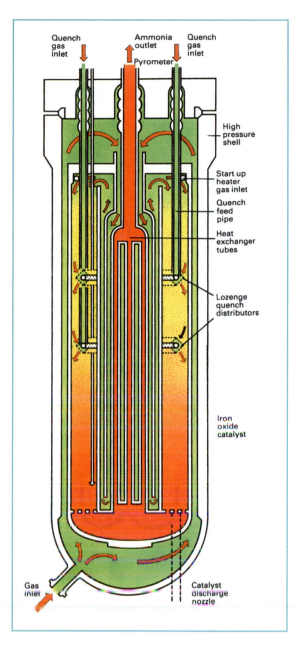

Quench gas inlet / Ammonia outlet / Quench gas inlet / Pyrometer / High pressure shell / Start up heater gas inlet / Quench feed pipe / Heat exchanger tubes / Lozenge quench distributors / Iron oxide catalyst / Gas inlet / Catalyst discharge nozzle

◀ Ammonia is produced by passing heated hydrogen and nitrogen through iron oxide in the Haber–Bosch process.

through a warmup heater before entering the converter. The ammonia gas formed is liquefied by passing it through pipes cooled by cold water.

Prior to the invention of the Haber–Bosch process, the more energy-intensive cyanamide process was used to prepare ammonia, where calcium cyanamide is sprayed with water to remove traces of calcium carbide and is then treated with superheated steam, which causes it to decompose into ammonia and calcium carbonate.

$$CaCN_2 \quad + \quad 3H_2O \quad \rightarrow \quad 2NH_3 \quad + \quad CaCO_3$$
calcium cyanamide $\qquad$ water $\qquad$ ammonia $\qquad$ calcium carbonate

SEE ALSO: ACID AND ALKALI • AIR • ATOMIC STRUCTURE • CATALYST • FERTILIZER • HYDROGEN • NITROGEN • REFRIGERATION

Ammunition

Ammunition is basically any explosive device, from the tiny cartridge in a starting pistol to a massive ten-ton bomb.

The word ammunition is derived from the Latin *munire*, meaning "to fortify," and originally meant fortifications and the tools of war. The modern definition states that ammunition is any military device that includes components filled with explosive, smoke-producing, incendiary (fire producing), or pyrotechnic (illuminating) compositions. However, this definition would exclude many other items, for example, shotgun cartridges, distress and signaling rockets, engineering explosives, chemicals weapons, aircraft ejection seat cartridges, and even fireworks, all of which can be considered as types of ammunition.

▲ The U.S. M60 general-purpose machine gun serves as a light machine gun when used on bipod, and as a heavy machine gun when on tripod. It was developed at the end of World War II and was used in Vietnam. Its ammunition is carried on a belt, which delivers a continuous stream of bullets to the firing chamber without the user stopping to reload.

Explosives

All ammunition contains explosive material in one form or another, and the way they function and release their energy may be precisely controlled.

Explosives are substances that can be converted into hot gases or volatile products and in the process exert a sudden pressure on the surroundings. The speed of the reaction determines the precise application of the explosive substance. High explosives react fast, usually within a few millionths of a second, and produce a sudden and disruptive increase in pressure that causes a severe shock wave. The tremendous power released by this detonation can be used to burst a shell into small, lethal fragments. Low explosives are slower, taking a few thousandths of a second to

react. The pressure produced can be used in a gun, for example, to propel a shell. Typical high explosives as used in shells, bombs, land and sea mines, grenades, and demolition work are trinitrotoluene (TNT), gelignite, hexogen, tetryl, and pentaerythritol tetranitrate (PETN). Nitrocellulose is a typical low explosive used in most modern guns as a propellant.

Gun ammunition

Ammunition for guns, whatever the size, comprises a propellant charge and a projectile. The two items may be secured permanently together (fixed), supplied as individual items and put together before loading (semifixed), or kept and loaded separately (separate loading). The deciding factors are, first, the method of gas sealing, or obturation, adopted and, second, the gun's barrel size, or caliber. The charge is sealed off in the gun's chamber either by means of a pad fitted to the breach or by enclosing the propellant in a cartridge case. Gas pressure from the burning propellant expands the pad or the case to seal off the rear of the charge completely. The projectile fits snugly in the barrel, preventing a forward leak of gas. As the bore (internal diameter) of the gun increases, the charge and projectile become heavier and more cumbersome to handle, and it is necessary to load them separately.

Components

A round of ammunition comprises the propellant, or charge, and the projectile, or shell. For a typical fixed round, the cartridge case is usually made of brass, 70 parts copper to 30 of zinc. The brass is pressed into shape in a series of stages, which harden and strengthen the metal. By alternately working and annealing, at about 1112°F (600°C), the case can be made thick and hard at the base to take the initiating cap and primer and to withstand the forces of loading and extraction. The center section is made softer, so it can expand and seal against the chamber wall, and the nose is harder so it can be crimped firmly to the shell. Other materials, such as steel, aluminum, and plastics, as well as cheaper methods of construction, are also in use today. The development of a small arms round with such durable propellant explosive that no cartridge case is necessary has resulted in ammunition in which the entire charge section is consumed when the round is fired.

The propellant may be in the form of small grains, short or long cords, or a solid block perforated by slots of holes to control the speed of burning. It is ignited by the primer. This comprises a small quantity of a very sensitive explosive that is initiated, or detonated, either when the striker pinches it between the cup and anvil or by an electric impulse. The flash is passed to a few grains of gunpowder that ignites to set off the propellant—the main charge.

The shell, or projectile, has three main components: the high-explosive filling, the driving band, and the fuse. Shells are normally forged from a good quality steel, and the final shape is the result of three or more operations and some machining to achieve the required tolerances. The projectile's shape is determined by a number of factors. For a stable flight, it should be no longer than five times the caliber. For low skin friction (the friction acting on the surface of a body moving through air), it should be smooth and the base should be streamlined to reduce aerodynamic drag. The driving band is a copper ring forced into a groove cut around the lower section of the body. Its tasks are to provide a good gas seal in front of the charge, to seat the projectile in the bore, and to engage the spiral rifling of the gun barrel to make the shell spin. The shell body is filled with high explosive, for example, TNT, by pouring molten explosive into the cavity, taking care to ensure no empty spaces are formed on cooling. A ratio of 15 percent explosive to the total shell weight is normal.

The explosive in the projectile is itself the propellant of the warhead. At the simplest level, it splinters its casing into lethal fragments of shrapnel, but even then, the case may be notched in sections to create a specific shape of shrapnel.

When a shell is used against armored fighting vehicles, the explosive may be distributed through the warhead in a way that is designed to direct all its force into a narrow channel capable of piercing armor plate. There are also cluster munitions, which carry a mass of submunitions to be released over the target.

Fuses

The fuse is the last component to be fitted to the shell. It can be the most dangerous component in the round and is designed not to explode during firing, when it is typically subjected to gas pressures of 20 tons per sq. in. (2.7 tonnes/cm^2) and accelerations of 20,000 g. Yet it must function reliably when the shell strikes the target. Like the cartridge, the fuse contains an explosive train: a striker sets off a detonator, the impulse is passed to a less sensitive but more forceful explosive contained in a pellet, and the detonation wave from this pellet sets off the main filling. Fuses are extremely intricate and are designed to respond to the forces of firing and flight. The mechanism can be likened to that of a combination lock: it is unlocked by the special signatures of the forces imposed by the gun, and no other stimulation is normally required.

Fuses may act either on impact or after a short delay, allowing time for the shell to penetrate the target. When attacking targets in the open, it may be advantageous to burst the shell above so as to deliver fragments and blast downward. This action requires a time fuse, which bursts the shell at a specified time after firing. Timing may be mechanical, electronic, or by the burning of a

▲ The projectile section of a 105 mm kinetic-energy round designed to penetrate armor plating.

◄ An array of the weaponry available to the European Panavia Tornado all-purpose warplane on its diverse range of missions.

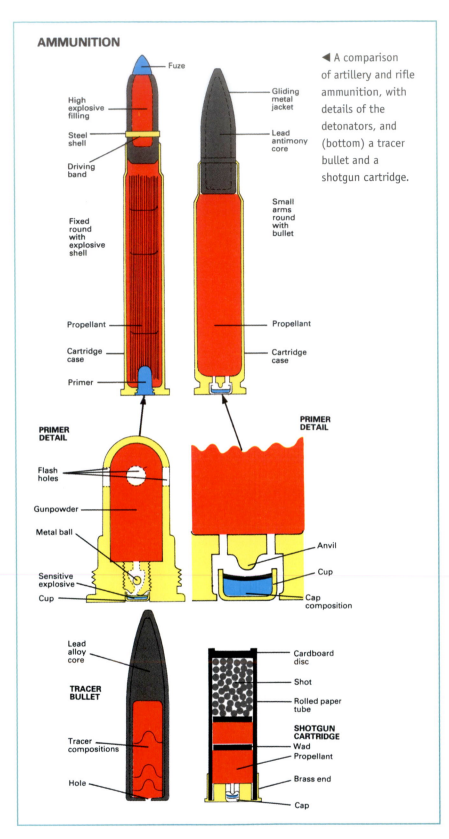

AMMUNITION

- Fuze
- High explosive filling
- Steel shell
- Driving band
- Fixed round with explosive shell
- Propellant
- Cartridge case
- Primer

- Gliding metal jacket
- Lead antimony core
- Small arms round with bullet
- Propellant
- Cartridge case

◀ A comparison of artillery and rifle ammunition, with details of the detonators, and (bottom) a tracer bullet and a shotgun cartridge.

PRIMER DETAIL
- Flash holes
- Gunpowder
- Metal ball
- Sensitive explosive
- Cup

PRIMER DETAIL
- Anvil
- Cup
- Cap composition

TRACER BULLET
- Lead alloy core
- Tracer compositions
- Hole

SHOTGUN CARTRIDGE
- Cardboard disc
- Shot
- Rolled paper tube
- Wad
- Propellant
- Brass end
- Cap

pyrotechnic train. Alternatively, proximity fuses may be used. They employ radar techniques to detect the target and burst the shell at the height for best effect.

Developments in gun ammunition

During World War II, Germany recognized that infantry fighting ranges were no longer about 3,000 ft. (900 m) or more, for which the first

metallic cartridges were designed, but were, in most instances, about 1,170 to 1,800 ft. (360 to 550 m) only. For such reduced range and for use in a new type of automatic rifle, known in Germany as the Sturmegewehr (assault rifle), Germany produced a new 0.308 in. (7.92 mm) cartridge with a shortened case. This new short-cased cartridge was ideal for the new class of rifle; it was lighter and produced less recoil. After World War II, several countries, including the former Soviet Union, Britain, and the United States, introduced similar cartridges.

During the 1950s, research carried out largely in the United States showed that the probability of hitting a human target fell off sharply once the engagement range increased beyond about 300 ft. (90 m). This investigation resulted in the first of a series of experimental, small-caliber, high-velocity cartridges. In the U.S. experiments, small caliber—0.223 in. (5.56 mm)—was combined with a relatively long case—about 1.77 in. (45 mm)—to produce a lethal, high-velocity cartridge. The bullet was reduced to nearly a third of the original weight of the 0.3 in. (7.62 mm) NATO cartridge so that it weighed only 55 grains (3.5 g) compared with the 144 grains (9.3 g) of the NATO ball bullet.

This reduction in weight helped to increase velocity but at the expense of range, which was less important. The muzzle velocity of the new bullet was about 3,100 ft. per sec. (970 m/s), a considerable advance on the 2,700 ft. per sec. (820 m/s) of the 0.3 in. (7.62 mm) NATO bullet. But most important, the new cartridge could be fired from a new, lightweight automatic rifle. Such a rifle was then developed in the United States, originally called the Armalite and eventually known by its U.S. Army designation of M16.

The main development in pistol-caliber ammunition has been in the area of bullet design. For antiterrorist use in urban areas, the target may be fleeting and there will not be an opportunity for a second shot. Accuracy and killing power are therefore of prime importance. A further important consideration is that, especially when hostages are involved or bystanders are at risk, the bullet should ideally not be able to continue and injure or kill the innocent.

Some designs have been produced to cope with this requirement. They are known under the generic term *effect geschoss*. The basic effect geschoss design has a nose cavity in the bullet, covered with a thin metal shroud so that the bullet seems to be full jacketed, or filled with a plastic plug. The intention is that the cavity causes the bullet to expand upon impact. Effect geschoss bullets are lighter than normal ball, or general-purpose, bullets and have a higher velocity.

Normal bullets are ineffective in stopping cars, and several alternative designs exist to cope with such targets. In one form, the bullet has a hard steel core inserted as a separate component. Alternatively, the bullet has a clad steel envelope with a normal lead core, but the envelope at the nose is specially thickened to form an armor-piercing cap. In the United States, it was discovered that all-steel bullets coated with Teflon had special piercing qualities. The Teflon provided lubrication and, therefore, improved penetration significantly.

Armor-piercing shell

Every advance in the design of tank armor is soon followed by improvements to the ammunition used to attack them. Even armor 10 in. (25 cm) thick is no protection against modern antitank shells.

The invention of the iron-clad warship led to the first types of armor-piercing shell, for coast defense and naval use, but it was the arrival of the tank that led to improved designs. Early weapons, such as the World War I Mauser antitank rifle, which fired a steel bullet capable of penetrating 1.1 in. (28 mm) of armor from a distance of 150 ft. (45 m), and the 2 pounder (pr), 6 pr, and 17 pr antitank guns used in World War II were all of the same type. They achieved their effect by punching a hole in the armor, relying on their mass and velocity for penetrating power. This attack is called the kinetic energy (KE) attack.

To obtain the maximum effect, the kinetic energy should be applied to the smallest possible area of the target. This end is achieved with a long, thin projectile, which can have a large mass and move at high velocities. The long, thin, heavy projectile is ideally suited to maintain its velocity as it passes through the air, but inside a gun, the maximum muzzle velocity is achieved by having the largest possible diameter shell, which will give the largest base area on which the gas pressure can act. So there is a contradiction in requirement —maximum diameter inside the barrel, minimum diameter while the shell travels through the air and strikes the target.

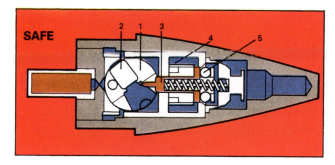
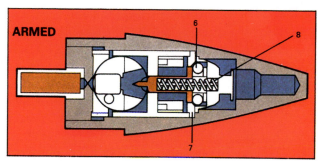
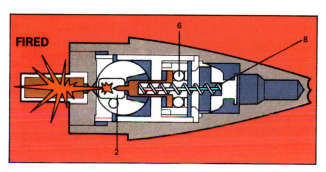

▲ The parts of a fuse: (1) shutter, (2) detonator, (3) firing pin, (4) flat spiral spring, (5) split collet, (6) balls, (7) support collar, and (8) firing pin spring. The shell is safe (top) when the shutter is locked. It becomes armed (center) when the spinning of the shell forces the balls up the support collar, pulling the firing pin forward and compressing the spring. It fires (bottom) when impact drives the balls back, freeing the firing pin to strike the detonator, which sets off the filling.

This contradiction was resolved by the British invention of the armor piercing discarding sabot (APDS) shell, which was first tried in the 6 pr and subsequently the 17 pr gun. It has since been used on the 20 pr, 105 mm, and 120 mm tank guns.

In the APDS shell, there is a small-diameter central core made of tungsten carbide, which is a strong and heavy material. The core is surrounded by a light magnesium alloy sleeve, or sabot, which produces a large diameter when the shell is loaded. When the propellant is ignited, a pressure of more than ½ ton per sq. in. (0.06 tonnes/cm^2) is applied to the large cross-sectional area of the core and sabot. The pressure gives the shell a large acceleration so that it emerges from the muzzle with a velocity of about 4,460 ft. per sec. (1,360 m/s). The force of the explosion breaks up the sabot into sections, but the confinement of the barrel holds it together until it reaches the muzzle. The sabot then separates from the core, which proceeds toward the target. At impact, there is a large kinetic energy contained in a small-diameter solid shot, which produces an extremely effective method of attack on armor plating.

In the 1970s, the fin-stabilized discarding sabot (FSDS) projectile was developed for use in smooth-bore tank guns. It has a long, dartlike subprojectile of either tungsten or depleted uranium (uranium containing less of the isotope U-235 than it normally does) with fins to stabilize it in flight. It is carried in a light metal sabot similar to the APDS shot and functions in the same way. The additional length gained by using fin stabilization increases the mass and thus the kinetic energy imparted to the target.

Unfortunately, all kinetic energy projectiles need a large and heavy gun, which although acceptable in a tank, cannot be managed by infantry who in battle have to maneuver the weapons into and out of action. To meet the need for a lightweight launcher, methods of attacking armor other than by kinetic energy were developed. Some other form of energy had to be employed, and the solution was found in chemical energy (CE) produced by the detonation of a high explosive (HE) charge in a shell—not the explosion produced by a conventional HE shell, which relies on blast and fragmentation, but a specifically designed shell that uses the controlled application of CE. The first CE shell was based on the hollow-charge, or shaped-charge, principle and is known as the high-explosive antitank (HEAT) round. The front face of the HE filling is hollowed out to produce a cone. A liner of copper or aluminum is placed in front of the cone.

When the shell hits the tank, the high explosive is detonated, and the energy produced is focused into a parallel sided gaseous jet—like light from a parabolic reflector. The jet, and the now molten liner carried with it, has a velocity of about 18,000 ft. per sec. (5,500 m/s). Together, the jet and liner weigh only a few pounds, but the high velocity produces a high kinetic energy, which forces the charge into the armor to a depth of about three times the diameter of the cone. A modern 84 mm recoilless antitank gun can penetrate 10 in. (25 cm) of armor plate at a range of about 3,200 ft. (1,000 m).

An alternative method of using CE is known as HESH—high explosive squash head. In this type of round, a large quantity of plastic HE is carried in a shell. When it strikes the armor plate, the HE filling spreads out on the armor face and is detonated by a base fuse. This system does not penetrate the plate. Instead, it relies on the shock wave from the detonation, which is transmitted to the tank interior. When the wave reaches the far side, it is reflected, overstressing the metal on the inside of the plate so that a large scab, often two-thirds of a meter across, is detached. This scab whirls around inside the tank at high velocity causing casualties and damage.

Grenade

A grenade is a small antipersonnel bomb filled with high explosives and used in close-range warfare. In the early days of their use, grenades took the form of spherical shells filled with large grains of black powder and resembled pomegranates with their seeds, hence the derivation of their name from the Spanish word *granada*, meaning "pomegranate." In the 17th century, each infantry company of the British Army included five grenadiers—soldiers armed with grenades.

Construction

Early grenades of the 14th and 15th centuries were made of bark, glass, or earthenware filled with black powder (a form of gunpowder) and were set off by a fuse of corned powder in a quill or a thin tube of rolled metal. Intended to produce an incendiary effect rather than a blast, they were not lethal, and grenades having spherical or cylindrical metal bodies soon succeeded them.

Field use of these grenades tended to be rather dangerous, because the fuses were unreliable: the powder burned sporadically and sometimes flashed through to the main filling with disastrous consequences for the thrower. It was not until the early 1900s that more consistent fuses were produced.

Modern antipersonnel grenades comprise three main parts: a pyrotechnic fuse and detonator initiated by the action of a spring-loaded striker on a percussion cap and giving about five seconds' delay; a filling of high explosives; and a fragmenting case made of wire or engraved steel. They weigh between 5 and 17.5 oz. (140–500 g) so they can be thrown to about 90 ft. (27 m) or projected from a rifle to approximately 1,300 ft. (400 m). Similar ignition and projection systems are used on smoke, tear gas, and signal grenades, but the appropriate filling is usually contained in a simple tinplate body.

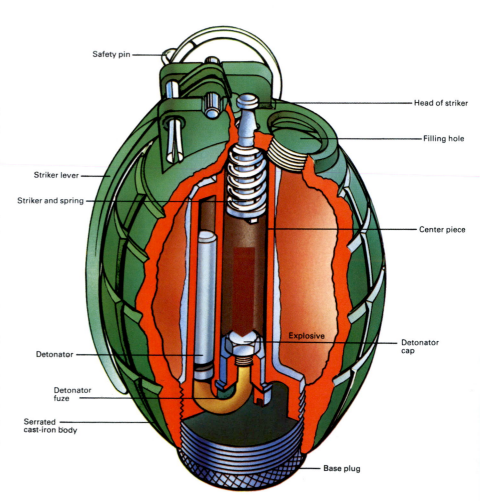

▼ A cutaway of a Mills hand grenade. The striker is held up by the striker lever. If the safety pin is removed, the lever flies free, the spring is released, and the striker hits the detonator cap. The detonator fuse is activated and ignites the explosive. During World War I, both the German and Allied armies used the Mills and similar grenades extensively. Many improvements were made and the grenade soon diversified so that it could be launched from rifles, specially designed weapons, and even spring-operated guns.

Safety pin

Head of striker

Filling hole

Striker lever

Striker and spring

Center piece

Explosive

Detonator

Detonator cap

Detonator fuze

Serrated cast-iron body

Base plug

SEE ALSO: Antiaircraft gun • Armor • Armored vehicle and tank • Automatic weapon and machine gun • Ballistics • Bomb • Explosive • Gun • Missile • Mortar, bazooka, and recoilless gun • Rifle and shotgun

Amphibious Vehicle

Amphibious vehicles, which can travel both on land and in water under their own power, range from specially adapted tanks to various designs of home-built swamp buggies.

Amphibious craft are mainly used for two purposes—pleasure and warfare. Farmers and foresters in wild country also make use of the versatility and toughness that they offer.

The current trend in nonmilitary amphibians is toward all-terrain vehicles (ATVs). Mostly built in the United States and Canada, they are usually based on two essential components: fat, ribbed tires at very low pressures and a transmission system using belts and tapered pulleys that adjusts the speed automatically according to the throttle setting. The softness of the tire, with pressures as low as 0.1 bar, lets the tread spread out to give maximum traction on land. The variable transmission relieves the driver of changing gear in normal forward use. Conventional gears are used for reverse and in some cases to give high and low speed ranges too. From the transmission onward, the mechanical principles are the same on most ATVs—an output pulley is mounted on a cross-shaft terminating at each end in clutch plates, which transmit the drive to the wheels on both sides of the vehicle. To steer the vehicle, one of the clutches on these drive shafts is disengaged and comes in contact with a disk brake to slow down the wheels on one side.

Most ATVs have six or eight wheels, which steer and drive the vehicle in water as well as on land. The vehicles' light weight and low center of gravity enable them to climb steep slopes easily and safely and the big soft tires mold easily round obstacles. Engines are usually single-cylinder units of around 15 cu. in. (250 cc).

The Amphicat is a typical ATV. It has a tough, lightweight plastic body and is powered by a Curtiss-Wright single-cylinder, two-stroke, air-cooled engine. It has expanding pulley and chain transmission with a high, low, and reverse range gearbox. A six wheeler, it weighs 400 lbs. (180 kg) and can carry 480 lbs. (220 kg).

Some ATVs, such as the Twister, have an articulated body with two separate watertight hulls that can move independently in response to the terrain to keep all wheels constantly in contact with the ground. Others have tanklike rubber tracks.

The problems of transport in the Everglades swamps of Florida led to the development of another type of amphibian, the swamp buggy.

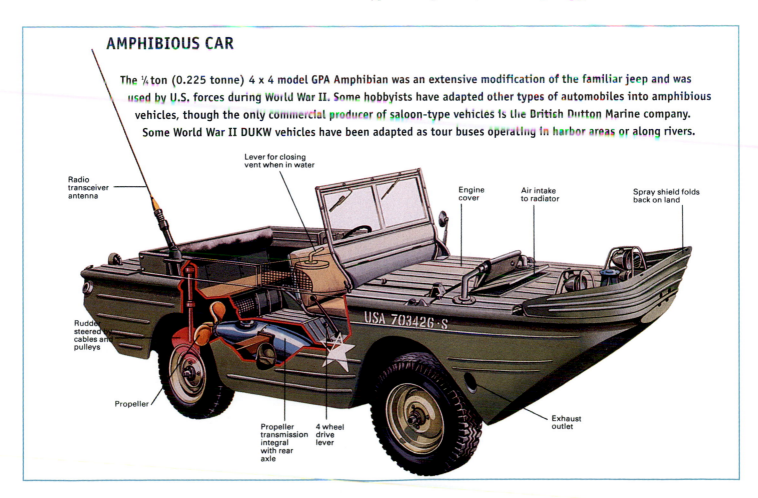

AMPHIBIOUS CAR

The ¼ ton (0.225 tonne) 4 x 4 model GPA Amphibian was an extensive modification of the familiar jeep and was used by U.S. forces during World War II. Some hobbyists have adapted other types of automobiles into amphibious vehicles, though the only commercial producer of saloon-type vehicles is the British Dutton Marine company. Some World War II DUKW vehicles have been adapted as tour buses operating in harbor areas or along rivers.

Radio transceiver antenna

Lever for closing vent when in water

Engine cover

Air intake to radiator

Spray shield folds back on land

Rudder steered by cables and pulleys

Propeller

Propeller transmission integral with rear axle

4 wheel drive lever

USA 70342G-S

Exhaust outlet

Swamp buggies ride on large truck, tractor, or aircraft tires, which support and drive them through thick mud and water. The Everglades is also home to an amphibious fan-propelled vehicle, which is steered and driven by a large fan at its rear that enables the light, small vehicle to ride easily over the mixed terrain.

More eccentric attempts at amphibians include an amphibious bicycle, shown at Lyons, France, in 1909. The front fork was linked by a rod to a rudder, and a small friction wheel at the rear drove a propeller. Cylindrical floats attached to the frame could be raised or lowered.

There have been several attempts at converting road vehicles into temporary amphibians, essentially, cheap alternatives to bridges or ferries. One, from New Zealand, consists of a floating platform onto which an automobile or truck is driven. The front wheels hang through slots into the water and act as rudders. The driving wheels rest on rubber-covered rollers that power twin propellers through a friction drive mechanism. Reverse gear provides a brake. Other similar devices have used simple rear-mounted paddles.

The advance of the air-cushion vehicle (hovercraft) reduced demand for amphibians. Most dual-drive amphibians waste time when transferring from water to land and vice versa, because they have to pause while they switch to another propulsion method. There are few amphibians with very good performance on both land and water—the price of their versatility.

Military vehicles

Military amphibians fall into several groups. First, at the basic level, are those that are primarily land vehicles that are able to take to the water for beach landings or river crossings. Next are land vehicles designed with built-in buoyancy that are capable of making limited trips without special preparation. Finally, there are surface-effect craft (hovercraft), which are more at home on the water but capable of overland transit.

The first group are all negatively buoyant and need preparation to gain enough temporary buoyancy to float or to crawl along the sea or riverbed. Techniques for floating tanks ashore go back to the major landings of World War II. It is essential that the main hull of the vehicle can be made watertight, with protruding shafts sealed at their exit points. A steel platform can then be welded around the upper hull and a waterproof screen raised from it supported by pneumatic tubes inflated by compressed air from the vehicle. No special water-propulsion unit is provided, forward thrust being generated by running the wheels or tracks, which act as paddlewheels.

Bottom-crawling is very common, particularly in Russian practice, for negotiating the many large rivers in continental Europe. No attempt is made to float the vehicle; a vertical air tube is erected from the turret hatch sufficiently high to project above the surface. On the French AMX 30 tank, for instance, the tube is 15 ft. (4.6 m) in length. The tank commander stands within the top and gives instructions to the crew below. Also necessary, of course, is a snort system, a temporary double pipe taking air down for running the engine and providing a route for its exhaust. This method can also be used to allow vehicles to transmit from landing craft to the beach where, say, an offshore bar prevents a close approach; the bottom must not be deeply rilled or the surf too heavy, or the vehicles may be swamped.

The second group, the truly amphibious vehicles, are becoming less common by virtue of the development of the third, the surface-effect craft. Most are thin skinned and transport personnel or cargo, but modern armor can be made from aluminum, plastic, or a sandwich of both, the result being of low enough density to permit the building of a buoyant tank. Such is the Russian PT-76, which incorporates a water-jet propulsion unit that obviates the need for shafts and propellers.

The Duck

The doyen of amphibious vehicles is the familiar Duck—more correctly, the DUKW (Duplex Universal Karrier, Wheeled. It was introduced in 1942 by General Motors as a development of their standard 6 x 6 truck chassis—six wheels, all driven. Topside it pioneered the boat-shaped hull, which once afloat, was propelled by a marine propeller clutched in as an alternative to the wheel drive. Its speeds of 50 mph (80 km/h) on land and

◄ The heavily armored U.S. LVTP-7, popularly called the Amtrack, is capable of transporting a payload of 19 personnel and their equipment.

◄ British Army amphibious bridging rigs on maneuvers. These rigs have stacked decking that is lifted across by gantries and coupled together to form bridge sections.

6 mph (10 km/h) afloat are rarely exceeded by current examples; indeed, many of the newer vehicles are so like the original that the basic design cannot be questioned.

Modern derivatives range greatly in size from the little Russian GAZ-46, a 4 x 4 (four wheels, all driven) with a useful payload of 1,100 lbs. (500 kg), enabling it to transport a patrol of five people, to the giant U.S. LARC-60. Another 4 x 4, this vehicle is 60 ft. (19 m) in length, weighing 37 tons (33.3 tonnes) empty and capable of floating with a payload of 60 tons (54 tonnes), though this can be considerably exceeded in an emergency. The LARC-60 (lighter, amphibious, resupply, cargo) is designed primarily to act as a ferry between the beach and ships lying offshore. It can unload its cargo directly onto the beach via its own bow ramp, or it can take the ground, engage the wheel drive and progress inland still loaded. Each wheel is powered by a separate engine, the pair of engines on each side being capable of driving one of two marine propellers set into tunnels below the hull.

Although most amphibians are wheeled, some, such as the Russian PTS, are tracked, improving their mobility in difficult conditions once ashore. Wheeled vehicles, in difficult conditions, commonly reduce tire pressures to improve traction.

Surface-effect vehicles are unlikely to replace the more conventional wheeled or tracked amphibians completely, but they are more numerous in a variety of configurations and can be many times larger than even the LARC-60. Rigid sidewall craft with conventional diesel/propeller propulsion are not truly amphibious; for progress ashore hovercraft need an aircraft-type propeller and flexible or combination skirts. Once ashore, its low air cushion limits its ability to negotiate the type of obstacle that would also hinder more conventional vehicles, but it will progress easily over marsh, deep snow, thin ice, or rapidly flowing water that would be otherwise impassable. It can be large, because unlike a wheeled vehicle, it is supported elastically over its entire underside by its air cushion. For instance, the British Hovercraft Corporation's nonmilitary SRN4 Mk 3 Super Four can transport up to 60 standard cars and over 400 passengers. It has a maximum speed of about 65 knots (120 km/h) and can cruise for about four and a half hours and would need little modification to be militarized.

The Russians in particular have recognized the hovercraft's potential in an assault role. Their Lebed, for example, is a 60-knot (110 km/h) craft with a 35-ton (31.5-tonne) payload, enough to lift a brace of the PT-76 tanks mentioned above. Like many more orthodox landing craft, it is sized to fit snugly into the well of an amphibious assault ship, such as an LPD. Thus, the Ivan Rogov class of ship can accommodate three preloaded Lebeds.

◄ Tracked landing vehicles are beached as troops are deployed. These vehicles weigh about 38 tons (34 tonnes) when fully laden and can carry between 25 and 30 occupants.

SEE ALSO: AIR-CUSHION VEHICLE • MARINE PROPULSION • TRACKED VEHICLE

Amplifier

In electronics, an amplifier is a device or circuit that increases or magnifies the strength of an electrical signal. This ability finds them use in audio and video devices as well as in other technological applications, such as computing.

The term *gain* refers to the factor by which an amplifier multiplies a signal. Most amplifier circuits are voltage amplifiers, and their gain is the proportional increase in voltage from the input signal to the output signal. In some circuits, however, gain is the increase in current or power. Some amplifiers have negative gain values, indicating that a positive input voltage is amplified to a negative output voltage, and vice versa.

An amplifier can be thought of as a variable switch. Instead of simply switching a current on or off, it responds to a low-amplitude signal by producing high-amplitude variations in output. All amplifiers rely on a power source, such as a dry cell or other direct-current (DC) supply.

Vacuum tubes

The devices at the cores of the earliest electronic amplifiers were vacuum-tube triodes, sometimes called valves for their ability to control the flow of current. A vacuum-tube triode contains a pair of solid parallel-plate electrodes—the emitter and collector—separated by a gap occupied by low-pressure gas that is essentially a vacuum. A third electrode—the base—is a metal grid between the other two electrodes and parallel to them.

The emitter is connected to the negative terminal of a DC power supply, and a heating filament causes its electrons to form an invisible "cloud" around the emitter. This reaction is a manifestation of an effect called thermionic emission, whereby thermal energy causes electrons to "boil" from hot metal surfaces.

The collector is connected to the positive terminal of the DC supply. Depending on the voltage of the base relative to the emitter, the electric field between the emitter and collector can pull electrons through the vacuum, causing a current to flow. A positive voltage of the base relative to the emitter encourages electrons to flow to the collector, whereas a slight negative voltage impedes that flow. The input signal causes a current to flow between the base and the emitter, but variations in that current are much smaller than variations in the flow of current between the emitter and the collector—this differential is the basis of the amplification effect. When the amplifier output is connected to a load, the current amplification results in a voltage amplification.

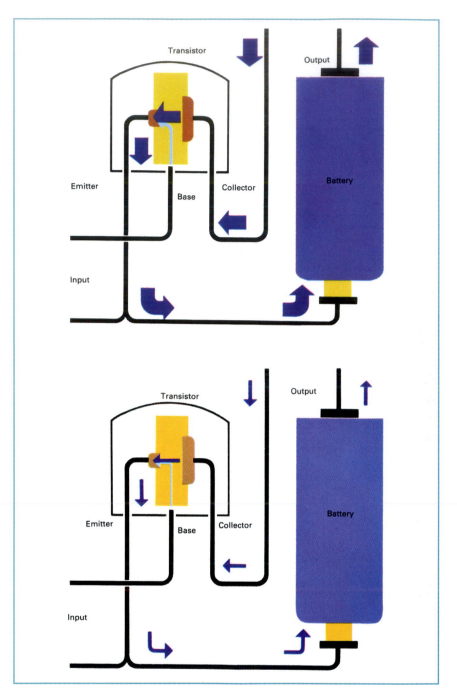

▲ An amplifier at two signal strengths. In the upper diagram, a relatively strong input signal (light-blue arrows) causes a much stronger output signal (thicker, dark-blue arrows). In the lower diagram, the input signal is weaker, so the output signal is also proportionately weaker.

Because vacuum-tube triodes can be built to withstand heavy current flows, they continue to be used for some high-power applications—the amplification of signals for radio and television transmission, for example. In most applications, however, semiconductor transistors take the place of triodes. Semiconductor amplifiers are more compact than vacuum tube amplifiers and more resistant to physical shocks and vibrations.

Bipolar transistors

The transistors in solid-state semiconductor amplifiers have three electrodes, just as the triodes in tube amplifiers do. If the transistor is of the bipolar-junction type, it consists of an *n-p-n* or *p-n-p* trilayer of *n*-type and *p*-type silicon. The emitter and collector electrodes connect to the outer layers of semiconductor, and the base electrode connects to the middle layer. The amplified current that flows through the emitter-collector circuit increases in proportion to the current through the base-emitter circuit.

Field-effect transistors

Some semiconductor amplifiers use FETs (field-effect transistors), in which case the electrodes have different names but perform similar functions to those of the base, collector, and emitter electrodes of triodes and bipolar transistors. In an FET, the amplified current flows between source and drain electrodes; the flow of current is controlled by the voltage at a gate electrode.

The source and drain electrodes connect to different layers of a bilayer of *n*-type and *p*-type semiconductor. The gate electrode is alongside the drain component of the bilayer but electrically insulated from it. When an appropriate voltage is applied to the gate electrode, the electrical field modifies the drain semiconductor, creating a channel through which electrons can flow. The "size" of that channel depends on the gate voltage, as does the size of the current that flows.

One advantage of FETs over bipolar transistors is that FETs need only an electric field—not a current—at the gate-source junction to cause a large current flow between the drain and the source. For this reason, FETs can produce far greater gains than bipolar transistors, and they have almost negligible input requirements.

Multistage amplification

A single-transistor amplifier with its associated power supply typically has a gain value between 10 and 1,000 and is called an amplification stage. Greater gains can be achieved by "cascading" two or more amplifier stages—that is, connecting the output of one transistor as the input of the next. The overall gain is the product of the gains of each stage, so a cascade of three amplifier stages with gains of 100 each give an overall gain value of 100 x 100 x 100 = 1,000,000.

The individual stages of a multistage amplifier may be coupled through capacitors or inductors. Both types of devices pass the alternating-current (AC) component of a signal to the next stage without any DC component, because there is no conducting path between the input and output of capacitors and inductors. Transformer couplings can also be used, but they are bulky in comparison with other coupling devices. Direct connections tend to be used only for amplifiers that

▼ The diagram at top shows the conventional symbols for an amplifier circuit based on a *p-n-p* bipolar transistor, whose emitter draws power from the positive terminal of a direct-current supply. For an *n-p-n* transistor, the polarity of the power supply would be reversed. The amplifier is bounded by the dotted line. The photo at bottom shows an integrated multistage amplifier circuit on the surface of a silicon chip.

must cope with low-frequency AC and DC signals, which capacitors and inductors handle poorly or not at all.

The junctions of transistors and other circuit components are extremely small, and complex amplifiers can be mounted on compact printed circuit boards. It is also possible to build integrated amplifier circuits on silicon chips for use in compact electronic devices such as desktop and palmtop computers and cellular telephones.

Operational amplifiers

Operational amplifiers, also called op-amps, are amplifier circuits capable of extremely high gain values; they are also characterized by having two inputs. An ideal op-amp would have an infinite gain; real devices have gains around 1,000,000. In practical uses, the gain of an op-amp is modified by the use of feedback, whereby part of the output signal returns to an input.

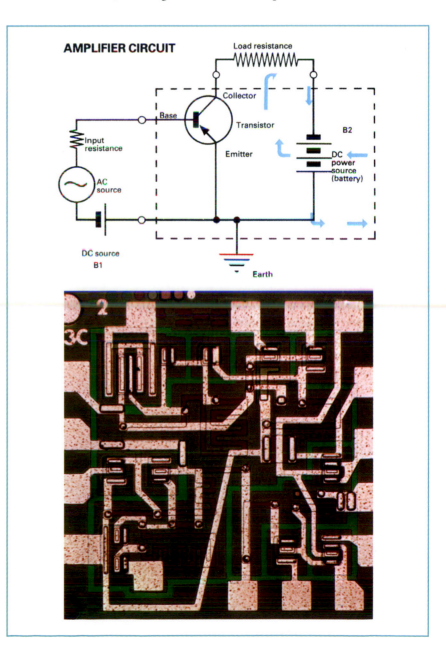

The circuit components of the feedback loop determine the behavior of the op-amp. Appropriate feedback circuits can make an op-amp perform mathematical operations, such as addition, subtraction, differentiation, and integration on the input signals. This possibility was exploited in analog computers and is the origin of the name "operational amplifier."

Distortion and its avoidance

Distortion arises when the output from an amplifier does not vary in exact linear proportion to its input. One form of distortion is clipping, which happens when the amplitude of an input signal is such that its peaks call for a greater output than the DC power source can supply. If viewed on an oscilloscope, the peaks of a sinusoidal waveform appear to have been squared off when clipping occurs, and such a waveform produces a harsh sound if used to drive a loudspeaker.

Other forms of distortion include frequency distortion and temperature distortion. In frequency distortion, gain depends on the frequency of the input signal; this distortion can degrade the natural balance of sound reproduced through an amplifier. Temperature distortion occurs when gain varies with the running temperature of an amplifier, particularly when overheating.

The solution to distortion is to use an amplifier with negative feedback. A small proportion of the output signal from the amplifier is inverted (has its sign changed) and is fed to the input. The input components that become overamplified have their input signals diminished to a greater extent than those components that are underamplified. Applying negative feedback reduces the overall gain, but it is easily restored by using greater gain in the early stages of a multistage amplifier, where distortion is less of a problem.

▲ Amplifier units are produced to meet a wide variety of applications, with the performance characteristics of the amplifier closely matched to the job.

▼ With public address systems, the amplifier is often built into a cabinet along with the loudspeaker unit to give an integrated assembly that can be quickly manhandled onto the stage and connected up ready for a performance.

Audio amplifiers

An audio amplifier is designed to amplify low-power signals from audio equipment, such as a compact disc or digital tape player, to such power levels that they can drive loudspeakers or headphones. For a stereo system, each amplification stage is part of a pair—left and right.

In some cases, preamplifiers (preamps) first boost the voltages of the input signals to a convenient level for filtering through equalizers or through balance, tone, and volume controls. Output signals from these filters are then boosted to the power necessary to drive speakers by power amplifiers (power amps). In other cases, combined multistage amplifiers, called integrated amplifiers, act as preamps and power amps.

The quality of sound from an audio amplifier is greatly influenced by the degree of distortion introduced by the amplifier. A high-quality audio amplifier might use negative feedback to ensure less than 0.2 percent distortion over a frequency range of 20 Hz to 20,000 Hz. The range of operating frequencies for which the distortion specification applies is called the bandwidth.

One of the other factors that detracts from sound quality is noise—a loosely defined term covers a number of phenomena. Part of the noise that affects amplified signals stems from the quiescent current—a steady current flow from the DC sources through the components. This aspect of noise can be kept to a minimum by using FETs, where no current flows from the gate electrodes, rather than bipolar transistors. A good amplifier might boast a signal-to-noise ratio of at least 70 dB, corresponding to a signal strength (power) at least 10^7 times greater than the noise level.

SEE ALSO: Capacitor • Electronics • Hi-fi systems • Loudspeaker • Radio • Resistor • Sound • Transistor

Analog and Digital Systems

Any physical quantity can be measured, recorded, transmitted, and displayed in either analog or digital form. Both forms of data have advantages: analog systems cater for continuous ranges of values between two limits, whereas digital systems cater for a finite number of values over the same range; digital data lends itself to more accurate storage and transmission, whereas analog data is more prone to corruption by interference.

Analog-to-digital and digital-to-analog converters (ADCs and DACs) are devices that translate data between analog and digital forms. They are used to record and reproduce audio and video data and for digital computers to communicate with analog input and output devices.

Displays

The same information can be displayed in analog or digital forms. The face of a clock or watch might be an analog or a digital display, for example. An analog face has hands that pass through an infinite number of configurations as they sweep around the face. One type of digital face has six display elements that have a limited number of configurations—from 00:00:00 to 23:59:59. This and other types of digital displays can represent no time between the possible configurations.

The differences between analog and digital displays have implications for how their information can be read. Since the hands of an analog face are in almost continual motion, their positions could be measured at any instant to determine the precise time at that instant. In fact, an analog stopwatch can be frozen in time to make such a measurement at the end of a race, for example. A digital clock display differs from an analog face in that it can show only the closest displayable value to the exact time at any instant.

When people read an analog face, they usually make a form of analog-to-digital conversion: they read an instantaneous value of time from the markings on the clock face to which the hands are closest at a given instant. A digital display could be converted into an analog signal by taking the instant at which one display value changes to the next as being the midpoint between those two values. Since time progresses in a linear manner between these points, interpolation to give time values between the midpoints is straightforward.

Properties other than time can be displayed in analog and digital forms. Conventional mercury and dyed-alcohol thermometers give a direct analog display of temperature as ends of their liquid threads expand and contract along marked scales.

Thermocouples—electrical devices whose output voltages vary in response to changes in temperature—can be used to drive either analog pointer-and-scale meters or digital displays.

Values of properties as diverse as pressure, displacement of an object, wind speed, and liquid level can all be represented in analog and digital forms by using a suitable transducer to convert a physical value into an electrical signal and using that electrical signal to drive appropriately calibrated analog meters or digital displays.

Computing

In general terms, a computer is a device that performs mathematical and logical operations on incoming data. The results of those operations form the output of the computer.

In analog computers, transistor-based circuits perform operations. For accurate results, the output signals from the transistors in such circuits must vary in exact proportion to the input signals. Distortion—deviation from this ideal behavior—is minimized by the use of operational amplifier circuits. Nevertheless, small errors at each operation can become compounded into larger errors in the final results of calculations.

In a digital system, the transistors in logic circuits behave as switches. That is, they have two states—conducting and insulating—rather than the continuous range of states possible for an operational amplifier. Unless a drastic circuit breakdown occurs, there is no way for one logic circuit to misread the output of another. For this reason, digital circuits have proven themselves more accurate and reliable than analog circuits.

▲ The operations center of a telecommunications network. Because this system uses microwave and fiber-optic links in conjunction with PCM, a single channel can carry many thousands of telephone messages, or hundreds of color TV programs.

Signals

A signal is essentially a stream of values that vary with time; in the context of electrical signals, the value that varies is usually voltage. In the analog signal from an oscillator circuit, for example, the voltage varies sinusoidally (in the form of a sine wave) over a continuous range between positive and negative maximum values. In the output signal from a microphone, several sinusoidal waves typically combine to form a more complex signal.

Over distance, and particularly if the signal passes through switches or complex circuits, the true analog signal becomes weaker and gets contaminated by noise—extraneous electrical signals caused by interference. Eventually, the original signal can be overwhelmed by noise or at least degraded to such an extent that the original data—an audio or video signal, for example—cannot be reproduced with satisfactory quality.

Digital signals differ from analog signals in that the voltage may take only certain values over a given range. The great advantage of such systems is that noise from interference is seldom of such intensity that it can change the signal from one "allowed" value to the next. If interference boosts an 8 V signal to 8.2 V or cuts it to 7.7 V, for example, a device that reads only whole-number values for voltage will recognize the original value of 8 V, so the effects of noise are eliminated. Digital systems are nevertheless susceptible to corruption if the intensity of noise is greater than the interval between allowed signal values.

Analog-to-digital converter (ADC)

It is often desirable to convert an analog signal, such as the output from a microphone, into a digital signal. The aim might be to produce a signal that is more resistant to interference during transmission or storage or to convert the signal into a form that is compatible with digital circuits.

The devices that read analog signals and encode them in digital form are called analog-to-digital converters, or ADCs. They work by a process called sampling, whereby a signal is inspected at regular intervals and its value at each sampling point is encoded in digital form. The output of an ADC can therefore be considered as a stream of digital "snapshots" of the analog signal. The quality of the digitized signal depends on the sampling rate—how often the analog signal is examined—and the amount of detail in each sample.

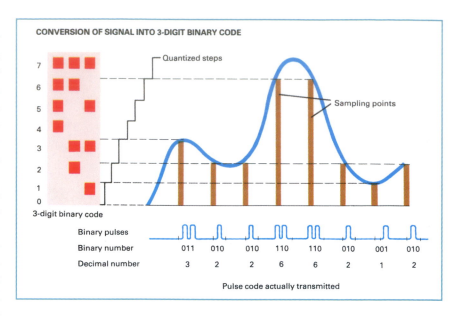

CONVERSION OF SIGNAL INTO 3-DIGIT BINARY CODE

	Binary number	Decimal number
	011	3
	010	2
	010	2
	110	6
	110	6
	010	2
	001	1
	010	2

Pulse code actually transmitted

▲ This diagram shows how an analog signal (the blue curve) can be digitized by sampling the signal at regular intervals and representing the sampled values as the closest integral values in binary code. The presence or absence of pulses at three time intervals can code for decimal values from zero to seven.

▼ This table shows how some decimal values translate into binary values. Such conversions are used to store and transmit, in the form of binary code, decimal values sampled from analog signals.

Pulse-code modulation (PCM)

Dating from the 1930s, pulse-code modulation, or PCM, is the oldest technique for analog-to-digital conversion. Although its theoretical worth was soon appreciated, the number of practical applications started to grow only with the development of integrated circuits and the boom in communications that took hold in the 1960s and continues to the present day. By the late 1960s, telecommunications engineers viewed PCM as being vital for the reliable transmission of audio and video signals.

A pulse-code modulator works by sampling an analog signal, such as a voltage variation that represents speech, and measuring its amplitude at each sampling point. The amplitude value is expressed in binary digits, or bits, so an amplitude of 6 on an arbitrary scale would translate to 110 in three-bit binary code (or 0110 in four-bit code, 00110 in five-bit code, and so on). In an electrical system, each bit is represented by a pulse of voltage in the output signal; in an optoelectronic system, the pulses would be of light.

The necessary sampling rate depends on the maximum frequency in the analog signal. A low-quality telephone system might aim to use PCM signals that are faithful to audio frequencies up to 4,000 Hz, for example. To transmit even this low-quality signal faithfully requires a minimum sampling rate of 8,000 Hz (8,000 samples per second) so as to read a 4,000 Hz signal twice in each cycle.

Each sample is converted into binary form by an analog-to-digital converter, which uses

TABLE OF 4 DIGIT BINARY CODE

Number	Binary code	Number	Binary code
0	0000	8	1000
1	0001	9	1001
2	0010	10	1010
3	0011	11	1011
4	0100	12	1100
5	0101	13	1101
6	0110	14	1110
7	0111	15	1111

capacitors in integrated circuits to store charges that correspond to the voltage at sampling points. The magnitude of each charge translates into a binary value that is stored in a device called a shift register. From there, the binary code leaves as a series of pulses ready for transmission.

Apart from the sampling rate, a second important factor in the quality of a PCM signal is the number of permitted amplitude values, or quantization levels, that can be expressed in the pulse code. The greater the number of quantization levels, the more faithful the representation of a smooth waveform can be. In telephone signals, seven-bit pulse codes allow for the expression of 128 (2^7) quantization levels; for high-fidelity audio and video signals, many more bits are required in each pulse of the coded signal.

Transmission

Additional benefits of pulsed digital signals become apparent in the field of telecommunications, where they are used to transmit information along channels, which might be wires that conduct electrical signals or optical fibers that carry pulses of laser light around networks.

One technique, called time-division multiplexing, or TDM, allows several digital signals to pass along a single channel without cross talk, or interference between signals. In TDM, each signal is converted into a binary form and fed to its own shift register. The shift registers are shifted in sequence so that sample one of signal one is followed by sample one of signal two, and so on, through to the last signal then back to sample two of signal one, and the cycle is repeated. At the beginning of each cycle, a framing signal (indexing pulse) is transmitted so that the receiver equipment can be synchronized, thus allowing the various signals to be separated.

The quality of signals can be maintained over long distances by the use of repeaters. These devices read the incoming signal and boost it for onward transmission so as to keep the signal strength above the threshold at which it would become susceptible to interference.

A problem with PCM is that the high rate at which the digital pulses have to be transmitted means that a much wider signal bandwidth is required for transmission of the coded data when compared with the analog form. However, several compression methods can be used to minimize the bandwidth requirements for transmission.

Digital-to-analog converter (DAC)

In many cases, a digital signal is an interference-proof means of providing information for a device that uses that information in analog form, such as

the loudspeaker of a telephone handset. In such cases, the receiver must be able to reconstitute the original signal from the digitized data. The device that performs this task is called a digital-to-analog converter, or DAC. Provided the sampling rate in the digitized signal is adequate to describe the original signal, the DAC reproduces the analog signal by calculating a smooth curve that joins the sampled values encoded in the digital signal.

Audio and video recording

For decades, the main storage systems for audio and video information were analog: they stored sound and images in the form of analog variations in the magnetization of magnetic tape. Sound was also recorded in the grooves of records that would produce analog vibrations in a pickup.

Since the 1980s, audio and video recordings have been increasingly dominated by digital media. In compact discs (CDs) and digital versatile discs (DVDs), pulses of digitized information are stored as pits in spiral tracks read by laser as the CD or DVD rotates. In digital audio tapes (DATs), the information is stored as discrete pulses of magnetization in the tape. Such recording media benefit from the resistance of digital information to interference caused by dirt or diminishing magnetization. Digital radio and television broadcasts also are finding increasing acceptance.

Modems

Although telephone networks are now largely digital, conventional lines between telephones and exchanges use analog signals. A modem is simply a combined ADC and DAC that converts digital signals from computers into analog signals for transmission through the analog line and converts incoming signals into a digital form compatible with computer circuitry.

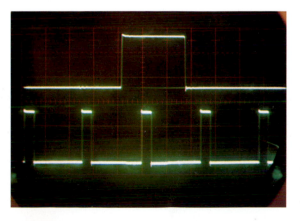

◄ Oscilloscope traces showing PCM pulses. Any random pulses superimposed on such a signal are not recognized as coded signals and not reproduced; noise is thus almost eliminated—a factor that is of special value when communicating across the huge distances to space probes.

SEE ALSO: COMPACT DISC, AUDIO • COMPUTER NETWORK • DIGITAL VERSATILE DISC (DVD) • FIBER OPTICS • MODEM AND ISDN • TELEPHONE SYSTEM

Anemometer

Strictly speaking, anemometers are instruments for measuring wind speed, but their use has also been extended to the measurement of fluid velocities. The type of anemometer used depends on the nature of the fluid, the range of velocities likely to be encountered, and the accuracy required. For the measurement of wind speeds, however, there are essentially three types of anemometer: the rotating cup, propeller, and pitot-static pressure tube.

▲ A combined rotating cup anemometer and wind vane used by meteorologists for measuring wind speed and direction.

Cup anemometer

The simplest type of wind speed indicator is the rotating-cup anemometer. This consists of three or four conical or hemispherical cups mounted at the ends of horizontal spokes that radiate from a vertical rotating shaft. The concave surfaces of the cups offer greater wind resistance than their convex surfaces, causing them to catch the wind efficiently and rotate. When the wind is steady, the cups rotate at a speed approximating that of the wind. By attaching a revolution counter to the shaft and counting the number of revolutions in a certain period, the wind speed can be calculated quite accurately.

Alternatively, a continuous indication of the rate of rotation (and hence the wind speed) can be achieved by coupling a small dynamo to the shaft. This method produces a voltage output proportional to the rate of rotation; wind speeds can then be read directly off a suitably calibrated voltmeter.

In gusty winds, the cup anemometer tends to overrate the average wind speed, because the rotating cups speed up at a faster rate than they slow down, and thus the overrunning errors pro-

duced can be as high as 30 percent. Nevertheless, this type of anemometer is a simple and inexpensive device capable of measuring wind speeds from 5 to 100 mph (8–160 km/h).

Propeller anemometer

Propeller anemometers are suitable for the measurement of low air speeds in the region of 1 to 25 mph (1–40 km/h). In this case, blades of a propeller, or fan, are attached to a horizontal rotating shaft directed into the wind by a weathervanelike tail fin. The speed of rotation is proportional to the wind speed and can be measured by the same methods as are used with cup anemometers.

Mechanical anemometers cannot be accurately calibrated simply from their dimensions, since factors such as friction vary from instrument to instrument. They must, therefore, be calibrated in the controlled conditions of a wind tunnel, the air speed being measured by a pressure anemometer.

Pitot-static anemometer

The pitot-static pressure tube anemometer is mechanically simple, having no moving parts, and has many applications; both wind tunnels and aircraft employ them as airspeed indicators. They may also be used to study the flow of liquids.

The main part is a probe consisting of two separate tubes aligned into the wind. The pitot tube is open at one end, allowing air to blow in and hence cause a pressure build-up. The pressure is the sum of the static air pressure and the dynamic produced by the flow of air into the tube.

The other tube is the static tube, closed and rounded at its upstream end with a series of holes around the tube some distance downstream. The airstream is effectively undisturbed by the rounded front of the static tube, so this tube contains air at the static pressure alone. Between the downstream ends of the tubes, there is a differential pressure gauge. This gauge measures the pressure difference between the two tubes, thus giving the dynamic pressure of the pitot tube.

Pitot-static anemometers cause some disturbance in the airstream and so are not suitable for velocity measurements in confined spaces where such disturbances may be significant. With modification they can, however, be used to measure supersonic air flow.

SEE ALSO: AIRCRAFT-CONTROL ENGINEERING • FRICTION • HYDRODYNAMICS • METEOROLOGY • PRESSURE • WIND TUNNEL

Anesthetic

Anesthetics are used to induce a temporary state of unconsciousness in a patient undergoing an operation—and with the complicated surgery being performed today, the patient may be kept unconscious for many hours.

The anesthetic is delivered by a machine that supplies the patient's lungs with a mixture of anesthetic gases, which are selected by the anesthetist according to the degree of unconsciousness required, the health and age of the patient, and the type of surgery being performed. Under anesthetic, the patient should be insensitive to pain and have no muscular reflexes that could interfere with the surgeon's delicate manipulations.

Halothane (2-bromo-2-chloro-1,1,1-trifluoroethane) and the flurane group (which includes sevoflurane, desflurane, and isoflurane) are gases commonly used for inhalation anesthesia, supplied together with oxygen (O_2) and nitrous oxide (N_2O) via a mask and a tube inserted through the mouth and into the throat.

Nitrous oxide is a nonflammable gas, stored as a liquid compressed into cylinders, used as the sole anesthetic agent in most dentistry. Because the gas is not irritating to the lungs, it is often used to induce unconsciousness before introducing a more pungent anesthetic, such as ether, when the patient is well and truly under.

Liquid anesthetic agents, such as ether and chloroform, are also widely used. To make them breathable, they must first be broken into droplets by a vaporizer in the machine. Trichloroethylene vapor is another popular gas.

Inhalation anesthetics work by targeting the nerve endings in the brain. In current practice, they are rarely used alone but are combined with muscle relaxants or analgesic drugs to provide "balanced" anesthesia. This approach allows the anesthesiologist to produce an effect appropriate to the part of the body being operated on and the type of surgery to be carried out.

Design of machines

The most basic anesthetic machine is Boyle's apparatus, introduced in 1917 and still very widely used in a much improved form. The com-

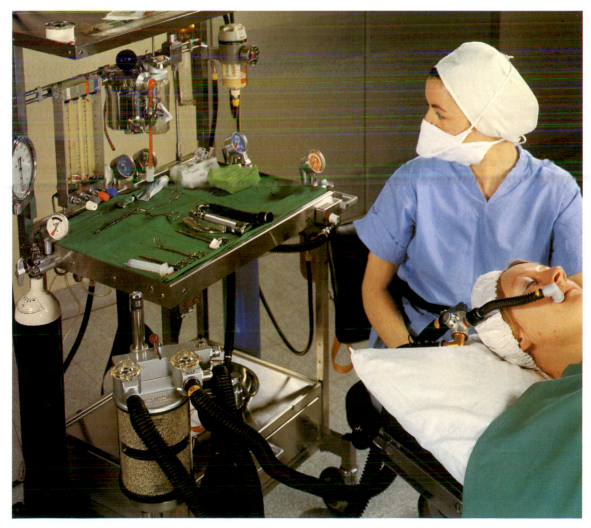

◄ The anesthetist must keep a constant check on the proportions of the gas mixture fed to the patient during the course of a surgical operation. As well as being trained in how to keep a patient sedated, anesthetists have to be able to bring a patient out of anesthesia quickly and safely.

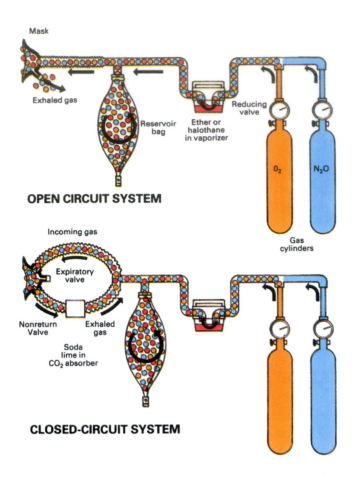

OPEN CIRCUIT SYSTEM

Mask

Exhaled gas

Reservoir bag

Ether or halothane in vaporizer

Reducing valve

O₂

N₂O

Gas cylinders

CLOSED-CIRCUIT SYSTEM

Incoming gas

Expiratory valve

Nonreturn Valve

Exhaled gas

Soda lime in CO₂ absorber

ponents are usually either supported on a moveable trolley or installed conveniently close to the operating table.

Gas is supplied from cylinders attached to the machine or by hoses from a bulk supply in another part of the hospital. In the latter case, the machine may have cylinders as a standby for use in emergencies. The normal complement of cylinders is two of oxygen (colored black with a white top, for easy identification), two of nitrous oxide (blue), one of carbon dioxide (gray), and one small cylinder of the anesthetic. Carbon dioxide (CO_2) is included for use as a stimulant, should breathing become weak during the operation.

Each type of cylinder and its accompanying hose has connections of different designs to prevent attachment to the wrong inlet. Reducing valves are fitted to the high-pressure O_2, CO_2, and N_2O cylinders to supply the gases at a suitably low pressure. Isoflurane, however, is already at the correct pressure and can be fed directly into the machine from its storage cylinder.

The selected gases are fed separately into flowmeters, which indicate the quantities of each in the mixture being delivered to the patient. These flowmeters are tapered tubes containing loosely fitting plungers. The plunger floats on the gas as it passes up through the tube, a more rapid flow being required to carry it to the top, where

▲ In an open-circuit anesthetic machine, the exhaled gases are vented to the air, whereas in a closed-circuit system, they are chemically scrubbed.

the tube is widest. The height of the plunger on the scale indicates the flow rate.

When vapor from liquid anesthetics is to be added to the mixture, the combined gas flow is directed through a vaporizer. This is a container holding the liquid anesthetic, which evaporates as the gas mixture is blown across the surface or bubbled through it. From the vaporizer, the mixture passes to a rubber reservoir bag, which fills with gas then deflates as the patient inhales and refills when the patient exhales.

The final anesthetic mixture passes along a wide corrugated-rubber tube to the mask, which is held over the patient's face. An expiratory valve is fitted to the mask to prevent exhaled gases from being forced back into the incoming mixture and causing carbon dioxide buildup and eventual suffocation. Exhaled gases leaving the expiratory valve are often ducted out of the operating room to prevent the surgical staff from becoming affected during the operation. In more complex closed-circuit systems, exhaled gases are not exhausted from the apparatus but pass through a cylinder containing soda lime (a mixture of sodium hydroxide and lime), which absorbs the carbon dioxide; they then pass back into the reservoir bag, from which the mixture is reinhaled.

If the patient's respiration is inhibited by deep anesthesia or by the use of muscle relaxant drugs, a ventilator may be used to assist breathing. This is a rubber bellows that pumps the gas mixture into the lungs automatically, and the patient exhales normally. There are, however, various models of highly sophisticated automatic ventilators, some of which are specifically for either adults or children. In addition, there are instruments that monitor the ventilator's output and raise an alarm should a malfunction occur. This information together with readings of blood pressure, pulse rate, and various other factors monitored on separate machines is available to the modern anesthetist at all times throughout an operation.

Local anesthetics

For short operations or procedures where the patient needs to be conscious, local anesthetics are used. Injections of synthetic cocaine compounds, such as Novocain, are used in dental work or for minor surgery. Another form is the epidural anesthetic used during childbirth, where the anesthetic agent is injected into the space around the protective membrane at the end of the spinal cord, dulling the nerves to the pelvic organs.

SEE ALSO: AMBULANCE • FLOWMETER • OPERATING ROOM • PHARMACEUTICALS • SURGERY

Aniline and Azo Dyes

Aniline and azo dyes are important classes of synthetic dyes manufactured from substances derived from coal tar and products of oil refining. Most aniline dyes range from pink through purple to black; a few are green or blue. Most azo dyes are red, orange, or yellow. Dyes are used to modify the colors of such substances as polymers and textiles; they are also used in inks and coatings.

Until the mid-19th century, the only available dyes were of animal or vegetable origin. These dyes include madder, a moderately strong red dye taken from the root of a herb of the same name and known to the Egyptians as early as 1500 B.C.E.; indigo, a dark blue dye with a reddish cast derived from indigo plants; cochineal, a scarlet dye and food colorant taken from the dried bodies of cochineal beetles; and saffron, an orange dye and spice extracted from dried stigmas of the purple-flowered *Crocus sativus*.

The rarest and most highly prized dye was purpura, a purple dye extracted from the *Murex* mollusk. Purpura was used to dye the robes of the Persian nobility as early as the sixth century B.C.E. and then the clothing of Roman nobility. In the late fourth century, Emperor Theodosium of Byzantium—now the city of Istanbul, Turkey—prohibited the use of purple-dyed garments by persons other than members of his family; the penalty for disobedience was death.

In the mid-19th century, purple clothing would again catch the interest of a ruler—this time the British Queen Victoria. The difference was that Victoria's preferred shade was that of the first commercial synthetic dye, mauveine.

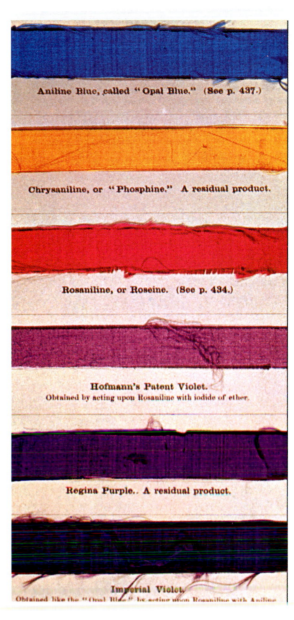

Aniline Blue, called "Opal Blue." (See p. 437.)

Chrysaniline, or "Phosphine." A residual product.

Rosaniline, or Roseine. (See p. 434.)

Hofmann's Patent Violet.
Obtained by acting upon Rosaniline with iodide of ether.

Regina Purple.. A residual product.

Imperial Violet.
Obtained like the "Opal Blue" by acting upon Rosaniline with Aniline

◀ A page from an 1864 science magazine showing a selection of early synthetic dyes, which enabled clothing manufacturers to produce brightly colored new ranges. Queen Victoria started a trend when she began wearing dresses colored with William Perkin's new mauveine dye.

Aniline dyes from coal tar

Following the development of coal carbonization by the British inventor William Murdock in the 1790s, an industry developed for the production of coal gas for lighting and heating. The industry produced large amounts of coal tar—a by-product that was at first thought to be of little use.

In 1832, Friedlieb Runge, the new technical director of a municipal gasworks in Oranienburg near Berlin, Germany, started a series of experiments with coal tar. In one of his experiments, he isolated an oil by standard distillation of coal tar and then steam distillation of the first distillate. When Runge treated this oil with a solution of calcium chloride in water, chlorine gas (Cl_2) was evolved and the liquid turned blue.

Runge found that this liquid, which he called *Kyanöl* (German for "blue oil"), left a yellow stain on pine. Furthermore, he found that moderately strong oxidizing agents, such as chlorine and nitric acid (HNO_3), could convert the blue oil into blue, red, violet, and even black dyes.

Runge foresaw the commercial prospects for these dyes, which were in fact the first synthetic aniline dyes. His plans to develop a dye manufacturing plant were stifled, however: the financial director of the gasworks saw Runge as a rival and refused financial support for his project.

A number of other German chemists were interested in the components of coal tar. Among them was August Hofmann, who purified the aromatic compounds benzene (C_6H_6) and methylbenzene ($C_6H_5CH_3$, also called toluene) and developed methods for converting those compounds into their nitrated derivatives, such as nitrobenzene ($C_6H_5NO_2$), and subsequently into amines, such as phenylamine (aniline, $C_6H_5NH_2$), which he had also isolated directly from coal tar.

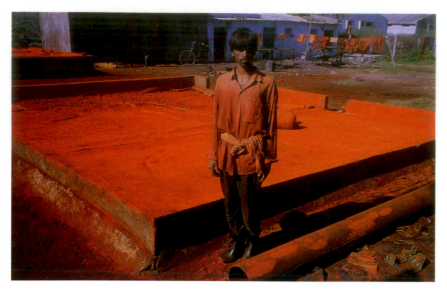

▲ A red azo dye powder left to dry in the sun at a chemical works in Gujarat, India. Although azo dyes are toxic, few precautions have been taken to prevent the powder from contaminating the workers or the surrounding environment.

Hofmann was invited to Britain to be the first director of the Royal College of Chemistry in London, which opened in 1845.

Perkin's mauve

Hofmann was keen to use the chemistry that he was developing to synthesize quinine—a malaria medicine extracted from chinchona bark. During the Easter vacation of 1856, the British chemist William Perkin, then an 18-year-old pupil of Hofmann, tried to synthesize quinine by oxidizing allylmethylphenylamine (allyltoluidine). Unfortunately, his first experiment produced only a reddish brown sludge.

Perkin repeated the procedure using aniline as the basis. This time, he prepared a black sludge, part of which dissolved in ethanol (C_2H_5OH) to give a mauve color. Intrigued by the color, he tried dyeing a piece of silk. So successful was the result that he immediately patented the discovery—mauveine, the first synthetic dye. Assisted by his father and brother, he went into commercial production within six months, building a factory at Greenford Green, London.

Mauveine-dyed clothing was an instant success, and its popularity was boosted yet further when Queen Victoria wore a mauve gown to the Royal Exhibition of 1862. The commercial success of mauveine stimulated intense development work in the field of dyes. Hence, it can be said that the profitability of fashion was a driving force behind the early development of organic chemistry and the chemical industry.

One of the first new dyes after mauveine was basic fuchsin, a deep rose-pink dye discovered by Nantaston in 1856 and made in 1859 by Verquin by heating commercial (impure) aniline with tin tetrachloride. By this time, the range of colors had increased to include Hofmann's violet, methyl violet, and iodide green, and Nicholson's blue.

Structures of dyes

Since the early days of dye development, analytical techniques have become available that allow chemists to "see" the structures of the compounds with which they work. From such observations, they have deduced the key structural components common to all dyes.

Dyes produce color by absorbing light from the region of the visible spectrum that corresponds to the complementary color of the dye, so a violet dye absorbs green light, for example. These absorptions happen because electrons in the dye jump to higher energy states, and the energy gap between the initial and final states matches the energy of a visible-light photon.

Aromatic compounds, such as benzene, are colorless because they absorb light in the ultraviolet region of the electromagnetic spectrum, so they have no effect on visible light. When the aromatic bond systems of several rings are linked together, the gap between the electronic ground state and the first excited state—the initial and final states in the absorption process—becomes smaller. This is why polycyclic aromatics have a yellow tinge: they absorb high-energy visible light, which is the blue part of the spectrum.

In a dye, one or more functional groups attached to the aromatic system bring the absorption frequency well into the visible range. The generic term for such a functional group is *chromophore*—from the Greek words *chroma* (color) and *pherein* (to carry). Other groups, called auxochromes—from the Greek *auxein* (to increase), boost and modify the frequency of absorption by a chromophore–aromatic system.

The main component of mauveine consists of four C_6 aromatic rings connected by –N– bridges. The unbound (lone) electron pairs on the nitrogen atoms connect the electron systems of the rings together, and an $–NH_2$ group acts as chromophore, bringing the absorption of the aromatic system into the yellow-to-green region of the visible spectrum and making the dye purple.

Triarylmethane dyes

The structure of the main component of mauveine is not typical of aniline dyes, however, which are better described as a class of triarylmethane dyes (the term *aryl* standing for a general aromatic group). These dyes are well represented by the example of a red dye called pararosaniline chloride. This compound consists of a carbon atom bonded to three aniline groups, $–C_6H_4NH_2$. Although the central carbon carries a nominal positive charge, that charge in fact spreads through and unites the aromatic systems of the three rings and is balanced by the negative charge of the chloride ion. Hence, the formula of pararosaniline chloride is $C_{19}H_{18}N_3Cl$. The three $-NH_2$ groups act as chromophores. Basic conditions can remove a hydrogen ion from one of the $-NH_2$ groups, disrupting the bonding system and making the compound colorless.

Pararosaniline chloride is a major component of basic fuchsin, and it is worth noting that its formation from aniline depends on the presence of an amount of toluidine to contribute the central carbon atom. The other components of basic fuchsin are rosaniline (sometimes called magenta I) and magenta II. These compounds have additional methyl groups attached to, respectively, one and two of their aniline rings.

The colors of triarylmethane dyes depend on the functional groups attached to the aromatic rings and the chromophores. Hofmann's violet, for example, is rosaniline in which an ethyl ($-C_2H_5$) group replaces a hydrogen atom on each of the $-NH_2$ groups. Other common substitutions include sulfonate groups ($-SO_3^-$) for one or more hydrogen atoms on the aromatic rings attached to the central carbon atom.

Azo dyes

In 1858, around the same time that Perkin was developing his aniline dyes, the German chemist Peter Griess discovered a reaction that would later find much use in the manufacture of another important class of dyes: the azo dyes. Griess made this discovery during his spare time while working at a brewery in Britain.

In the first part of the Griess process, dilute nitrous acid (nitric (III) acid, HNO_2) and hydrochloric acid (HCl) convert an aromatic amine into a diazonium salt:

$$ArNH_2 + HNO_2 + HCl \rightarrow ArN_2^+Cl^- + 2H_2O$$

where Ar is an aromatic group. This reaction is performed at around 32°F (0°C).

Diazonium salts attack other aromatic compounds, displacing a hydrogen atom from the ring and replacing it with a diazo coupling, $-N=N-$. The diazo structure links together the aromatic systems on either side of it, as well as acting as a chromophore. Hence, azo compounds of the general formula $Ar-N=N-Ar^*$, where Ar may or may not be identical to Ar^*, are strongly colored compounds that can be used as dyes.

Azo dyes have three great advantages over aniline dyes. First, the coupling reaction can be applied to numerous pairs of aromatic systems to produce a wide variety of dyes. Second, the coupling reaction is smooth and efficient and gives products of high purity rather than a complex mixture. Third, the coupling reaction can be done

within a fabric: one component is soaked into the fabric, and then the second component is added to complete the reaction. The product of the reaction is often much less soluble than the reagents, so the dye becomes trapped within the fibers.

Dyes and medicine

Some dyes are used as stains to highlight certain types of tissues and bacteria on microscope slides for which they have a pronounced affinity. At the start of the 20th century, the German bacteriologist Paul Ehrlich realized that certain bacterial illnesses could be cured by applying a dye that had an affinity for the bacterial pathogen of the illness and that was also toxic to that pathogen.

Using that approach, Ehrlich discovered in 1904 that tryptan red was toxic to the bacteria that cause African sleeping sickness. The dye is also toxic to humans, so its use was restricted to extreme cases. Experiments with other dyes led to the discovery in 1910 of the antisyphilitic drug Salvarsan (arsphenamine), in which toxic arsenic replaces nitrogen in a dye that attacks syphilis.

In the 1930s, a team led by the German bacteriologist Gerhard Domagk screened a large number of dyes for therapeutic activity. The result was the invention of sulfonamide drugs, which are effective against various streptococcal infections.

◀ Natural dyes produce mellow reds and browns, colors that were difficult to produce with the early aniline dyes but were later achieved with azo dyes. However, it can be difficult to use natural dyes with many of today's synthetic fabrics. Synthetic dyes often have a better colorfastness than natural dyes and can withstand modern laundry processes.

SEE ALSO: CHEMISTRY, ORGANIC • CLOTHING MANUFACTURE • DYEING PROCESS • FABRIC PRINTING • TEXTILE

Animation

Animation is a technique for making inanimate objects appear to move before the eyes of the viewer. It is mainly used in the making of cartoons but has found new applications since the advent of the computer and the sophisticated graphics software that has been developed to run on fast, memory-rich machines. In fact, the full-length animated feature film probably owes its survival to the introduction of computer technology, because the increasing costs of hand drawing every frame were making animated films expensive and uneconomical to produce. Animation techniques have also been used to provide special effects in other films, for example, the human–cartoon interaction in *Who Framed Roger Rabbit?* and the pod race in *Star Wars*, and are now commonly used in computer games and on Internet websites.

Early animation techniques

The simplest animation relies on the principle of persistence of vision. Most people will have attempted to make a simple animated cartoon by drawing a series of pictures of the stages in an action on the successive corners of a wad of paper and flipping them with a thumbnail. If done quickly enough, the human eye perceives the action as a continuous movement. The first commercial device to achieve this effect, invented in 1832, was a spinning cardboard disk called a phenakistoscope, which gave an illusion of movement when viewed in a mirror. It was followed in 1834 by the zoetrope, a rotating drum lined with pictures, which was adapted in 1876 so that it could be projected in front of an audience.

The major leap in the production of mass-viewing animation came with the introduction of sprocketed-roll film and the movie industry at the turn of the 20th century. Drawings could be shot as individual frames on a film and passed rapidly in front of a projector. Another technique, stop-motion animation, in which objects are photographed then repositioned and photographed again, also began to appear. Early cartoon characters such as Gertie the Dinosaur and Felix the Cat quickly became favorites with cinema audiences.

Perhaps the biggest impact came with the introduction of synchronized sound to accompany film. Walt Disney was the first to exploit its potential in animation with his 1928 feature *Steamboat Willie*, which helped to make cartoons more lifelike and turned Mickey Mouse into an international star. Disney gradually introduced other advances in filmmaking, such as synchronized music, Technicolor, and the multiplane camera to make his cartoons more realistic, culminating in full-length features, including *Snow White and the Seven Dwarfs* (1937), *Fantasia* (1940), and *Bambi* (1942).

▲ Stuart Little is the latest in a long line of animated mice. Like his ancestor Mickey Mouse he represents a breakthrough in animation history. Where Stuart differs from Mickey, however, is that he looks exactly like a real mouse and is completely believable when mixed with human actors.

Animating cartoons

An animated cartoon is a motion picture created from a series of individually drawn still pictures, each one varying very slightly from the last. If these pictures are shown one after the other very quickly, the small differences merge into one another, and the illusion of movement is created. It is the same technique, in fact, that is used to make any moving picture—a movie film consists of a huge number of still photographs (frames), each capturing a split-second of the moving action, joined together so that they can be shown at the rate of 24 frames a second. To make an animated film, therefore, the usual technique is to use a standard movie camera to photograph the animation pictures one frame at a time, with the picture being changed between each frame. So just one minute's animation can require a staggering 1,440 different drawings.

After selecting a story, the first stage of the work is to produce a storyboard. This resembles a giant comic strip and consists of rough sketches portraying the action of the story and the accompanying dialogue. Once this and the directing animator's preliminary sketches are approved by the key personnel, the storyboard, music, and dialogue are recorded. The sound track is then translated on to a track sheet to break down the exact length of each consonant, vowel, and sound, and this information is then presented on a bar sheet—a ruled length of paper with one division for each frame and a column apiece for character action, background movement, and dialogue. At the same time, preliminary sketches and character model sheets are prepared to reveal the visual nature of the characters, color, design, and general appearance of the film.

Then, a team of layout artists works with the director to set the scenes and action and produces drawings to guide the two groups of artists who do the actual animation—the background artists and the animators. The background artists draw all the backgrounds for the film. Backgrounds include everything that will appear on the screen except the characters.

The key animators, while working within the framework of their technical instructions, are primarily responsible for the creative vitality of the film. They draw the key phases of movement—the ones that determine the life and expression of a character—while their assistants complete the in-between phases.

The background artists must work closely with the layout artists and animators, because film motion is achieved by both background and character movement. When a character walks, for example, it is usually the backgrounds that move while he or she walks a treadmill.

With the animation complete, the drawings are traced onto sheets of punched, clear celluloid, or cels, in ink (a more expensive process involves copying the drawings directly from paper to cel). They are then sent to the painting department, where the appropriate colors are applied to the reverse side of the cels, leaving a clean, black outline on front. The completed cels are then sorted into scenes and sent to the camera department, where they are photographed frame by frame over the proper background onto the film strip.

Computer systems have been employed increasingly over the years to speed up these laborious processes. Perhaps the simplest form of help came with the computer-controlled animation, or rostrum, camera, consisting of a camera poised directly above a flat board, the camera table. The camera can be raised or lowered in a precise series of tiny steps; the table can also be moved back and forth or rotated.

Normally, the cameraman follows a precise sequence of camera or table movements to achieve the effect of pans, zooms, or cartoon movements. For example, a cartoon figure might be photographed in a sequence of running movements. To add realism, a background cel is moved backwards in precisely calculated steps so that the cartoon figure appears to be moving forwards during a sequence.

By allowing a computer to operate the rostrum, a far more precise sequence of movement can be achieved. The result is laborsaving and gives smoother, more realistic motion. The device also opened up the field for complex special effects in films, such as those in the early *Star Wars* and *Superman* movies.

Computers are used in animation, however, to do much more complex work—including the

▼ A sequence of frames from a cartoon film. It will last only one-quarter of a second when viewed at the standard speed of 24 frames per second.

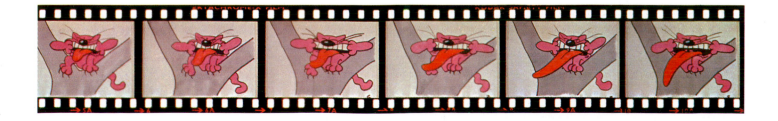

actual drawing and animation. But before a computer can work on or store a picture, it is translated into computer language. That is, the image is broken up into a mosaic of tiny squares of tone, and each square, or pixel (picture element), is then assigned a number that represents its tone level. Thus, the artist's drawing becomes, for the benefit of the computer, a string of numbers.

Computer graphics imaging

Even with computers to aid the process, most animated feature films remained two-dimensional until the mid-1990s. The challenge for computer graphics designers was to create the impression of three dimensions on the computer in the same way that television and movie film can by tricking the brain using perspective and lighting.

To create a character using computer graphics imaging (CGI), a "wireframe" is set up. If the character is a humanoid, it is often formed by an actor wearing a black bodysuit to which reflective markers are attached at key movement points on the body. The actor then performs key actions from the storyboard, while a digital camera records the movements of the markers and stores them as coordinates in a computer. For other objects or animals, a set of linked points is generated that increase or diminish the farther or closer the object is from the screen. The model is then tested by the designer to ensure that it moves in the right way.

Once the wireframe has been generated, a surface is added to give the object a firm shape. This surface is made up of polygonal shapes that link the points on the wireframe. The more polygons that can be drawn, the smoother the final outline of the shape. Animators choreograph the movement in each scene by defining the key frames or highlights in the action. The computer then draws the frames between these reference frames, which can be amended by the animator if necessary. Textures, finishes, and colors are then added to the surface to give the desired covering, whether feathers, fur, skin, metal, or wood grain.

The final stage is to light the scene using ray-tracing, in which the positions and intensities of light sources in the shot are decided. The computer then calculates how much light would be seen by the viewer from every point on the surface of the objects in the scene. Key, fill, and bounce effects are used in the same way as movie lighting to create shadows, reflectance, and ambient lighting in the scene.

When the director is happy with the scene, the sequence undergoes a process called rendering. Powerful software draws the image by computing every pixel using information from the model, the texturing, and the lighting settings. The final image can then be transferred to a variety of formats, including film, DVD, and video. This is the most demanding part of the computerized process, as each image can take between 1 and 20 hours to compute, depending on how complicated the scene is.

Animated films undergo the same postproduction processes of editing, adding retakes, dubbing the dialogue, incorporating special effects, and adding music as conventional movies do. When these processes have been approved, the audio and visual tracks are married, and titles and credits are added to the start and finish of the film.

The first animated feature film to be generated entirely by 3-D computer imaging was Pixar Studio's *Toy Story* in 1995 for which Pixar developed its proprietory Marionette software. Since then, more 3-D animations have been produced including *A Bug's Life*, *The Lost World*, and *Antz*. A new generation of computer software has sprung up to provide more realistic visual effects for these films, including 3D Studio Max, Maya, Softimage, and Aftereffects.

Digital computer animation is increasingly being used to provide backgrounds and special-effect action sequences in conventional movies like *The Matrix* and *Star Wars: The Phantom Menace*. One example is the film *Gladiator*, in which an entire arena was filled with computer-generated images instead of using thousands of extras. A small group of people were filmed, then had their hair, clothes, positions, distances from the camera, and perspective changed and replicated numerous times to give the impression of a huge crowd. Blending tools prevented the harsh outlines of earlier films, like *Mary Poppins*, where the actors were filmed against a blue screen and the animation was dropped in afterward.

▼ The light path through the lenses of an optical step printer. This device—essentially a projector and a camera—is used in conjunction with a computer to create a wide range of optical effects, such as the battle sequences in *Star Wars*. By moving the camera frame by frame, images may be enlarged, reduced, or flipped at will.

▲ In this scene, the animators have to make Stuart appear to be walking across the floor between these two feet. A frame from the movie is used to reference the exact position of Stuart and the geometry and perspective of the shot.

A CLOSE-UP OF STUART LITTLE

Bringing Stuart Little to the big screen was an enormous challenge that required many new computer-imaging tools to be developed especially for the project. Although an entirely digital creation, Stuart needed to be as realistically like a mouse as possible and interact with the actors and scenery in a convincing way.

First, hundreds of sketches and 3-D images were made based on real mice but caricatured to give him a personality and a look. Once this had been established, a mime artist was used to act out Stuart's movements so that they could be captured by the animation team and used for the key frames of each action sequence.

One of the more difficult aspects of making Stuart look believable was creating his fur and his clothing, and new software had to be developed especially for the purpose. Every hair on his head is computer generated—a half a million hairs in total—and his whiskers and dimples had to be designed and added separately. Making his clothes was equally daunting, as they had to be digitally tailored not only to fit his body but also to bend and crumple like real fabric when he moved.

Like a human movie star, Stuart even had his own lighting team to make him look his best. Again, software was developed so that his fur would have the same sheen as real fur and react to light in the same way. The lighting also had to look the same as that shining on the actors in the scene, a process that took many hours. Finally, to make Stuart look as if he was present in a scene and reacting to what he could see, a silver ball was photographed in each set, and the reflection was digitally incorporated onto his eyeballs.

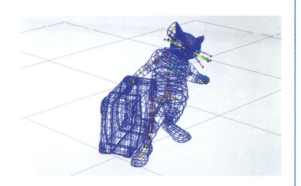

▶ Next, the wire-frame model of Stuart is generated and his position on the floor established.

▶ Polygons are used to provide Stuart's wire frame with a firm surface. The model is overlaid on the film to check that he looks right against the human actors in the scene.

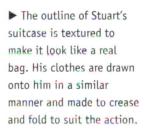

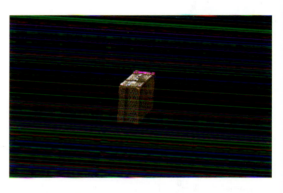

▶ The outline of Stuart's suitcase is textured to make it look like a real bag. His clothes are drawn onto him in a similar manner and made to crease and fold to suit the action.

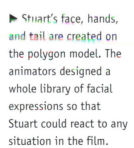

▶ Stuart's face, hands, and tail are created on the polygon model. The animators designed a whole library of facial expressions so that Stuart could react to any situation in the film.

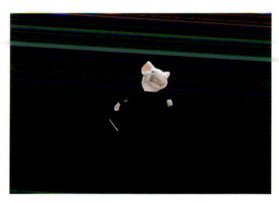

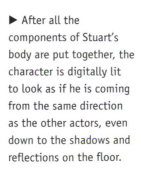

▶ After all the components of Stuart's body are put together, the character is digitally lit to look as if he is coming from the same direction as the other actors, even down to the shadows and reflections on the floor.

◀ *Count Duckula* is an example of a cartoon drawn on celluloid and colored by hand. Nowadays, computers draw many of the intermediate images in an action shot, saving time and the cost of having to redraw and color the fractional changes as a character moves an arm or leg. Animators of celluloid cartoons could produce, on average, 3 seconds of film a week. Computers have speeded this process up considerably.

Stop-motion animation

Stop motion, one of the earliest animation techniques, has undergone something of a revival in recent years, since the success of Aardman Animations' *Wallace and Gromit* films. This type of animation uses plasticine characters or puppets, which allow animators to change the action for each shot. A stop-motion camera can be paused between each frame of a scene to permit the animators to make slight alterations in the object's movement. With 24 frames of film per second, this may result in each character having to be repositioned 24 times. For Aardman's *Chicken Run*, an 80-minute feature-length stop-motion animation, tens of chickens at a time were moved. For some scenes, as many as 40 animators were used to position the characters between frames. Large numbers of spare body parts had to be available, as plasticine is easily damaged. In particular, a variety of different beaks were made to make it easy to change the shape according to the dialogue or expression of the character. Aside from positioning the characters, other aspects of films like this—such as lighting, scenery, and special effects—have to be set up in exactly the same way as in an ordinary movie.

Anime and manga

Despite the advances made in 3-D animation, there is still interest in producing 2-D cartoons. The Japanese in particular developed the distinc-tive style of the *anime* cartoon, which was based on their *manga* comic books. A similar style was used in the United States by Hanna-Barbera for *Yogi Bear* and *The Flintstones*. Designed for television, the animation is less smooth than cinematic cartoons, and the story lines are based on science fiction or fantasy subjects. Much of this type of animation is now made for the home video market, and some titles have cult followings. A further boost to the 2-D cartoon has come with the emergence of shows like *The Simpsons* and *South Park*, where the quality of the animation has become less important than the story and consequently has attracted a loyal following among adult audiences.

Web animation

As with any new media, applications have been found for animation on the Internet. Many Websites have animated images, and interactive games make great use of CGI and virtual-reality techniques based on wire frame images. Advanced software, such as Macromedia's Flash and Shockwave packages, have enabled home computer owners to produce their own animated images, complete with sound and interactivity, that can be accessed by millions of people.

SEE ALSO: COMPUTER GRAPHICS • MOVIE CAMERA • MOVIE PRODUCTION • MULTIMEDIA • SOUNDTRACK • VIRTUAL REALITY

Antenna

An antenna is a device for transmitting or receiving radio waves. Antennas may be tiny—as in miniature transistor radios—or massive dishes, such as tropospheric scatter antennas.

A transmitting antenna converts the electrical signals from a transmitter into an electromagnetic wave (a wave of electric energy), which spreads out from it. A receiving antenna intercepts this wave and converts it back into electrical signals that can be decoded and amplified by a receiver, such as a radio or television set. A radio transmitter produces its signal in the form of an alternating electric current, that is, one which oscillates rapidly.

Electromagnetic waves

The oscillating current in the transmitting antenna produces an electromagnetic wave around it that spreads out from it like the ripples in a pond. This wave sets up electric and magnetic fields. The lines of the electric field run along the antenna and those of the magnetic field around it. Both the electric and magnetic fields oscillate in time with the current.

Wherever this wave comes into contact with a receiving antenna, it induces a small electric current in it that alternates back and forth along the antenna in time with the oscillations of the wave. Although this current is much weaker than the one in the transmitting antenna, it can be picked up and amplified by the radio.

The air is full of radio waves at all frequencies, which the antenna picks up indiscriminately. Each radio or television set has a tuner with which the desired frequencies can be selected.

Each frequency is associated with a wavelength, because the waves, as they radiate out from the antenna at a certain frequency traveling

at the speed of light, space themselves a certain constant distance apart. The higher the frequency, the shorter the wavelength (the product of the two is always equal to the speed of light—186,282 miles per sec., 299,792 km/s). A transmission with a frequency of 1,000 kHz has a wavelength of 984 ft. (300 m).

Electrical waves travel along a wire at a similar speed. It will therefore greatly increase the efficiency of an antenna if its length is correctly related to the wavelength of the signal it receives or transmits—ideally one-half or one-quarter of the wavelength it receives or transmits.

Receiving antennas inside domestic radios cannot be even one-quarter as long as the wavelength and in any case have to work over a wide range of different wavelengths. Fortunately, the

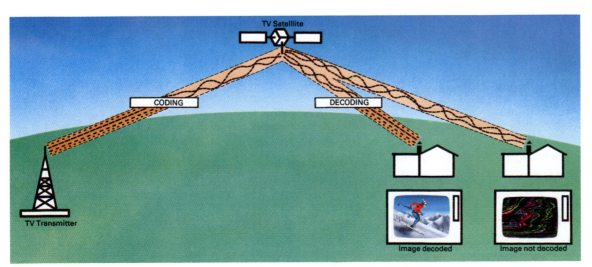

signal from a public broadcasting transmitter is so powerful that it can be received on a relatively small antenna.

Types of antennas

The same principles apply to transmitting and receiving antennas. The simplest form of antenna is a single elevated wire with an earth connection. This type of antenna was introduced in the early days of radio by Italian physicist Guglielmo Marconi, who found that by using a wire instead of a small metal cylinder, as he had done previously, he increased the range of his transmitter from 100 yards (91 m) to 2 miles (3.2 kilometers).

This type of single-element antenna is called a monopole. It is connected to only one terminal of the transmitter; the other terminal is connected to earth. This arrangement does not stop the current from flowing in the antenna; it streams between the antenna and the ground, as if across a capacitor, and sets up an electromagnetic field between the two. The ground here is said to be used as a counterpoise. Automobile radio antennas, portable radios, and mobile phones all use monopole antennas. Automobiles use the vehicle body as the counterpoise, while mobile phones and radios use their casings.

Antennas called dipoles are also used. These consist of two rods of equal length (again half or quarter wave) set end to end a few inches apart. The rods may be arranged either in a straight line or in a V shape. One rod is connected to each terminal of the transmitter, but they are not connected to each other. The field forms about both rods, linking them. No grounding is needed, since the rods counterpoise each other; they are said to be balanced-fed.

Dish antennas are used to send and receive radio waves and microwaves. Satellite television uses these antennas to concentrate the received signal—the dish focuses the signal on a receiver held above the center of the dish.

Directionality

Antennas radiate or receive better in some directions than others and are said to possess directionality (sensitivity to the signal angle).

The directionality of an antenna is very clearly illustrated in the comparatively inefficient internal antennas used in portable radios. They may be of two types: the loop antenna, a length of wire wound many times around the interior of the radio cabinet, and the ferrite rod antenna, wire wound around a magnetic material, thus increasing the antenna's efficiency. For the best reception, the plane of the loop, or a plane at right angles to the ferrite rod, should pass through the transmitted signal.

Reception of a radio broadcast may sometimes be impaired by interference from another transmitter with nearly the same frequency. Medium- and long-wave radio signals follow the curve of Earth by reflecting off the ground and the ionosphere and can travel hundreds or even thousands of miles with comparatively little loss of strength, and therefore they can cause serious overcrowding problems.

The shorter wavelengths of very high and ultra high frequency (VHF and UHF, respectively) transmissions, which are used for hi-fi radio and television broadcasts, tend not to reflect off Earth's upper atmosphere, so reception stops shortly beyond the horizon. Thus, a large number of VHF and UHF transmitters can cause reception problems to someone halfway between two transmitters sending different programs.

Both problems can be solved by using a strongly directional receiving antenna lined up with the desired transmitter. The classic type of highly directional antenna is a domestic television antenna. It consists of a half-wave dipole antenna—the part of the UHF band used in many countries for color television has wavelengths ranging from 25 in. (64 cm) down to 13 in. (35 cm). The dipole is lined up with the transmitter. In front of it (as seen from the transmitter) there is a row of directors, which are plain metal rods approximately the same length as the dipole but not electrically connected to it or the set. Behind it is a reflector, which is similar in appearance but at right angles to it.

The directors and reflectors pick up the signal, causing a slight current to flow in them so that they re-radiate the signal, though very weakly and with a changed phase—positive for negative. As a result, the reflected waves coincide exactly with the direct waves, thus reinforcing the received signal.

▲ The trans-horizon station at Mormond Hill, Scotland, provides oil platforms, 200 miles (320 km) offshore, with direct worldwide links.

▼ A receiver dish such as this may be used to receive satellite television signals. The signals can then be sent to the surrounding area using microwave transmitters.

SEE ALSO: AIR • CAPACITOR • CELLULAR TELEPHONE • ELECTROMAGNETIC RADIATION • ELECTRONICS • RADIO • SATELLITE, ARTIFICIAL

Antiaircraft Gun

Antiaircraft (AA) guns were first used in World War I, when they were adapted from equipment designed for other roles. Their job was to prevent enemy aircraft from flying at such a height that they could observe, photograph, range artillery, bomb with accuracy, or attack troops at low level. They also prevented hostile aircraft from flying in formation, thus preventing the enemy from using the power of a combined defensive armament against counterattacking aircraft. This technology persisted until the end of World War II, by which time the great speed of jet aircraft made AA guns impractical against high-flying targets.

The AA problem

Once the AA shell has left the gun muzzle, it is set on an unalterable ballistic trajectory. At the same time, as it is traveling upwards toward the target aircraft, the target is itself traveling through the sky. For a guided missile, which can change course and maneuver as it homes in on its target, this travel distance is not of ultimate importance, but for a shell, it can affect the accuracy very considerably. For example, a target traveling at the now modest speed of 200 mph (320 km/h) would travel almost 1¾ miles (2.8 km) during the 30 sec-

ond flight of a 3.7 in. (9 cm) AA shell. The position of the target is known at the moment the gun fires, but once the shell starts on its way, no further control can be exercised over it. Thus, certain assumptions must be made about the behavior of the target during the time of flight of the projectile: that the target will maintain a constant course, height, and speed shortly before and during the flight of the shell and that, if any of these variables change, it will be at a constant rate. The higher and faster the aircraft is flying, the longer the time of flight of the shell and the less likely are the assumptions to be justified.

Predictor

The apparatus developed to pinpoint the future position of the target is called a predictor. Although extremely complex in design, it is simple in principle. The predictor follows the path of the target and measures the bearing (direction) and elevation. The change in bearing and elevation in a short period of time enables the course and speed to be calculated and this information, with the height supplied by a modified range finder, gives all the target data. Initially an optical range finder was employed, but it could not be

▲ A twin-barrel 3 in. (8 cm) 50 radar-controlled antiaircraft gun on board a U.S. Navy troop carrier.

used at night and later was replaced by radar. The trajectory of the shell depends on its initial velocity, the retardation due to its shape and diameter, and its weight and stability in flight together with the meteorological conditions at various altitudes through which it passes. All these factors are fed into the predictor. The business of prediction is now carried out by computer with data-processing techniques so fast that it can deal with attack by the fastest low-flying jets.

In the U.S. Vulcan Air Defence System, the Vulcan 20 mm Gatling gun (which could spew out bursts of fire at 3,000 rounds a minute) used a computer to offset the optical sight to allow for the distance covered by the target while the shells were on their way to it. The computer gained its information from a range-finding radar and the movement of the gun as it tracked the target, with the gunner using optical sights. Because air attack is made at such speed that unaided target analysis is impossible, the Vulcan was designed to be used as part of a larger system in which early-warning radar gave notice of approaching aircraft and IFF (Interrogation Friend or Foe) radar could recognize signals emitted by friendly aircraft. This system relieved the gunner of the problem of identifying aircraft as hostile or not in the split second available to him.

The Vulcan's sheer weight of fire gave it a high probability of hitting the target, but for guns that fired at a slower rate or for some missiles, the probability of achieving a kill was increased by a proximity fuse system that detonated the warhead in the target area. A proximity fuse works by using a radio device built into the shell to detect when it is near the target. The strength of the signal determines when the fuse should detonate the shell.

In the 1980s, it became increasingly clear that the Vulcan system could not compete with new technological developments and so was phased out by the U.S. Army Air Defense Artillery (ADA) and replaced with the Stinger missile.

Antiaircraft missiles

Although some AA guns are still in use, guided missiles are now preeminent in the modern antiaircraft arsenal—particularly against distant or high-flying targets. There are a variety of ways of guiding SAMs (surface-to-air missiles) to their targets. The simplest are those contained within the missile itself and therefore impossible to jam by using electronic countermeasures to disorientate the guidance system. In this category are the infrared, or heat-seeking, weapons that home in on aircraft exhausts. This sort of guidance is very popular in the lightest, most portable SAMs, such as the U.S. Stinger. The heat-seeking sensor indi-

◀ The Rapier antiaircraft missile system provides an ideal defense against a surprise attack.

cates the direction of the target, and the missile's onboard control system alters its flight path accordingly either by turning its wings or by deflecting the thrust of its rocket motor by blanking off one of its exhaust nozzles.

In more complicated guidance systems, the missile can be made to change direction in response to radio command generated by control systems responding to information from radar, laser, or TV camera. Radar illumination is another system in which control is carried onboard the missile, but radio commands are needed in radar-command guidance, which employs two radars: one radar tracks the target and another tracks the missile, and their information is fed into a computer that causes signals to be transmitted to the missile so that it will intercept the target.

Only one radar is needed for beam-riding guidance. The beam stays locked onto the target, and the missile rides down the beam until it strikes. Laser beams can be used as an alternative to radar if the target is within sight of the controller. Radar has an advantage at night or at distance, but the laser designation is impossible to jam or deflect with countermeasures. In the same way, TV cameras can be substituted for radar sets in conditions where radar is less effective, such as in low-level air attacks on ships.

A hostile aircraft is not a passive target for guidance systems. It frequently carries sensors that indicate to its pilot when it has been picked up by radar. At this point, countermeasures can be activated to discharge chaff to clutter the radar or to transmit radio signals that will confuse missile guidance. The aircraft can also drop flares to deceive heat-seeking missiles and maneuver violently. The development of stealth technologies has improved the ability of aircraft to go undetected by missile-guidance systems.

SEE ALSO: AMMUNITION • BALLISTICS • GUN • LASER AND MASER • MISSILE • MORTAR, BAZOOKA, AND RECOILLESS GUN • NUCLEAR WEAPON • RADAR • STEALTH TECHNOLOGIES

Index

Page numbers in **bold** refer to main articles; those in *italics* refer to picture captions.